Beyond Grief

Pippa Vosper

Beyond Grief

Navigating the Journey of Pregnancy
and Baby Loss

First published in 2022 by HEADLINE HOME
an imprint of HEADLINE PUBLISHING GROUP

3

Cataloguing in Publication Data is available from the British Library

Hardback ISBN 978 1 4722 9200 1
eISBN 978 1 4722 9202 5

Designed and typeset by EM&EN
Printed and bound in Great Britain by Clays Ltd, Elcograf S.p.A.

Headline's policy is to use papers that are natural, renewable and recyclable
products and made from wood grown in sustainable forests. The logging and
manufacturing processes are expected to conform to the environmental
regulations of the country of origin.

MIX
Paper from
responsible sources
FSC® C104740
www.fsc.org

HEADLINE PUBLISHING GROUP
An Hachette UK Company
Carmelite House
50 Victoria Embankment
London
EC4Y 0DZ

www.headline.co.uk
www.hachette.co.uk

To Axel and all the babies who couldn't stay

Contents

Introduction

At five months pregnant, I delivered my healthy son in our bathroom at home. He was alive at birth, passing away shortly after. When I lost my baby, I found it difficult to connect to other's words. I read page after page, but I needed to find another way to talk about my loss.

I have brought the voices of many people with different experiences to this book, to provide solace and empathy to those experiencing the same trauma. Along with the detailed, very personal story of the loss of my own baby, my book features others' stories of pregnancy loss, grief, and how lives change afterwards. I have included many different perspectives in order to make this book accessible to as many women, and men, as possible.

When I lost my son at five months into my pregnancy, I was made to feel fraudulent when referring to my son as my baby and not a miscarriage. Within my research, many who have experienced pregnancy loss agree that referring to baby loss as a miscarriage, at any stage, feels clinical and outdated. I want you to feel confident in speaking of your own pregnancy or baby loss, and not a miscarriage, should you wish. Although the medical terms for pregnancy loss are unlikely to change, my hope is that my book will give you the confidence that I did not have, to refer to your baby in the way you choose.

This book offers practical discussion of expert opinion on causes of pregnancy loss, because 'why?' is such a common and urgent question. I have also explored what comes after loss: grief, burial and memorial, along with the short- and longer-term emotional and physical effects of pregnancy loss.

I want all readers to relate to the content, to see themselves somewhere in the book. I hope those reading this book will feel as though they are not a forgotten minority within the wider conversation of fertility.

What I have also noticed through my research is that there is seldom a hopeful ending to the personal stories out there of pregnancy loss. This is fully understandable, as it's difficult to find any hope after this level of trauma. Most stories end very soon after the loss of a pregnancy, with few words of encouragement that things do get easier. I wanted to find a message of hope from those who have shared their stories, to explore the ways in which we can move beyond grief. Although traumatic and something we all wish had never happened to us, I want to give other parents the hope and encouragement that life will not always feel as painful as it does after pregnancy loss.

As with anyone who is given a positive result from a pregnancy test, no one expects to have their pregnancies end prematurely. I have always considered myself to be a lucky person, an optimist. I never once considered that any pregnancy I was fortunate enough to experience would be taken from me. But it happened. After my pregnancy loss, I had to find a way to live alongside an experience that ripped my entire world apart. The grief I experienced after losing my baby was beyond anything I thought I could feel. But through the first months and then years that followed, I found there was life beyond that grief, something I was unsure I would ever be able to understand. When you lose a baby at any stage of pregnancy, it can feel as though your grief is inescapable. Within the pages of this book, I hope you can find a pathway through that grief.

I always knew that, when I wrote this book, I would ask those who had been so open with their experiences to share their words on the pages. When I lost my baby, knowing there were others out there who had felt this intense pain, and lived through it, gave me hope. I needed to know that, in time, I would be okay. Nothing will ever feel as it did that night, but sometimes I am hit with a memory so vivid it feels as if I am reliving the pain all over again. It has been an intense, raw few years, where I have had to rebuild myself from within. I have felt a lot, learned a lot, and come to understand better many of my strengths and weaknesses. Nothing can prepare you for the emotional journey you face, but I hope the shared stories on these pages will give you the connection and hope I so urgently needed when my baby died.

Above all, I hope that, in sharing my story, the stories of others, and a wealth of information from experts in pregnancy loss and grief, you will find the words and comfort you need to navigate your own journey of pregnancy and baby loss.

The night I lost my baby

In January 2017, I found out that I was pregnant. My husband and I had spent almost three years trying to conceive naturally, eager to give our son, Astie, a longed-for sibling. With my fortieth birthday approaching, we had agreed it was time to explore IVF. It's a gruelling process, with multiple scans, blood tests and rounds of injections, so when we were successful at the first attempt, I was elated.

My first pregnancy had been fairly straightforward (bar pre-eclampsia and the resulting emergency caesarean), so it didn't occur to me that this one might be any different. My twelve-week scan had showed the baby was developing as expected. All-day nausea aside, I had been feeling otherwise well.

I announced my pregnancy news on Instagram, with a picture of my barely-there bump. Reading each congratulatory message, from both friends and strangers, was heart-warming. My morning sickness waned, and I finally figured out how to dress my expanding bump. I was excited about the future.

Five months into my pregnancy, I noticed a pink-toned mark on my underwear. With the natural pregnancy fears any mother has, I immediately researched what these marks could mean. From all the information I read on various medical sites, this fluid was completely normal. Often there are signs of blood. I could clearly see that I didn't have anything as serious as blood spotting, so didn't feel any need to go to A&E to have myself checked over.

I told my husband what had happened and we both agreed it was minor, but that I should call my doctor. My doctor advised me that, should my symptoms worsen, I should head to A&E as a precaution. She said she would call the hospital in the morning and arrange for me to be booked in for a general scan, but for now I shouldn't worry.

Later that afternoon, I was feeling slightly worse than I had earlier, but still no alarm bells had gone off. I questioned myself on whether we should drive to the hospital. It would be an opportunity to check that the baby was fine and put my mind at ease. Looking back, of course we should have driven to the hospital. With further internet searches and my doctor not seeming overly concerned during our earlier conversation, I instead chose to go home and rest. I felt sure that by the following morning I would feel fine.

I had the most ill-judged reasons for not going to A&E that afternoon. I didn't want to be a pain or waste the nurses' time. Not listening to my instincts and worrying what others would think of me would prove to be a painful life lesson.

By 10 p.m., I was feeling weaker than I usually did at this time. Evenings were harder due to being naturally more tired through the pregnancy, but I remember it being a more intense exhaustion. I went to bed, still not thinking that my situation was serious enough to bother my husband, wake our son, and have them drive to the hospital with me. I will regret this decision for ever.

I woke at 3 a.m. with pains akin to mild period cramps. I am an eternal optimist, but I knew instinctively that my baby was going to die that night.

I reached under the covers and placed my hands on my stomach. My hands moved downwards along my stomach to just above my pelvic bone. That is when I began to panic. There was a large raised area above my pelvic bone that I hadn't felt before. I stroked my skin, lovingly holding who I knew was my baby under the surface. I knew my baby shouldn't be there, his position was too low. Sick with fear, I woke my husband and told him something was very wrong, and that we should go to the hospital immediately. I was holding the area where my baby was with one hand, while trying to get dressed with the other. My husband went upstairs to wake our son. As it was the middle of the night, we felt we had no option but to take him with us.

I had a sudden, very strong urge to use the bathroom. Unbeknown to me at the time, the period-like pains I was experiencing were contractions. The pressure I felt, which I assumed to be a need to use the loo, was my baby coming. Due to Astie being induced when I was forty weeks pregnant, I didn't know how it felt to go into labour naturally. Previously, my experience of birth had been controlled by medication, nurse's schedules and an epidural.

As I walked into the bathroom, I turned back to face the door and could see my husband in the other room. I was still standing when a gush of water pushed out of me. My waters had broken. I will never forget the terrified look on my husband's face as his eyes fixed on the space between my legs. I looked down and could see a tiny pair of legs hanging between my own. Our baby was here.

We will be forever grateful to the lady who answered our emergency services call. My husband placed the phone on speaker, resting it on the side of the bath. We were instructed on how to deliver our baby on towels on the floor.

I bent my knees, while lowering myself to the floor. I pushed only once, then felt my baby come out of me and into my husband's hands. And there he was – a perfect, tiny copy of my elder son. And he was alive. I loved him instantly, and I know he felt my love as I kissed his hands, while my husband listened to the advice on the phone and started mouth-to-mouth.

Astie was woken by the ambulance outside, and my husband protected him from seeing me, as I continued the efforts to breathe life into our baby. My fear in those brief moments is indescribable; in shock at having just given birth, I was now responsible for keeping our precious boy alive.

I remember two paramedics standing above me. Their presence seemed to fill the room as they gently advised me to stop the resuscitation. My baby was too young to live, they said. His lungs couldn't cope with the outside world. In front of me lay my beautiful son, his arms slowly moving. As I watched him, I experienced a moment of extreme calm amid all the madness: my baby and me understanding what had just happened to us. It may seem strange to some, but it is those brief minutes – those moments that belonged just to us – that fill me with the most love.

Parts of those early-morning hours are unclear, but I know that, as I went from my home to the hospital, from A&E to the recovery room, I must have repeated the words 'My baby died' at least a hundred times. Astie and my husband had followed the ambulance in our car. I was unable to stop the silent tears that came when our confused little boy asked why I was in hospital. I told him his baby brother had died, but that everything would be fine. He was upbeat as friends came to collect him, not understanding the enormity of what had just happened.

Doctors, midwives and nurses crowded my cubicle bed as questions were asked, forms were ticked and my placenta was pushed out (thankfully an easy transition – I overheard a doctor discussing taking me to theatre if things didn't go smoothly). And then it went silent. I had been wheeled into a dimly lit room, and now it was just my husband beside me. It was then that it really hit me: I had gone into labour;

my baby had been delivered; he had died. My husband and I held one another and cried more deeply than I could have imagined possible. Tears came first, then wailing, then painful, gut-wrenching, uncontrollable sobbing.

Outside our room, I could hear a baby crying. By the piercing tones I knew the sound was that of a newborn. In my delirious state, I was convinced it was my son. At this moment, I truly believed the doctors had managed to save our baby. I looked at my husband, who hadn't registered the sound outside, and pressed the bell for a midwife to come. It wasn't my son, they explained, we were in a room on the labour ward.

I couldn't comprehend why I had been taken to the labour ward. It felt wildly insensitive to be placed so close to other mothers giving birth. I wanted to scream, but was unable to verbalise anything that day. I was too weak and too broken to voice any opinion. The mental torture continued for hours, as I heard other babies being delivered on the ward outside our room.

Once tests had been done and an intravenous drip inserted into my hand, a midwife came to ask the question that hadn't entered my mind: Did I want to hold our baby? I did. When the midwife laid my son, Axel, in my arms, concealed inside a tiny blanket, I thought I would break from my physical longing for him. We gently unwrapped the blanket, and there was our baby. I had been scared of how he might look, but he was perfect, his body small but perfectly formed.

I didn't know how long it was since I had last seen him – we had arrived at the hospital in the dark, and now the sun had been up for some time. I willed him to open his eyes.

It wasn't strange to kiss his cold body; it was the lightest feeling that filled me with an overwhelming love for him. I kissed his soft face for much of the two hours we spent together.

The hardest part was the final goodbye. Soon after my son had been carried out of the room, forms were placed beside me with choices to be made about a post-mortem and a funeral service. We would be attending our baby's funeral – another part of this surreal story that was not supposed to be happening to me.

After Axel was taken from us, I didn't want to be in the hospital a moment longer. I didn't want to be touched or tested one more time. My son had died and now I just wanted to be left alone. I requested to be discharged, but the level of blood I had lost meant I would have to stay in the hospital until the doctors were comfortable with my condition.

The midwives and nurses were kind, listening patiently as I talked about my baby. Every time someone would come to check on me, I would tell the story over and over again in disbelief.

We arrived home late in the evening. Astie was with a family friend. She had let herself in while Astie was at nursery and removed any trace of our home birth from the bathroom. The blood-stained towels had been washed, new ones hanging on the rail above where I had given birth to Axel that morning.

For days after my baby's death, I just sat on the sofa and cried. I didn't eat and I barely slept. Whenever I saw the hospital's number on my phone, I truly believed that they were calling to say they had good news, that they had managed to revive our son and that he was waiting for us to collect him.

I started to tell my wider group of friends, my mind so hazy that I have no recollection of speaking to some. But they know the entire story, repeating parts in a way that only I could have told them, so I must have. In the weeks that followed, I felt somehow fraudulent when I spoke of 'my baby dying', but the term 'miscarriage' didn't – and still doesn't – feel like a word that conveyed the depth of the suffering I was experiencing.

Why had he died? Of course, I blamed myself: maybe I shouldn't have done that spinning class; perhaps it was the stress of starting a new business. But it was neither of those things. Specialists have repeatedly assured me that working out and working hard do not cause pregnancy loss. I just got really, really unlucky. An incompetent cervix was recorded as the reason my son had died. I questioned whether this made things easier, to have an explanation of just why my son hadn't made it past five months. It didn't, it just created further questions as to how I could have done more to prevent this from happening.

Each day after Axel died I received at least one email or online comment regarding my bump. I knew I had to stop the well-meaning enquiries. One Sunday evening I sat alone and wrote what I felt was a fitting tribute to my baby and, adding the image of his tiny footprints to my Instagram feed, I hit 'share'. Within seconds, comments began to appear. I turned off my phone and didn't turn it on until the following lunchtime. I dreaded seeing my words again, reading the kind comments from friends and strangers. I hadn't wanted to share my news like this, it was so unbearably private, but

I knew it would be the fastest way to let people know that I was no longer pregnant, to stop many of the thoughtful questions about a bump that was no longer there.

The days that followed opened my eyes to heartbreak that wasn't only mine. Email after email arrived in my inbox from women telling me that they, too, had lost a baby. Some had lost theirs later than me, some earlier, but it was the same pain. I had known some of these women for many years, yet there had never been any indication that they had experienced anything so traumatic.

But I'm not surprised that I didn't know about my friends' pain. There is little mention of pregnancy loss outside hospital walls, and for most people it remains an incredibly difficult subject to broach.

I'm unsure whether I will ever be able to fully accept what happened, but I know that I'm grateful for what Axel gave me. When Axel died, my heart broke in a way that I would find impossible to describe, but he also changed my world in a way that I will thank him for for ever.

My path did change. I changed. I didn't notice it at first, but, as time passed, the weight that had once occupied my mind and body was no longer a heaviness but a grounding: I was stronger. I am lucky to have had that night with my son, when he came into my life, and for a small moment everything was quiet.

ONE

Pregnancy Loss

Loss at any stage is significant

After the experience of early pregnancy loss, often women are expected to recover almost immediately. In many cases, there is still a startling assumption that a loss in the first weeks of pregnancy is something that should not be taken too seriously. I have heard the words 'insignificant' and 'minor' attributed to losses that take place in the first weeks of pregnancy. Some may recover quickly from an early loss, but we can't discount the fact that the majority of women who experience early pregnancy loss will be greatly affected.

Whatever stage of your pregnancy, you were carrying *your* baby. There will be those that don't accept or understand that your baby should be past the twenty-four-week stage to be called 'your baby'. People's beliefs differ; some are rigidly sticking to medical terminology, some have a spiritual outlook. I simply knew that once I had seen a positive result on a pregnancy test, I was carrying *my baby*.

Recently, a friend confided in me that she had experienced a pregnancy loss at six weeks. She then apologised, saying she felt self-conscious telling me, as her experience 'wasn't as bad' as mine. This was not the first time I had received an apology for someone's loss being earlier than mine. Discounting your pain in early pregnancy loss is not uncommon, but the pain of those experiencing loss in the first weeks of pregnancy should not be hidden.

My own fertility challenges made me focus heavily, almost obsessively, on my age and the time I may have left to conceive. Although I longed for another baby, I did have a son. I had not experienced any known pregnancy losses prior to this. When I lost my baby at five months into my pregnancy, my journey to that point had been fairly straightforward. Not the way I would have planned it, but, equally, there were no moments of trauma. For the woman who lost her baby a few weeks into her pregnancy, she may have had multiple pregnancy losses, years of IVF treatment, a situation where she was not able to access IVF, or any number of situations that accentuated her grief to an almost unbearable point. We can never truly know the extent of another's grief and longing. The experience of loss will be different in many ways, but it is impossible to make assumptions or comparisons when considering others' pregnancy loss experiences.

I asked Gubby Ayida, Consultant Obstetrician and Gynaecologist MA FRCOG DM (Oxon), how parents can better understand the significance of their loss, at any stage in pregnancy.

> It's understanding that pregnancy loss is a bereavement of a loved one, even though you had never met them. Sometimes women cannot fully express that bereavement. If you have a bereavement of a loved one, a child, people know, can see and understand that loss. With pregnancy loss (especially if early), it can be that only the mother feels that loss. That sense of loss of something you never had. For some women there is no difference between early and late pregnancy loss, but people may say 'at least it was early' when the loss was in the first trimester. These types of comments can be

hurtful. From the minute women know they are pregnant, they have started planning. From twelve weeks, you are saying 'next summer with the baby', or 'next Christmas'. Even early on, you have started adjusting. Do I take that job, do I take that trip? You have to consider there is a loss of all of that planning, all of that future that others may not see. It's not just the physical baby, it's also the loss of what could have been. It can be hard to explain this to others, so the mother can feel very alone in her grief. I often say to mothers that there will be up days and there will be down days. There is support out there even in maternity units. Most hospitals have a bereavement team. There is someone you can contact, who knows what you are going through and can help or signpost to helpful resources.

Jools Oliver, designer and author, on her grief following five pregnancy losses and how she connected on a deeper level with her family through the experience.

I got pregnant with all my children fairly quickly. I had easy pregnancies and always wanted a large family, so we decided to try for baby five. I was forty-one when I fell pregnant with our fifth child and everything seemed to be going well, as it had with my other children. It was only after a scan when I was close to three months pregnant that I was told my baby's heart had slowed at nine weeks, allowing our baby to grow slowly to eleven weeks. It was the first time there had been any cause for worry in any of my pregnancies. I knew about pregnancy loss, but never thought it would happen to me. It was a huge shock.

I was almost three months pregnant when I began to bleed heavily. I knew a sanitary towel wouldn't be able to hold the level of blood, so I used one of my young son's nappies and placed tissues inside too. The blood just wouldn't stop, so I knew I had to go to A&E. I saw a gynaecologist that I had never met before. He used the words 'let me see what I can get out', which I found surprising. This was all new to me, so I didn't think to say anything. I just accepted this wording, even though it felt awful to hear. He began taking what he could from my uterus, taking my baby's surroundings to a sink in the hospital room. It felt so wrong.

The doctor wasn't able to bring my baby out, so I was told to go for a walk to see if my baby would come naturally. Nothing happened, so I went back. I was given the choice of taking tablets to allow my baby to come, or have a D&C. I chose the tablets and was told to go home. There wasn't much in the way of advice, but it was explained that my baby may come out on the way home, or over the next few days. I thought it would all be simple, that I would go to the loo, my baby would leave me and then I would recover. In many ways I wish everything had been explained, so I would know what was to come.

Over the coming days, the surroundings of my baby left my body in stages. One evening, when I was alone, I went to the loo and felt something quite large come out of me. I was unsure at the time if this was my baby, but now know it must have been. I did the only thing I knew to do, and that was to flush. I chose not to look down, I was in absolute shock.

I'm so sorry, Jools. Did your body recover easily, as you had expected it to?
I continued to bleed heavily for over a month. I was weaker than usual due to the extreme blood loss and my mind was constantly occupied by not only my loss, but my physical state. As I reached week five of the bleeding, I made the decision to go back to the hospital for a D&C. My body hadn't recovered. I told everyone around me that I was fine, that I was okay to go alone. Why do we all do this? Why do we say we're fine when we're really not?

We say we are fine, when we are screaming inside for someone to understand. Did you go on to have other children after this first pregnancy loss?
I became pregnant with my second son and assumed that my pregnancy loss was a one-off experience. I had a son after losing a baby, so I thought everything would be fine going forward. I thought that my first pregnancy loss was something that happened and I would never have to go through it again. After my

second son was born, I became pregnant again and, for the first two months, everything seemed fine. Only then I began to bleed quite heavily.

I went to the hospital and was told my baby had died. Rather than taking the tablets this time, I chose a D&C. What seems crazy now, but very normal then, was that I planned my D&C around my son's violin performance and my daughter's birthday. I was on autopilot and wanted to keep my word to my children. I scheduled my D&C for the following week, after their events. It was while I was at the concert that I felt blood begin to come out. As I sat there watching my son on stage, I knew exactly what was happening. I shouldn't have been at the concert, I should have been at home, but I didn't want to let anybody down.

How were you feeling in the time before your D&C?
With a second pregnancy loss, I felt more nervous for my health, so, before my D&C, I booked a mammogram. I wanted to feel some security that another fear, cancer, wasn't a part of my life. Blood began to come quite heavily on my way to the appointment. Even though I felt I was concealing my emotions, it was clear that I was pre-occupied. When the man checking my boobs asked if I was okay, I told him I was going through the loss of another baby. The conversation was a little awkward and he suggested I get to the hospital as soon as I could.

As I made my way to my car, blood began to literally pump out of me. Everything felt out of my control. This time I didn't have anything with me to absorb the blood, just tissues. As I began driving to the hospital, I knew what was happening was serious. The blood was everywhere and I was feeling faint. I stopped my car and called an ambulance. I then called the hospital and was told my appointment was hours later and could I hold on until then. Blood was seeping through my trousers and I told them I needed urgent help, that I was dying.

Although I was quite close to the hospital, there were roadworks and heavy traffic, so they sent someone with a wheelchair to collect me. As I reached the hospital, the doctors then saw my condition and the level of blood loss. I was told I needed to go to theatre, that I could die if they didn't operate immediately. I received such incredible care from the hospital, there is no question that the doctor I saw that day saved my life.

My husband arrived at the hospital. Due to the emergency of my situation, everything had happened so quickly. There had been no time to clean anything around me and blood was everywhere. He was understandably upset by the trauma and all that had happened. I can't think about that day without questioning: 'Did that really happen?' That's the PTSD. The trauma that you block out.

Did you have a strong support system of friends around you?

Some friends were amazing, but a lot of my friends didn't understand the depth of the pain. It's hard to explain. I felt that there were other people thinking I shouldn't go on about it, that I had children at home and I should feel lucky. Which I do. But I also lost babies. Whether a loss was early or late, there was a baby.

With the traumatic second pregnancy loss, how did you approach wanting to become pregnant again?

My family had concerns, but when I fell pregnant again, we were all excited. Then I had a feeling something was wrong when I was between seven and eight weeks. I was on the way to a school drop-off. I began bleeding heavily in the car, so knew that, after I had dropped my children to the school gate, I had to take myself to hospital. By now I knew what to expect. The doctor and I discussed my choices and we agreed to a D&C that day.

I was able to compare this D&C to my first and realised the care that this doctor had shown made a great difference to the handling of my experience. The doctor from my first pregnancy loss had not been entirely considerate of how I felt, both emotionally and physically. I realised then how important the care you receive is to your recovery. My hand was held throughout the D&C during this third pregnancy loss. I felt so cared for. Feeling the compassion and more gentle way in which my body was treated made a huge difference in how I lived with my experience after.

How did you make the decision to try for another baby after you had experienced three losses?
Knowing the possibilities of what may happen, I knew I was mentally strong enough to try to get pregnant again. I longed for another baby and knew how much it would bring to our family. I became pregnant after a few months of trying, but weeks later felt the familiar dread that something was wrong.

I saw discharge that had a slight pink tone to it. Trying to convince myself nothing was wrong, I found a torch to shine a brighter light on my underwear to see whether there was anything to worry about. A few days passed and the colour of my discharge was getting darker. I booked a scan. As a family we are very open, so I spoke to my eighteen-year-old daughter about my fears that day. She wanted to come with me to my scan and I felt that, at eighteen, if she wanted to be with me, she could. I knew she was also worried about me, knowing this could be a possible fourth pregnancy loss.

It was confirmed at the scan that there was a faint heartbeat, but that my baby wouldn't stay alive for more than a few days. There was little I could do, so we slowly walked back to the car. My daughter cried as we began our drive home. I told her I was fine, but

I don't know if I was convincing myself I was fine, or if after four losses I really was fine. I still don't know. We spoke of the fact that the baby still had a heartbeat. I knew there was little we could do, but she held on to the hope that the baby might survive. A week later, she came with me for another scan. My baby had died and she was understandably upset all over again. It was, in some way, beautiful to have gone through this with my daughter. She said she now understands what I went through during my pregnancy losses. To have her say she understood pregnancy loss was a huge moment. She may experience loss in the future, or her sisters, or best friend. It's important to know the reality of what happens during pregnancy loss. We were always close, but it brought us closer. Through all of the losses over the years, I also became closer to my husband. I know that doesn't always happen and I know how lucky I am that our relationship became stronger.

Did the trauma of four losses make you reconsider a future pregnancy, or was the longing for another baby still very much with you?
I knew I wanted another baby. I did become pregnant again, although I experienced another loss. My fifth pregnancy loss was a more private experience. I chose to live through the loss by myself. I didn't want to put my family through the pain again. They would have been fully supportive, of course, but I just felt as though this was something I had to do by myself. We

are so close as a family that all my pregnancy losses are part of our lives. Although I lived through this experience alone, I told my family about our fifth loss after I had been to the hospital. This fifth pregnancy loss became another part of our story.

Is there a special way you remember the babies who couldn't stay with you?
We moved to the house we're in now before one of our pregnancy losses. I was pregnant and I made plans for the new baby's nursery when we first viewed it. We saw this as the home we could spend the rest of our lives in. A space for all of us. This house holds a special place for us, as we planned to move here before we lost our baby. When we moved in, I knew I wanted to have a place to remember our baby. All of our babies we lost.

We went as a family to a garden centre and chose a young blossom tree. We planted it in the garden. Planting the tree became a small ceremony for us, for the children to know I was fine and a way to have the memory of our babies with us always. I see the tree growing and can't help but think of what life would have been like if our babies had survived.

Why do we diminish the importance of our experience?

When I first wrote openly of my pregnancy loss experience, I received hundreds of messages via my private inbox on social media. I received calls from friends and emails from those I work with. There was a running theme in the majority of the messages from those who had also experienced pregnancy loss – the need to minimise how much their loss had affected them. 'I was lucky, really, I was only five weeks' read one. 'I can't compare my loss to yours, as mine was much earlier' was the opening line of another. These messages continued, and, at the time, I could only think to read and accept their words. Months later, I returned to the messages. While reading the words of others, I felt a deep sense of sadness that these mothers had felt the need to lessen the intensity of their experience in this way. Yes, I had lost my pregnancy at five months, but that they felt the need to diminish how their own loss affected them seemed to be an unconscious conditioning stemming from their experience. The need to always play down their pregnancy loss was clearly ingrained.

I spoke to doula and author Latham Thomas about why she feels people diminish the experience of those who have gone through a pregnancy loss.

> I think it's uncomfortable for people to witness those they love in pain. When it's something so profound and when there's no way to explain why a baby passes away, you have nothing to hold on to. The people who have to watch you move through that suffering aren't capable

of supporting you through the suffering, of being with you through the silence. They may find it uncomfortable watching you cry without trying to stop you from crying because they don't know how to handle your emotions. That's why people suffer in silence, because they feel they're going to burden others with their emotional response and their grief. Everything in our culture turns us away from emotion, so you don't have to feel anything. There's a pill you can take for every sensation so you don't have to feel. Being in such a visceral experience of grieving is challenging and most people will try to find a way to escape grief.

Grief has its own timeline. That period of grieving can be three months, three years, it could never end. Someone could find themselves years after an event suddenly experiencing waves of sorrow. If we don't know how to support, we tend to turn our head the other way and pretend it's not happening. Sometimes people gaslight or centre themselves to try to make you feel better. It's often the case of people wanting to relate and find common ground. The appropriate response is to listen, and often listening means there's pockets of silence that are uncomfortable, and that doesn't mean they have to be filled. Sometimes people just want to be heard, and held; they don't want to be talked at. Sometimes it can be they want their head held and for them to be able to cry over your shoulder. That might just be all they need, to be rocked and held.

If you haven't seen the baby, I think it's much easier to objectify the experience. If I lay eyes on someone, there's more of a connection. Regardless of whether people have met the baby or not, the excitement around the new family member from the whole community is one of extreme joy and anticipation. When it goes in a different direction, people who are closest are obviously crestfallen, but they often don't know how to be in a relationship with you. Losing a child is a completely different type of loss.

The way we are almost expected to play down the intensity of pregnancy loss needs to change. In most societies, the loss of a pregnancy is still not considered to be worthy of the level of sympathy a grieving parent often needs at the time. It is also the case that the subject of pregnancy loss causes many to feel uncomfortable, resulting in a barrier in relation to the opportunity to discuss the trauma. Harbouring this grief and feeling unable to talk about the loss of a pregnancy leaves little chance to come to terms with the enormity of the experience. In many instances, mothers convince themselves that their loss wasn't a big life event. By expressing that their loss wasn't late, or that they can try for another baby in the future, they are often simply conforming to what society expects of them.

You have lost a pregnancy. Your plans for a future with this baby have been taken from you. You should feel absolutely free to express your sadness at what has happened. Why should we hold our pain inside for fear of being judged, for fear of making others feel uncomfortable? Pregnancy loss happens, it is a huge life event and society needs to understand its emotional significance. There is a lot of talk of the conversation opening up, which is positive, but from someone who regularly speaks about pregnancy loss, the clear discomfort the subject creates shows that we have a long way to go. I often question why pregnancy loss is still such a misunderstood subject.

I spoke with therapist Claire Bidwell Smith, who explains her theory as to why we are caught in the cycle of diminishing the effect of pregnancy loss and the continued misunderstanding of those around us.

We do that because most of us struggle to deal with death and grief in general, we are always pushing it to the side. Pregnancy loss is a very hidden grief, the loss itself isn't visible, so the people around you are not experiencing it the way you are, it's very personal. They didn't meet your baby, so it's very different on that level. It's just as big a loss as any other, but it becomes so insular. We push our grief aside as that's the message we receive from others. And culturally we're not good at grief, so the people around you who aren't really recognising it as a loss, or feeling it as a loss themselves, are sending you a message of not acknowledging the grief. We don't want people to feel uncomfortable and so if those around us are not acknowledging the grief, we're not going to throw it in their face. They will initially think what has happened to you is terrible, they will be sorry for you, but then it goes out of their minds. As they're not acknowledging it, you start to feel as though you shouldn't either. The cycle continues.

Why do we often stay silent following pregnancy loss?

Feeling alone is something most of us experience following pregnancy loss. The conversation can be uncomfortable for those who have not been through this trauma, while those who have may not be immediately open about their own loss due to the stigma attached to the experience. These factors keep the continual wall of silence surrounding pregnancy loss in place.

Being unaware of the shared experiences of those around you can contribute to your belief that you are the only person in your circle of friends and family who understands this pain. It is not a conversation you will likely have with colleagues or associates, so this too will compound your belief that it is just you who understands the reality of your loss.

Another factor of the silence and shame is that pregnancy loss is not widely acknowledged as a trauma, particularly in the early stages of a pregnancy. Women often feel as though they are overreacting, making too much of their experience. With the silence and lack of understanding that often surrounds pregnancy loss, women can become confused about the reality of their grief. Being told they should try to move on, or that at least they know they can get pregnant, can inadvertently reinforce this unhelpful belief. Many women mask their distress for fear of being judged for a perceived exaggeration of what many assume is simply a minor blip. This only works to conceal their trauma, and those in a state of grief withdraw further.

Within most friendship groups, there will be others who

have experienced pregnancy loss. Almost certainly, within any working environment, there will be those who have lived through the pain of losing a baby at some stage in pregnancy. You may never become aware of those around you who know first-hand what you are going through, as the opportunities to initiate conversations around baby loss are rare. It can be extremely helpful that those who have lived through pregnancy loss hear of others' experiences. These stories validate the extent of their own grief and confirm that their pain is real. These conversations can also be a way to hear how others navigated their way through their own experience, a chance to understand that it will not always feel so painful. The opportunity to speak of your experience – the longing, grief and possible depression – can be the difference in beginning to navigate your way out of the grief, or being faced with a prolonged period of low mood or worsening depression.

I spoke to Kitty Galsworthy, on how she found support by talking to friends and family through pregnancy loss and the further challenges her family faced.

I had two early losses and one late pregnancy loss before I had our three children, followed by another early loss after them. Despite investigations, I've never discovered why my babies didn't make it. The little girl we lost almost five months into my third pregnancy was declared perfect following the post-mortem.

Knowing you're pregnant before anyone else does is such a strange feeling. I always felt it was written all over my face and carrying on as normal seemed so odd. With my first two pregnancies, this was made more bizarre when, in the first few weeks, I was scanned after some spotting and told to go away and return a week or two later when progress, or lack of it, could be measured. Sadly, in each instance there was no heartbeat and I had an operation under general anaesthetic, returning to work the same week.

How did you navigate the first months after each loss?
The hardest thing was the adjustment. Our lives were so full of plans and work. Each pregnancy had set us up with dates, assumptions and expectations for the year ahead. With each loss came a disappointing shift, which was then exacerbated as friends and people around us became pregnant and were able to fulfil those expectations. Feeling any negativity towards those people and their happiness really made me feel so conflicted.

Was there any indication that anything may be wrong before the next pregnancy loss you experienced?
There was nothing to make us think anything would happen in this pregnancy. When I got to twelve weeks, it was a relief. We were confident those early miscarriages had simply been very bad luck. At around seventeen weeks, I started to feel my baby kicking

and had the start of a bump. One Saturday morning, the week of my twenty-week scan, I lay in bed trying to feel the baby and couldn't. After a call to my midwife, my husband and I drove to the hospital to have a check-up. We were told that they couldn't hear a heartbeat. A scan confirmed that our baby had died.

Did you stay in the hospital from that point, or return home?

We were sent home and asked to return twenty-four hours later, so that I could be induced. I was induced on a labour ward, which was traumatic. I didn't feel prepared for labour. I'd been so sure I wanted a natural birth that I resisted any pain relief. With no happy ending, I was persuaded to have an epidural and our tiny girl was born. Our amazing midwife encouraged us to see and hold our baby. We were given footprints and a photograph to take home.

Leaving the hospital initially, before the induction, was hard because we knew we had to break the news to family, friends and work. But we still had our baby with us, inside me. After having the delivery, that was far harder than leaving hospital days before, knowing our baby had died. I didn't want to go without her, to leave her there and to no longer be pregnant. It felt like wading through mud just to walk out of the doors and go home.

Did you have a strong support system around you?
Our belief that there was nothing life could throw at us that we couldn't face together got us through a really tough time. As a couple, we still felt lucky. I went back to work the following week, but it was too difficult and emotional, so I took more time, which allowed me the space to grieve properly.

I found talking really helped. I was so lucky to have the most incredibly supportive friends and family. I'm also a great believer in the power of the mind. I used alternative therapies and became really interested in hypnobirthing. It helped me to feel I was taking positive steps towards a successful pregnancy. Having experienced pregnancy loss, I have an amazing appreciation for every miraculous baby. Motherhood suddenly seems to me a gift, not a given, and that makes it all the more special.

How do you look back at your experiences of loss?
After our losses, we had three babies in three years: Isadora, Rafe and Eddie. I have learned a lot about myself in the process. Eddie was diagnosed with leukemia when he was eighteen months old. In a way, we feel that the loss of our baby at twenty weeks prepared us for the traumatic shock of this diagnosis and the brutality of the long treatment he faces. We know we've already dealt with something so hard and that together we can face this too.

When my baby died, I wanted to talk of every moment of my experience, from the pain, blood loss and birth, to holding him in my arms hours after he had passed away. But I often felt I couldn't. Not with more than a handful of my closest friends anyway. It's not the lightest of conversations, but all that happened was a part of my experience and I wanted to share it. I had lost my son, and wanted to speak of his birth and all that came before it. I found that speaking about him brought him closer to me in many ways.

When I was first asked to write of my experience for *Vogue*, there was no hesitation. I agreed immediately. I knew that by sharing my own experience, this would, I hoped, allow others to speak more openly of their own pregnancy loss. I hoped that by speaking of my son in an open and honest way, others would also further connect with their own loss. I hoped that those who had previously been shielded from the reality of this loss would gain a greater understanding of the trauma. It is impossible to fully understand any trauma that you have not lived through personally, but the understanding from those around us when it does happen is crucial. We need a support system and for friends, family and colleagues to know that this is not a small thing that we will get over in a short space of time.

To no longer feel the need to keep a pregnancy loss a secret can help to connect us on a deeper level with others. I found that, once I had spoken openly of my experience, with those I knew, on social media and then in a magazine, I formed greater relationships with those who had shown compassion. There were changes in friendships, mostly all positive, and I was not only comforted by those who contacted me via social media, but I was made to feel embraced by people I may never meet in person. This show of care was something I hadn't expected. I began to understand that I wasn't alone in my grief.

Why does shame play a part in pregnancy loss?

As depicted in films and perfectly executed social media announcements, pregnancy is often portrayed as something that comes very easily to most. Those who have not experienced pregnancy loss often assume the parenthood journey is as simple as having a healthy sex life and excellent forward-planning skills. Which is why it makes losing a pregnancy that much harder to admit to. We want the happy ending. We anticipate the birth announcement, the first images of the baby, the excitement from friends and family. When the future plans with a baby are cut short, it can leave us feeling unexpectedly exposed. And ashamed.

After years of unexplained infertility following my first child and with the positive result of an IVF pregnancy, at the three-month mark I proudly announced my news on Instagram. Behold, I was bearing a second child. I was proud, happy, apprehensive and tired. But mostly I was thrilled that I was able to show my body was finally working as I had hoped it would. I was among the many thousands of women who put pressure on themselves to create another life. And here I was for all to see, cradling a small bump, with the late-afternoon sunlight perfectly framing the shot. See, I fell into the trap of that perfect pregnancy announcement too. I don't regret it. It was a lovely picture. But it was another part of the pregnancy story I would look back on with a feeling of sadness.

A few days after Axel died, I looked at the image of my pregnancy announcement on Instagram. A sudden feeling of shame came over me. What would they think? 'They' being those I knew and those I didn't. Would they think it was my fault? I was certain most people would assume I had caused the death of my baby. There was also a feeling of shame that my body clearly wasn't equipped to carry a child to term. And what of my husband? Would they pity him for being with me? These were the main, but not the only, negative thoughts that went through my mind. Why had I been so concerned with what others may think?

Therapist Claire Bidwell Smith gave me her thoughts on why many of us focus on others' reactions to our loss:

> In general, we do that with grief because most people don't know how to bring up a loss to other people. It makes people feel different and separate to go through a loss, and people around them don't know how to talk about it. There tends to be shame and guilt around loss, which is irrational, but that is why we tend to stifle it. We worry that people will wonder what happened, what caused the pregnancy loss. Was it something that the mother did? The shame and guilt that we experience is often irrational and unconscious. And shame is a big silencer.

Those who have experienced IVF may also find separate forms of shame. It is not uncommon for women going through IVF to feel as though their bodies have failed them. There are the additional thoughts of money that has been spent, or the IVF drug-induced mood swings that may have affected a partner. Creating a life with the help of assisted fertility is nothing to be ashamed of, but in a world where our bodies are expected to work miracles, there can be a lot of unwarranted shame involved in the process.

And what if an IVF cycle doesn't give you the pregnancy you longed for? Whether you have gone through IVF alone, or with a partner, you cannot place blame on yourself for an IVF cycle not resulting in a pregnancy. With any guilt you feel concerning the disappointment of a partner, it's important to remember that having a baby with someone is a joint effort, joint longing and involves joint finances. In the case of an IVF embryo not embedding in the uterus, or the loss of a pregnancy after an IVF transfer, your main focus should be on how to deal with your grief at that time. If possible, try to shift your thinking to the present, rather than allowing the additional shame of the money you spent, or the emotional struggles through the process, to add extra emotional strain. With six IVF cycles behind me, it's easier said than done, I know.

Why do we blame ourselves?

When lying in the hospital bed on the day I lost my son, my mind swirled with thoughts of just how I had caused the death of my baby. There was little consideration of other factors that could have resulted in my baby's premature birth. As the one carrying my baby, I was the first to blame myself for my loss. I continually questioned medical professionals on the possible causes. I was unable to accept that my baby's death wasn't directly related to something I had done. I constantly questioned myself on whether I had walked too far, stood too long, lifted something that was considered too strenuous for my body. I spent many hours considering the ways in which I may have caused Axel's death, asking myself what I could have done differently.

I spoke to Alexandra Stedman, writer and editor of The Frugality website, about feelings of personal blame and guilt, and the grief of losing her conjoined twins

I remember at our scan, when we were told they could see two heads. It was a surprise. I thought I was going to have three children under two. Then the sonographer saw they were conjoined twins. They were joined by the chest and there was only one heart. There was quite a lot of fluid within my babies. Their heart wasn't pumping hard enough.

I always think something I did contributed to them being conjoined. I have been told it couldn't have been caused by anything I had done, but I still thought in some way it could have been my fault that they were conjoined.

What happened after you were told your babies were conjoined?

Over a week, we had a series of scans. Firstly, we were at the hospital where I had given birth to my daughter, then we were sent to a more specialised unit at another hospital, who were more experienced in difficult pregnancies. I had a lengthy scan appointment and was given my options. I was told that I could continue with my pregnancy, but that my babies were unlikely to survive to full term. I was told that if I did reach full term, my babies would most likely be stillborn. The last option was that my babies may be born alive at full term, but that the probability of surviving longer than a day was extremely low. Every outcome was terrible.

How did you make the difficult decision to end your pregnancy?

I was torn. Should I let nature take its course? Should I hug them when they were born at full term? It was so awful. I remember the day we decided to end the pregnancy; I felt like I had given up on my babies. In the end, my husband and I made the choice to end the pregnancy while our babies were still alive, still together. So they had each other and they didn't know anything. I felt that, if they survived until full term and died after a day, they would feel pain. I didn't want them to know any pain and I wanted them to be together.

How have you coped with your decision, knowing this was the best thing for you and your babies?

With all the research I did and what we were told by the doctors who saw us, for my babies to survive for even a day was one in a million. This, in some way, made the decision easier. To know that they would never have survived, no matter what decision we had made at any stage in my pregnancy.

For a long time, I still felt like I had let my babies down. I kept thinking that miracles do happen. I feel like I don't have a right to talk about baby loss. I made a decision to end my pregnancy.

You do have a right. You lost your twins through no fault of anybody.

In many ways I was made to feel like I was doing the wrong thing. The medical care and aftercare made me feel as though I had no choices, that my mental health and my babies were not really considered.

How was your experience in the hospital?

As my twins were conjoined, I had to deliver in the hospital. I begged for an operation, I didn't want to deliver my babies naturally. I didn't think I could go into labour and go through that. I was told that, if I didn't give birth, that there was a chance my babies wouldn't come out in their full form, that parts of them may be left inside of me. I felt I had to accept what the hospital said. I was given medication to induce labour.

The nurses that saw me didn't know why I was there, my notes were either not correct, or they hadn't read them. As I lay on a bed in the hospital, I was congratulated by a nurse on my pregnancy. It was so traumatising. As my babies were going to die, I was allowed morphine, but I could still feel the contractions. I was in so much pain.

Before delivering my babies, I needed a wee. First I sat on a chair and that's when my babies came out. I laid back on the hospital bed, and my babies were still attached to me. It was over thirty minutes before anybody came back with a clamp for my umbilical cord. For half an hour I lay on my side, my babies with me on the bed. I felt I couldn't look at them. I just held my husband's hand, hoping it would all be over soon. I was asked by a nurse if this was my first baby. I was lying on a bed, my twins had clearly died, and I was asked this question. It was traumatising.

Alex, I'm so sorry you went through this.
The umbilical cord was finally clamped and cut, then the doctor I had seen when I was admitted came back. I asked to see my babies. I wanted to see my children. A friend's baby had been brought to her in a blanket when the baby died at five months, so I wanted the same for my babies. I asked to see them.

I was told my babies were in the bathroom. I asked to see them, but never thought what happened next was ever going to happen. A nurse brought out a bucket. My babies were in a bucket. I hoped they would have been cared for, cleaned, laid in a blanket, no matter how small they were. But they were in a bucket.

The nurse lifted the lid of the bucket, and there were my babies, covered in blood. I was so shocked. This was not how I wanted to see them. I was so nervous that I didn't have the courage to say anything, to say that they should have cared for my babies and not placed them in the bottom of a bucket.

The doctors were acting as though my babies were not important, so I didn't have the courage to ask questions. I felt silly. They were tiny little things, but they were my babies. I was grieving and then had to deal with a hospital experience that made me feel embarrassed to ask questions and ask to see my babies.

I went home from hospital the same day. I felt so guilty that they were alone. I wanted them to be wrapped up warm.

Did you find you were able to talk to friends and family about your experience?
Nobody really talked about what had happened. Everybody was quite closed off. I find the terminology difficult. Our experience is described as a termination, essentially an abortion. But to me it wasn't an abortion.

My babies were cremated three months after they died. I still don't know where they were during this time. We didn't get to have their ashes. Under a certain number of weeks in pregnancy loss, the hospital we were at cremated babies together, but we didn't get our twins' ashes. The ashes were scattered on our behalf. I know where the ashes are, I go there on Mother's Day.

Do you have any physical memories of your babies?
I asked to take a photo. It wasn't suggested to me, but I asked. I asked for the bucket they were in; if it was all I was going to be able to take away with me, I wanted something. The bucket was brought to me, dangling there as I looked inside like it was a goldfish bowl. My babies were covered in blood, the hospital kept the bucket at arm's length from me. The photo isn't beautiful. I wish I had a photograph of them, of me holding them in a blanket. I wish I had been told it was possible for me to take a photograph with them. I have a small blanket too. I was only given one, which was upsetting. I had two babies. My daughter has this blanket in her room, she uses it to cover a dolly that's the same size as my babies were when they died. I always think about my twins when I see the blanket.

How did the experience of losing your twins change you and how you view life now?
I had never really known loss like that before, something so lonely and so invasive. It hit me hard, but it also made me much more empathetic to so many others' pregnancy loss and fertility stories. I don't feel uncomfortable discussing it with a friend, or anyone really. Before I would probably have been scared to bring up the topic. I hope my openness can help others.

I asked Gubby Ayida, Consultant Obstetrician and Gynae-cologist MA FRCOG DM (Oxon), why she feels so many of us question our role in the loss of our pregnancy.

There can be a level of guilt associated with loss. Should I have taken time off of work? Should I have rested more? Was I travelling too much? I often explain that whatever the mother did, thousands of mothers have done this before them, that what they did wasn't the cause of their loss. Many mothers blame themselves for pregnancy loss. I always say to write down all the questions that come to mind, so you can ask these questions when we meet. This can help to dismiss some of the unhelpful thoughts that a mother has concerning the loss of her baby. It can help with the 'what if' and 'was it because' that go around in the mother's mind in the middle of the night. By answering these questions, I can give parents the assurance that it was not because of such and such that your baby died. By asking questions, you can demystify women's assumptions and put those nagging concerns to bed.

Weeks later, my weakened cervix was recorded as the reason my son had been born too early. Only then was my mind able to release the other possible scenarios of how I could have directly contributed to my son's death. This is not to say I completely let myself off the hook, as, on discovering my cervix was the cause, I then began to blame myself for not thinking to have increased scans.

I was given an answer, but what of the parents who are left without any explanation of why they experienced a pregnancy loss? Therapist Claire Bidwell Smith suggests why we often blame ourselves, and how we might navigate not knowing the reason we experienced our pregnancy loss:

> It's an existential crisis really. It touches on everything. You can wonder about every single thing you have ever done, you can wonder about your ancestry, you can question your faith. It's so enormous. It eventually comes down to learning how to sit with uncertainty, sit with not-knowing. That becomes the only place you can go to eventually, which is a very Buddhist way of being. Before you can go to that place, you sort through everything you can possibly sort through, and it's a very intense process. This is something people misunderstand with this kind of loss – it's very much with child loss as well – they can be similar and have an overlap. Parents wrack themselves with what did I do, where did this come from? They're going back, reviewing life choices, everything. Your mind will go everywhere trying to find a reason, until it settles in a place where you accept you cannot know the answer. Then it becomes how do you sit with not-knowing? Ultimately, this can lead to really beautiful places. It can lead to a spiritual awakening, a relationship with religion or spirit, or something bigger than ourselves, which I think is a really important part of the grief process.
>
> Self-compassion and self-forgiveness are at the root of all the work I do. I don't know why we are so hard on ourselves when we are going through something difficult. To have compassion with yourself, to forgive yourself for whatever you think you did, is one of the most difficult things, but it's so important.

Reasons for pregnancy loss

Sometimes there is no single, discernible reason for pregnancy loss. When I experienced my loss at five months, I urgently needed answers as to why I had lost my baby. Without the knowledge I have now, my mind created ways in which I could have caused the loss of my pregnancy. I laid blame on myself and assumed I was personally responsible. Hours of internet searching each day gave varying information as to why it may have happened. Mostly, the internet searches were confusing, overwhelming and unable to help me identify the cause. Only weeks after I had lost my son, when I met with an obstetrician, was I able to understand the reason for his death.

Only a medical professional can confirm the reason for a pregnancy loss, although in many cases a reason cannot be given, such are the varying possibilities and circumstances. This information will not be able to confirm the reasons for your own personal loss, but may help you to gain a better understanding of why pregnancies can end prematurely.

Main forms of pregnancy loss

Anembryonic – Anembryonic loss happens early in pregnancy and is one of the most common causes of early loss. During an ultrasound scan, a pregnancy sac will show no embryo. It is thought that either an embryo never grew at all or the pregnancy sac once contained an embryo, but the embryo did not grow past a certain stage.

47

Chemical – A chemical pregnancy occurs when a fertilised egg doesn't fully implant in the uterus. This form of pregnancy loss is most common within the first month. Due to the higher hCG levels in your body during this time, you will see a positive chemical result on a pregnancy test, but you may have already lost your pregnancy.

Ectopic – An ectopic pregnancy occurs when a fertilised egg implants and grows outside the main cavity of the uterus. Most often, an ectopic pregnancy occurs in a fallopian tube, although the embryo can begin to grow in other areas, such as an ovary, abdominal cavity, or the cervix. It can be life-threatening for an embryo to continue to grow in these locations, if left untreated.

Threatened – Vaginal bleeding and/or stomach cramps often happen ahead of a doctor confirming a threatened pregnancy loss. It is usual that the mother will have a scan, which most often shows that everything is in place as it should be. The mother may be advised to have more regular scans, but vaginal bleeding is common in pregnancy and blood spotting is not always a cause of huge concern for most doctors. The appearance of blood does not always lead to the loss of a baby, although it is advisable to see a doctor immediately if blood loss is combined with abdominal pains.

Inevitable – Often arising as a later stage of threatened miscarriages, inevitable loss generally means that heavy blood loss and abdominal pains are combined with the opening of the mother's cervix. Once the cervix has opened, the natural course for the baby is to be birthed by the mother.

Whether the baby can be saved will depend on the month and circumstances of the pregnancy.

Missed – When an embryo/fetus dies in the uterus without you having any serious symptoms that follow, you will be told you have experienced a missed miscarriage. You may have experienced blood spotting or mild cramps, which may not lead you, or your doctor, to assume you have lost your pregnancy. A later routine scan will then show that you have experienced a missed pregnancy loss.

Incomplete – If there is remaining pregnancy-related tissue within the uterus following pregnancy loss, a hospital may suggest expectant, medical or surgical management, depending on how far along in the pregnancy you are, or how much tissue is left behind. The surgical procedure is preferred if there is heavy bleeding or concerns about infection. The surgical procedure is called a D&C (dilation and curettage) or ERPC (evacuation of retained products – a term many of us do not appreciate and one that is thankfully being phased out of medical terminology), where the cervix is dilated to allow entry into the uterus, then the remaining tissue can either be removed via suction or by scraping away from the uterus.

Molar – A molar pregnancy (also known as hydatidiform mole) is caused by the unusual growth of trophoblasts, the cells that would develop into a placenta, and occurs when there are irregularities in fertilisation. A complete molar pregnancy occurs when an empty egg from the mother is fertilised with sperm and forms no fetal tissue. An ultrasound scan will likely show signs of swelling and the formation of fluid-filled cysts. A partial molar pregnancy occurs when two sperm fertilise an egg. In this instance, there are usually early signs of a fetus, but there is too much genetic material and so the fetus does not develop into a baby..

Recurrent – Recurrent pregnancy loss is thought to affect 1% of women. Presently, three or more consecutive pregnancy losses are defined as recurrent. It is often suggested that medical advice is sought following several consecutive losses, as there could be an identifiable medical factor that is contributing to the losses. There are questions as to whether women should wait for three pregnancy losses before being tested (UK standard), as it could be that an earlier diagnosis of possible issues could prevent losses from happening in the first instance.

I spoke to author Charlotte Sinclair on recurrent pregnancy loss, further medical complications and how she took back control of her fertility narrative.

I first discovered I was going to have difficulties getting pregnant aged thirty-two, when a test showed I had a very high egg reserve due to PCOS. My husband and I started trying for a baby naturally, but were unsuccessful, and eventually we were diagnosed with unexplained infertility. We decided to try IVF and, on the first cycle, I became pregnant with my son. The pregnancy was straightforward, so I had no reason to believe it wouldn't be as easy again in the future.

When my son was two, we did another round of IVF. Again it worked first time. At every stage of the IVF I was constantly monitored and scanned and everything was on track. Then, at my thirteen-week scan, there was a pause. The sonographer went back and forth with the wand, and in that pause the oxygen was sucked out of the room. She cleared her throat and asked me whether it had been a 'normal pregnancy' and I knew.

How did you navigate the following days after being told of your loss?
The shock was brutal. I was told to come back the next day to figure out next steps. I walked out of the hospital in a daze. At home I lay down on my bed and just roared into my pillow. The day before we had received the results of the Harmony Test; everything was perfect, I had been pregnant with another boy.

The next morning, we went to the early pregnancy unit. It felt so insensitive to be placed in a waiting room with half a dozen pregnant women. I sat there radiating ill-will towards them: why were their babies alive and ours wasn't? The consultant gave us our options: take a pill and let the pregnancy pass naturally or have a D&C operation to remove it. I decided I wanted to have a D&C. I respect anyone who chooses to do it the other way, but we were into the second trimester and I couldn't get my head around the bleeding.

Were you seen immediately, or did you have to return some days later?

I had to wait another five days before I got an appointment to have the surgery; time crawled. I felt like my body had betrayed me, that it was punishing me for going into this too blithely. Returning to hospital was a process of re-traumatisation, constantly having to tell my story to new people. When I burst into tears having the canula fitted into my hand, the nurse asked me why I was crying. The operation was pushed back as other cases took priority until eventually I was forced to stay overnight. On my way to surgery the following morning, I was asked to take a pillow to theatre. I remember holding it to my stomach as I walked through the hospital corridors as if it might protect my baby from what was about to happen.

After the operation I felt completely empty, as if everything had been taken from me. Not just my pregnancy but my trust in myself, in the idea of being able to have future children. A few nights afterwards there was the most extraordinary thunder storm, lightning cracking every few minutes, the whole sky in torment. I remember standing in front of the window and thinking, yes, this is exactly how this feels.

When did you choose to explore IVF again?

Seven months later we did IVF with one of the frozen embryos we had from our initial round. I got pregnant, but it was a very different feeling. Since they had never discovered what had happened with the first miscarriage, there was no reason to my mind that it wouldn't happen again.

Again we went for a scan at thirteen weeks. As we arrived at the hospital I mentioned my misgivings to my husband but he reassured me that everything would be all right. The sonographer began moving the wand over my stomach and within seconds there was the same drop in oxygen. We were dispatched to the early pregnancy unit where I had another scan. This new sonographer spoke softly but directly and not once did they squirm under the awkwardness of the moment. You remember the awful people in these situations but the people who treat you beautifully are equally indelible. 'No heartbeat,' she said. 'The fetus is completely normal.'

I was rattling with sadness afterwards, but I was also furious and the anger was incredibly sustaining. Surely the IVF clinic had missed something? The fact I had lost both pregnancies at the same time, that I had given up the progesterone injections and blood thinners at week twelve and then a week later suffered another loss: there had to be a connection. I know correlation does not mean causation, but *surely* there was something there.

How did you move through the experience of your second loss?
I chose to have another D&C, but, a week after the surgery, I began to get back pain. I was working on my

computer at a café when I looked down and saw my left leg was swollen. I knew that deep-vein thrombosis was a possible outcome of surgery, so I went straight to A&E. I was a mess, the receptionist had to tell me to stop crying so he could understand me. It just felt more than I could handle. By the following morning I was back on the ward, and about to undergo a different kind of extraction, this time for a thrombosis deep in my abdomen. It had been caused by the surgery but also a pre-existing genetic condition of which I'd been unaware. I had been growing a baby, but I had also been growing a clot – which, with brutal irony, they had to diagnose via an ultrasound scan on my stomach. I was told the DVT was a life-threatening event and I would have to have emergency surgery. The upside to this sudden, surreal crisis was that the sadness I had felt just a few hours ago had been eclipsed. The operation was a success, but I was put on blood thinners and told under no circumstances to get pregnant for at least a year. At this point I just laughed. They tested me for every blood disorder, but everything came back negative.

In waiting a year, did this change the way you approached IVF and the narrative surrounding your fertility?
I knew that if I could get pregnant before, I could get pregnant again. At the end of the year we went back to the IVF clinic, but this time I took control of the conversation, asking for more progesterone support

and blood thinners throughout. Pregnancy loss happens *to* you, IVF happens *to* you, but if you can claw back some modicum of control, it's a chance to regain your autonomy. The IVF worked, we got pregnant, but it wasn't a safe place. I had to steel myself for each scan, explaining carefully what I wanted to happen – the heartbeat confirmed within the first few seconds, please.

There were days when I was convinced the baby I was carrying was dead. Right up to the day he was born I thought something would happen for us to lose him. Infertility and pregnancy loss makes you understand that the process of getting pregnant and, crucially, getting an actual baby to show for it at the end, can be outrageously cruel. I'm always looking for the cloud in the silver lining. Sometimes you anticipate the worst and the worst *does* happen. But the opposite can also be true. I know I have pockets of darkness in me that didn't exist before. But maybe those hollows hold the space where those babies once were. I hate thinking about what the experience taught me because why should these little beings be saddled with providing life lessons? I'd rather be ignorant and have managed to keep them alive. It's just something to be got through, while keeping your sanity and relationship and life intact, and out to the other side, whatever the other side looks like.

Septic – Following a pregnancy loss, such as missed or incomplete, the tissue will have been present for a prolonged period and thus becomes infected. This can cause an internal infection, which can spread into the blood. The loss will be described as 'septic'. The infection is usually contained in the uterus but can spread if untreated. In more severe cases, the infection can result in secondary infertility.

Sporadic – Also referred to as a spontaneous pregnancy loss, this form of loss often happens due to unpreventable chromosomal irregularities. In many cases of sporadic loss, a new embryo will have more or fewer than the twenty-three chromosome pairs it is meant to have to be able to grow healthily. In fewer cases, sporadic loss can be caused by the mother contracting a severe infection.

Termination for Medical Reasons (TFMR) – I don't love the word termination when it relates to pregnancy loss, but, for medical accuracy, I will continue to use it here. Termination for Medical Reasons is the assisted end of a pregnancy when it has been confirmed by a doctor that the baby has severe irregularities concerning their genetic or physical body condition. These irregularities mean the baby may not survive outside of the uterus, or will need a lot of supportive care and may result in a very poor quality of life for the baby. When being told of a baby's condition, it will be the choice of the parents, with guidance from medical professionals, whether they choose to end the pregnancy.

Most common causes of pregnancy loss

The information within this section is limited to the most common causes of pregnancy loss, but by no means covers all causes. It is always advisable to speak to a doctor to get detailed information on any causes that may lead to pregnancy loss.

Antiphospholipid syndrome (APS) – Antiphospholipid syndrome is an irregularity in your immune system that increases the risk of blood clots and often leads to recurrent pregnancy loss. APS prevents embryo implantation and growth in the uterus. APS is sometimes referred to as Hughes syndrome. Daily doses of aspirin or heparin, or a combination of both, are the most effective medications used for those with APS during their pregnancy to prevent loss.

I spoke to Simi Lindgren, founder of beauty site YUTY.me, about her multiple pregnancy losses and how a diagnosis of APS led to a longed-for baby.

I became pregnant with my first son with relative ease. Because of this, I assumed that would be the case with a second pregnancy. In a way, it was. It was with relative ease that I became pregnant on four separate occasions, although I experienced pregnancy loss on three of those occasions. During a total of nine months in one year, I was pregnant three separate times. Through that year, I did mother my babies for a time, if only for a trimester with each.

How did you navigate the experience of these losses happening in such a short space of time?
I entered a new year with a toddler and a growing bump. Although I knew it might be challenging, there was no apprehension, no fear. All I could think about were the two little boys I now knew were in my belly and the one outside. Some weeks into my pregnancy, I began to bleed. I had bled in my first pregnancy from about thirty weeks, but this time it felt far too early. I remember sitting with my sister in the hospital soon after the bleeding had begun. She told me everything was going to be okay, but I knew that it wasn't. The scan confirmed my worst fears. Silence and more blood. It was over.

Did you want to start trying again immediately after your loss?
One morning soon after my loss, I received an email update about my current stage in pregnancy. I hadn't unsubscribed from the pregnancy site. I couldn't breathe. My pregnancy was over, but, as I continued to stare at the email, I thought that, if I could get back there, if I were pregnant again, then I would feel whole. The shock of reading that email dissipated into hope.

I was anxious to get home, have the work day be done so my husband and I could start trying again. I was still bleeding from my loss, the pregnancy test showing as positive while my hCG levels were still high. We would have to wait.

Were you able to conceive soon after your loss, as you had hoped?
Yes. I told myself that nothing could go wrong with this pregnancy. I just needed to keep healthy, stress free and positive. I was anxious and completely neglected to acknowledge that my fear was being driven by the loss I had experienced only a few weeks earlier.

At eight weeks, I began to bleed again. I had bled in the later stages of my pregnancy with my son, but as with my first loss, this felt too early. This time I wasn't overcome with grief, I was confused. I had done absolutely everything right from the start. I returned to seeking answers on the internet, and there, in the dead of night, I read how breastfeeding could trigger a drop in progesterone. I inaccurately deduced that breastfeeding had caused the loss of my pregnancies. I promptly stopped breastfeeding. Along with breastfeeding, I found other unproven reasons why I had lost my pregnancies.

How did you process your losses?
Having back-to-back losses left me mentally and physically exhausted. I had hidden my feelings deep

inside, and been secretly tracking the progress of the pregnancies I had lost. I sat on my bed surrounded by pregnancy tests that I had taken, labelled with the due dates. I knew at that point I had to come to terms with the losses, and made the decision to mourn. I needed to take care of myself, not only for me, but for my son, my husband and those close to me. I had gone beyond losing pregnancies, I had lost myself.

You experienced a third loss. How did this loss compound all the emotions you had faced to that point?
After being just a few days late for my period, I had taken a pregnancy test, and it was positive. Only, after six weeks, I experienced a chemical pregnancy loss. After this third loss, I resigned myself to the idea that I just lose babies, that my body just wasn't going to be able to hold another pregnancy. I couldn't face the emotional rollercoaster any more, so I stopped trying. I had lost all hope. I wanted a child, but it wasn't happening.

Was there a point where you consulted an obstetrician about the possible reason for your losses?
After many tests, the reason for the losses was made clear. I was diagnosed with Antiphospholipid Syndrome (APS), an autoimmune disease that causes the blood to clot too quickly. I found it hard to process that APS is completely treatable with blood-thinning medication. Had I known, I would likely never have

experienced my losses, but until something happens, why would any of us think we would need to be tested for these conditions?

Some months after my third loss, I had returned to the hospital armed with my research on APS. I wasn't expecting to learn something else that day in the clinic. I was pregnant. I cried for the first time in a really long time. I had been pregnant three times. I had lost three times. I was pretty certain that I had been through enough. My weakened and shorter cervix would most likely need stitches, and I would need blood thinners throughout my pregnancy, but we were going to have our longed-for baby, a sibling for our son. In spring of the next year, our daughter arrived into the world.

Chromosomal irregularities – During fertilisation, the sperm and egg each bring twenty-three chromosomes together to create matched pairs. This is a complex process, and a minor irregularity can result in a genetic or chromosomal abnormality. While some chromosomal irregularities are compatible with life, other chromosomal disorders are not, in which case a pregnancy loss is likely to happen.

Congenital anomalies – Neural tube irregularities and heart defects are the most widely recognised congenital anomalies. These sometimes fatal diagnoses can be inherited, so a mother with a family history of any previous congenital anomalies may be advised to have additional scans and testing in a new pregnancy. An unborn baby who has a congenital anomaly may also have been affected by other factors, such as the mother experiencing a severe infection.

I spoke to lawyer Anna Walker about the grief of losing her son at full term to a condition she is certain could have been diagnosed with more thorough testing early in her pregnancy.

At my twenty-week scan, the sonographer explained they had noticed Choroid Plexus cysts, which are a marker for Edward's Syndrome. We were referred to see a consultant, but after another scan, the cysts didn't show and therefore he didn't feel there was anything to worry about. Instinctively I felt something was wrong, but as our baby was growing well, I chose to listen to the specialists and didn't go any further with additional tests. Hindsight is an amazing thing.

Did your pregnancy continue without further concern?
Yes, there was no reason to think anything would go wrong. Then, one morning, I remember not feeling great. My son, who was four at the time, had a cold and was lying on the bed next to me. I told my husband I had a feeling I was going into labour and asked him to blow up the birthing pool in our home. As my son was unwell, he had fallen into a deep sleep and,

as soon as I was sure he was asleep, I went into labour. My body had somehow waited until I knew he was sleeping.

My husband called our midwife. She was still on her way when I gave birth on our bed. My son, Jasper, arrived very quickly. As Jasper was born, my husband looked at him, then me, and I knew something was wrong. Our front door was locked, and I could hear the midwife knocking. My husband let her in and brought her up to our bedroom. I was holding Jasper in my arms when she arrived. She put a blanket around me, as I was shivering, and gently led me to the bed. I repeated the words 'I'm sorry' over and over again. Looking at him, I feel Jasper had been dead for a day or two before he was born, his colour wasn't that of a newborn. He looked just like my older son, which I found very difficult.

Through your shock, do you remember what happened after you had given birth?
A second midwife arrived and helped me into the bathroom. Soon after, paramedics arrived, and they confirmed Jasper was stillborn. The paramedics needed to check both of us were okay. They left soon after they were sure I didn't need to be admitted to hospital.

The midwives spent a long time trying to get the placenta out. Because Jasper hadn't been well, my placenta wasn't healthy at this time either. Delivering the placenta was one of the hardest things I have ever done. My midwives were determined that they would get every bit out so that I didn't have to attend the maternity ward at the hospital.

I asked if my baby died because of something I had done. The midwives told me I had kept him alive, that the factors that caused his death had nothing to do with how I had been as his mother. The midwives opened Jasper's clenched fists and showed me his hands, which were not how I would have expected them to be. Jasper had no obvious disabilities, which is why consultants hadn't been concerned through my pregnancy.

Did you spend time with Jasper at home after his birth?
The midwives wrapped him up and encouraged me to hold him. I had all the same feelings I had as with my first son's birth. All this love for him. I was so proud of him, I wanted to show him off. He was wrapped in his 'going out' blanket.

Some hours after Jasper had been born, the midwives asked if I wanted to go to hospital. I knew I would be taken to the labour ward. I didn't want to be there, I didn't want to be put through anything else. It was much later when one of the midwives took Jasper to hospital. He left in his 'going out' blanket, which was monumentally important to me, that he had left the house in the right clothing. I couldn't control anything else, but I could control that.

How did you get through the first days after Jasper died?
The day after he died, two police officers arrived at our door. We didn't know their reasons, until they explained they had come to interview us about the circumstances of our baby's death. As we were alone, without a medical professional in attendance at the exact time Jasper was born, we were under suspicion of causing the death of our baby.

My husband and I had to be interviewed separately, to be sure our stories matched. It was harrowing to be questioned on the reasons behind our baby's death, to be a suspect until proven innocent. My husband was interviewed in Jasper's nursery, where our baby was laid out hours before. I was taken to another room in our house. We called our midwife to have some support, to have a witness to what was happening. The police were both men, which somehow made the situation worse. They were lacking a level of compassion. We later found out being interviewed by the police is common practice in the UK if you give birth to a still-born alone, without a medic with you.

Later that day, I called the hospital to make sure Jasper had a teddy with him. I needed him to not be alone. I asked the hospital chaplain to see him for me; it was all that mattered, I had to have him blessed and for him to have his teddy. Knowing my baby was alone, in a cold room, was the hardest part for me. I struggled the most with this part. With my baby leaving, and never coming back.

> *Were you given the reason for Jasper's death?*
> Eventually, yes. We finally got a copy of Jasper's post-mortem results. It was confirmed that there had been chromosomal irregularities, that Jasper had Edward's Syndrome. I was angry that we had been advised against a Harmony Test and that we hadn't been sent for more tests after the cysts had initially shown up on the first scan. We booked an appointment with a leading consultant in London, where we were told that I should never have been advised to carry Jasper to full term and that his condition was also dangerous to my health. It was traumatic to hear. In telling my story, I hope this will allow for others to know they must ask questions, they must listen to their instincts when they suspect something isn't right.

Infections – It is not uncommon to get an infection during pregnancy; a common cold or urinary tract infection (UTI), for example. For more severe or longer-lasting infections, with early detection and medication, in most cases there will be no effect on the fetus or baby. Infections that can lead to pregnancy loss and/or congenital anomalies include rubella, malaria, cytomegalovirus, parvo virus and severe genital herpes. There are also bacterial infections that can lead to pregnancy loss, such as listeria, gonorrhea, syphilis, chlamydia and salmonella.

Polycystic Ovary Syndrome (PCOS) – Along with affecting fertility, Polycystic Ovary Syndrome can cause recurrent

66

pregnancy loss due to the hormonal imbalance the condition creates. It is estimated that women with PCOS are three times more likely to experience pregnancy loss. The most usual causes of PCOS-related pregnancy loss are elevated levels of insulin in the blood, raised LH levels that can cause irregular follicle development and increased androgen levels.

Weakened cervix – If your cervix is naturally weak, has been affected by a previous birth, or medical procedure, you may not be aware prior to a pregnancy loss. Around the time of the second trimester, your baby will be heavier and therefore more likely to push down on a weakened cervix that cannot hold the baby's weight, leading to the possibility of a premature birth. Blood spotting, backache and abdominal cramps are all signs of a threatened pregnancy loss. When a cervix is shown to have irregularities via a scan, a doctor will most likely suggest having a cervical cerclage fitted. A cervical cerclage is a procedure that use sutures or synthetic tape to reinforce the cervix during pregnancy, minimising the risk of losing a baby.

TWO

What Now?

Navigating life soon after pregnancy loss

Your experience will likely have similarities to others who have experienced pregnancy loss, but everyone will have their own journey and ways they will cope with the trauma. I had to live through a period of overwhelming grief in my own way.

When you are carrying a life inside of you, there is a connection so great that it is almost impossible to describe. Whether you choose to call an early pregnancy a fetus, a baby, or any other word, you know your body is carrying the possibility of a future baby. Unlike the death of a friend or family member, nobody else is able to fully understand. As much as you try to describe your pain, as I did, I believe it is impossible to convey just how losing a baby feels to someone who hasn't experienced it. There is something about having a life inside of you die that there are just not enough, or the right, words for.

Some parents get to hold their baby who died. Many parents do not have this experience. The grief of an early pregnancy loss and a late pregnancy loss are no less valid, but in many ways they are very different. The levels of grief cannot be pitted against one another. Due to varying circumstances, one cannot be deemed worse than the other, but there are differences.

It is a common assumption that an early loss cannot possibly be as traumatic as a later loss. We can never know this, as we cannot feel the pain of the parents. There are so many circumstances that I explore in this book, but to put this particular view into context, I will use my own experience and that of a friend to explain just why we cannot assume anything when it comes to the effects of pregnancy loss.

When Axel died in 2017, I had an almost six-year-old son at home, Astie. This didn't lessen my pain, but it did force me to get up, leave the house and try to be the best mother I could be at that time. I had experienced years of unexplained infertility, but had become pregnant after my first round of IVF. I hadn't known the effects of a lengthy labour and emergency caesarean section with my first pregnancy would result in a weakened cervix. My baby died after my weakened cervix was no longer able to hold his weight, and my waters broke too early. I continued to try to conceive naturally, while also having another five rounds of IVF in between. Our daughter, Audrey, was born as a result of our sixth round of IVF in 2019. There are many negatives, but looking at the positives, I *did* get pregnant, IVF *did* work on two occasions, and I *did* discover the reason for Axel's death. Within an experience I wish had never happened, there are these positives.

In contrast, my friend has been trying to get pregnant for almost eight years. Medical examinations and many tests over six years (the time in which she has sought medical help) have given her at least some results. She knows the most likely reasons as to why she and her husband are unable to have a baby. Over the past eight years, they have experienced multiple pregnancy losses, all in the first trimester. There is nothing to say that she will not be able to carry a baby to full term, so they keep trying to conceive. Each time my friend loses a baby, the longing, hope and cumulative grief is accentuated. Their marriage has been tested at times, but the experience has also brought them closer together. My friend's depressive periods are longer and more intense with each loss. The realisation that a baby may not be a part of their future in the way they had planned becomes more apparent as each year passes. Her hope vacillates depending on how she is able to look at her future.

If we are looking at the above based purely on the facts of bringing a child, or children, into the world, then it is apparent just how different the stories are. It is clear that we cannot view one story as worse than the other. There is no less empathy to be placed on my friend's story than mine. The stories are different, but are no less painful.

Your partner and pregnancy loss

Each person has their own timeline of grief. While I was in the deepest stage of my own grief, it appeared to me as though my husband's emotional state was lifting considerably. I asked him if he was beginning to recover, at which point he replied that he was. I was so angry with him. I questioned how he could be feeling as though life was worth living. I accused him of forgetting our son. My husband and I grew very close through our shared grief, but this was the one period that temporarily divided us. I wanted him to be hurting just as much as I was. When it appeared as though he was rising out of the darkest times, I became resentful. But another person cannot experience our grief for us, with us, or because of us.

In the first months of my grief, I don't recall thinking of anything other than myself, my baby and, as much as I could, my then five-year-old son. I don't remember asking my husband how he felt, or if he needed my support during that time. I hope I did, even though I could barely support myself emotionally. Although my husband and I have had conversations about the night Axel died and the months that followed, I have often wondered how he really felt about that time. I have been apprehensive to ask him, fearing he may say he remembers that period very differently to me. I want our memories of Axel to align with each other, as if that time was a story we told together. I have an almost dreamlike vision of those months now, choosing to soften the memories of the pain and trauma. My mind has chosen to softly coat my memory of the summer of 2017, making Axel's death far more gentle than I know it was in reality. It is a way to lessen the trauma and remember my baby fondly, rather than repeatedly visualising the traumatic night he died and the months of grief that followed.

As I began to speak to parents who had lived through pregnancy loss for this book, I wanted to know more about my husband's journey through his own grief. I realised the time had come to ask him how he really felt. Instead of asking him questions, as I had with other contributors, I asked him to write a piece for my book.

My husband, Nils Andén

The night Axel passed is no longer constantly on my mind and hasn't been for some time, although it was for a number of years. Pippa and I discuss on occasion how everything unfolded and our memories of that fateful night. It is not strange how strongly etched those hours are into our minds, but, even so, my perspective is different than my wife's. We remember different things of that time. I find that it helps me, both in understanding and accepting, to talk through what happened on a recurring basis. Not as a means to wallow in sorrow, but rather to reinforce our healing path, a way to de-dramatise something very tragic.

The memory that will stay with me for the rest of my life are the minutes after we delivered Axel on the bathroom floor. I had a lady from the emergency services on the speaker phone and she instructed me to give mouth-to-mouth to this tiny human being that had just emerged. Trying to breathe life through his tiny mouth, while I could see him unsuccessfully trying to take a breath into his unformed lungs was truly heart breaking. I realised it was a futile effort, because poor Axel's chest didn't move as I continued mouth-to-mouth. In hindsight, I see it almost as a beautiful moment, and I like to think that, as he passed, he was as close to us as he could ever be and felt our love in those last moments.

Once the paramedics arrived, our son Astie woke up due to the commotion and I left Pippa and Axel to go and care for him. Pippa was led out to the ambulance, which subsequently disappeared without any notification. That was a very scary moment, as I was standing alone with my son trying to figure out where we should go and assumed they had left due to concerns for my wife. I managed to get Astie into the car and started calling around to hospitals without any luck. I finally decided to drive to the hospital where we had planned to deliver the baby. Luckily that was where the ambulance had gone, and my relief was palpable once we managed to get to Pippa in the A&E department.

The hours that followed were both incredibly sad but also cathartic. Once we were alone in a room, with the adrenaline disappearing, we began to realise what had happened. This is when the overwhelming sadness started to set in. Once the midwife brought Axel in, all we could do was just sit with him and hold his tiny hands and look at his perfect little face. He looked peaceful. Having him with us in that time really helped me, in a way, in starting to heal. I would have regretted not being able to have him next to us and trying to make him feel he was part of our family. It also brought home the reality of the situation. Giving him back to the midwife was one of the hardest things I have ever done. I wanted to stay in that room for ever, with Axel by our side. Leaving the room was very hard, because outside was a life that hadn't stopped. My son still had to be picked up from nursery, dinner had to be organised. I also had to start informing friends and family of what had happened. How can you effectively convey something so practical, yet so emotional? It was also abundantly clear that not everyone understands the trauma that comes with a tragedy like this, which does not make sharing easier.

The following weeks are still a blur to me, it felt like we had gone into isolation. I think we did what we could to stay afloat, but there was such a sense of lethargy. Having a funeral for Axel stands out to me, though I am aware not everyone chooses this route, but I felt it was a beautiful event that really provided some further help in me reaching closure.

One of the challenges for me in the time that followed was the fact that we were coming to terms with what had happened at a different rate. It is natural in any journey through grief, but is, of course, further corroborated by the fact that I had just the emotional scaring, whereas Pippa had to deal with both the emotional and physical impact. This is something that can be difficult to articulate and, as time moved on, I felt I was healing quicker than my wife, but how do you bring that up without feeling guilty? Everyone reacts differently when grief hits you, but I want to emphasise that presence is more important than anything else. Remember that even though the loss of a baby is something you both share, the experience is not the same. It can be very hard to step out of your own grief and be supportive, but, if anything, this is the time to do it. I am a very solution-oriented person, but at a time like this it is important to not look for ways to explain what happened, to not think about how we could avoid this happening again once we were ready to start trying again. It helps to process what happened and support your wife as she goes through the incredibly tough hormonal rollercoaster that follows any birth, and the subsequent navigation through the process of grief.

There is no silver lining to an event like this, but I feel Pippa and I came through this stronger as a couple. The fact that we managed to navigate the journey together and support each other as much as we could showed we could handle anything. There were, of course, bumps in the road, but I think they were mostly related to the fact that we were healing at a different rate. I was not always able to maintain the required patience in allowing Pippa to continue her processing when I wanted to move on. It helped that we had incredible friends around us, who supported us and were very understanding. That gave us a vent that was outside of our family unit and gave both of us an opportunity to continue our healing journey at our own pace. I feel very thankful and fortunate for this.

As a final thought, I want to say that losing a baby is not an experience that anyone should have to live through, but, if it happens, remember that you can get through it together, but it requires patience and understanding and there are amazing resources out there to help. Don't feel afraid to ask for help, but also allow each other the space and time to heal in whatever time is required.

I read my husband's words and realised I shouldn't have feared him saying them out loud. I knew he had begun to move forward in his grief sooner than I had, but it still stung a little to hear this as the truth. I wanted to hear that he had felt how I did through that time, but I understood that, by not carrying our son, he couldn't understand the physical longing and prolonged grief I carried with me. We worked through it together, which I am grateful for, and I am grateful for him.

With not being able to consider anybody other than myself in the immediate period of grief after losing Axel, I asked Consultant Obstetrician and Gynaecologist Gubby Ayida, MA FRCOG DM (Oxon), if there was an effective way for those supporting the grieving parents to initiate the conversation of loss with the partner.

Partners are grieving too, but often feel they have to be brave, to be seen to be the rock. There is that consideration, the treading on eggshells around the mother. But who is looking after them? They have lost all those dreams as well. Partners can often suffer in silence. It's making sure they also have an opportunity to talk about the loss. It can be wrongly assumed that, because the partner wasn't carrying the baby, they are not suffering greatly too.

It can be difficult for partners, as there can be a feeling of 'will we ever move on from this?' As they did not carry the baby, there is naturally no actual physical connection and often less of an emotional connection. They can often begin to move forward in their grief sooner than the mother.

We need to give partners an opening to talk. Just asking how they are, how has it been for them. Sometimes this is when the mother gets to hear how their partner feels for the first time. They often start with explaining all they are doing to look after the mother, but then we need to ask specifically – 'how are you?' As the partner starts talking, it can be a surprise, as it might be the first time they have been asked how they are themselves. Giving them the space to talk and explain their feelings is important, not only for them personally, but for how the couple cope with their grief together.

These words confirm what so many think, that there needs to be immediate communication with the partner to give them the opportunity to express their feelings following loss. There is kindness towards the partner, but, in most instances, more understanding of the partner's emotional needs would be a way to help them through their own initial stages of grief.

In the majority of cases, the partner will move through their grief sooner than the mother who carried the baby, and there needs to be greater understanding within the relationship of this too. I spoke to therapist Claire Bidwell Smith about the difference in how parents may grieve following pregnancy loss.

It's one of the toughest parts. You're going through it together, but for the woman carrying the baby, it was very different. It was her body, the baby was inside of her, it was happening to her. In pregnancy, the partner doesn't fully connect with the baby until it's there, so they often do move through the grief sooner. It makes the woman feel so alone and she can question whether she's grieving too long. Couples therapy can be incredibly helpful. It's so helpful to hear each other's experiences. It's often in therapy where they hear for the first time how the other is really feeling. They can be in very different places in their grief – one can be angry, while the other is in a place of total guilt – so for them to understand each other and make space for each other is so important. They have to get to know each other in a new way, with the addition of this kind of grief into their relationship. It's important to talk to each other, to understand where you are in the grief, to explain why it feels different to you in many ways. You can miss who the other used to be before the loss, this can be another form of grief that comes from pregnancy loss. The grief of who you were as a family, and how your future looked.

I spoke to Kate Bryan, author, television presenter and art curator, on how she navigated pregnancy loss with her husband and how an egg donor changed their life.

My husband and I got married young, I was twenty-five, he was twenty-four. Afterwards, we moved to Hong Kong. I think we were scared of being conventional, so thought if we moved away that would give us an adventurous life, which it did. At one point, we really thought we probably wouldn't have children. What was important, though, was that we genuinely knew we could have an amazing life without children.

I came off the pill while we were still expats in Hong Kong and it took me about a year to get any semblance of normal periods back. When I was twenty-nine, we moved back to London and decided this would be a good time to try to have a family if we wanted to. We were having plenty of sex, but it never occurred to me to ever take a pregnancy test. I wasn't having periods, so, in my naivety at that time, it didn't seem a possibility. But after I had been off the pill for a year and a half, my periods had returned and, as I wasn't getting pregnant, I began to do some research.

We went to the doctor, my husband did a sperm test, and it was found to have some issues. I felt for my husband so much. All I could think was that, as long as our marriage is fine, I don't care about children. He's my soulmate and I hated to see him feeling as though he had let me down.

Did you have any plan in mind of how to move forward with getting pregnant?
At this time, we were properly trying. Thankfully, although it sounds intense, I wasn't obsessing, it was more like a fun project.

We had further investigations, which revealed that there was also a problem my side. I had a very low egg count despite being so young still. It was quite traumatic being told that; it was one of the worst moments actually. The tables were then turned and, when my husband said he didn't care, that he only wanted us to be happily married, I believed him as I knew exactly what he meant.

It really felt like the clock was ticking. We did our first round of IVF, and we got just two eggs: one never made it to an embryo and the other was our first failed cycle. I hated the IVF process. One of the huge problems was that I didn't talk about it to anyone, it felt like a dirty secret. Things have changed now. Thankfully people talk more openly and mental-health issues are very much on the table.

At this time, did you have a clear idea of the next steps you wanted to take?
We were young and we didn't want the emotional drain to put a strain on our marriage. The doctors mentioned egg donors, but back then the success rates were very low. We just instinctively knew we should stop the ride and take a break. We had this reckless kind of freedom, so decided to move to Rome for a year.

When we were there we really made our peace with not having children. We moved back to London because I got my dream job in the art world. Then I got to the end of our first month living in London again and realised my period was late. Five years of not being on the pill, and finally I was pregnant. I couldn't believe it happened after making the decision to have a child-free life and getting my dream job. I remember it being like I was back when I was trying to get pregnant years ago, it all felt so furtive.

I had never been pregnant, so was nervous. I paid to have an early scan at almost seven weeks. The nurse who scanned me explained there wasn't a beating cell, which would later be considered the heartbeat.

It was early in my pregnancy, but she told me there were other irregularities and that, if I went back in a week, it was highly unlikely my pregnancy would have progressed. It was totally unexpected that we had got pregnant, but I was still really upset.

How did you navigate life soon after losing your pregnancy?
I had what's called a missed miscarriage. It was so painful and so devastating and I just curled up on the sofa in pain for a few days. It was so distressing. For the first time in my life I felt really sorry for myself. I didn't really let myself grieve, I think I was really tough on myself. I understand why I was doing that, it's a form of self-preservation, but I couldn't let myself acknowledge that this was a really painful thing that was happening to me. Less than a year later I got pregnant again, this time I didn't miscarry until nearly twelve weeks.

Was this loss more emotionally painful than with your first?
The first time I only really had a week to consider myself pregnant. The second time I had known I was pregnant for a few weeks, which is enough time to change your mind about your entire life. It was really hard to lose this pregnancy: it was a baby to me.

I remember going for a Christmas hike with my husband and breaking down climbing up a hill. We sat on a bench and I told him I couldn't continue with my life unless I knew we had given it a proper shot. That time I was really grieving, I was bereft, I wanted a baby.

What happened on that bench was so special. We told each other we would stay completely madly in love and we were going to give it a two-year time limit to have our baby. We were going to throw everything at it.

With your two-year limit, did you then consider doing another round of IVF?
We went back to the same clinic after a few years away. I was only thirty-five, but was told my eggs were the quality of someone more than ten years older. I just felt it was a very risky prospect to try to make them deliver me a healthy baby. We discussed our options and really looked into egg donation. Success rates were now much higher than when we had looked into it before. I also had friends, gay and straight, who had used donors and had so much respect and love for their journey.

We went to therapy, we were shown children's books of how to explain it to the child. I found it very moving, it was beautiful. Donors in the UK are doing full IVF, but don't do it for any other reason than altruism, they just get paid their expenses.

Before it wasn't so much the concept of it, it was the riskiness of it not working. Once I saw the improved success rates, and knowing I could physically get pregnant now, we decided to go ahead with an egg donor.

How was your experience of finding a donor?
We did more research and signed up to an egg bank where we could choose our donor. There were no

photographs, just descriptions, which included hair colour, eye colour, interests and education.

It made sense to try to find an egg match that was as close to me as possible, although, in hindsight, I wouldn't care less now. We acquired six eggs, and five defrosted successfully. Of the fertilised eggs, four became embryos.

What was the process of IVF with a donor egg?
It was very similar to IVF, you just don't do the egg harvesting and retrieval. You still take all the medication to prepare the uterus to improve your chances of the embryo latching. We did the embryo transfer, had a six-week scan and all looked fine. Shortly before going on holiday, I asked to have a seven-and-a-half-week scan just because I was nervous from my past experience. Sadly, we were told there was no longer a heartbeat. That was a world of pain. I had done the egg donor, so, in my mind it should have worked. My husband was amazing. He reminded me we were going to give it two years and we had to keep going.

How did you cope?
We went on holiday and I wept and wept and wept. I really broke down, but I came back fortified and ready to do it again. We had another frozen embryo transfer and my daughter was born the following year on July 4th.

Do you think about the egg donor?
When I was pregnant, I was just really grateful to the woman who had donated her eggs. I knew I was going to tell my daughter, I knew I wanted it to be part of her story. When my daughter is eighteen, if she chooses to, she can contact our egg donor in writing. In sixteen years, there's a possibility that we could meet our egg donor, which I would love, so I can thank her. She changed our life. That woman went through a lot of hormones to give this gift to us. She's not a part of our family, but, on a spiritual level, she's like a fairy godmother. Every now and again when I was pregnant, I wondered what I should say if people tell me my baby looks like me. And it's funny because people say that she does non-stop. I had done a lot of research through pregnancy on all aspects, and things kept coming up that comforted me. For the first months of pregnancy, she was entirely fed by me and they recently discovered that DNA would have been passed in the amniotic fluid. And it was always my water, my blood, my food, my exercise, my air, my thoughts, my heartbeat. An egg is one thing, and its miraculous, but I spent nine months making our baby. Even if you're not in the mix on a DNA level, you're so in the mix through nurture, through the way that the baby is. A parent teaches their baby to smile, how to walk, they mimic your gestures – you teach your baby everything. Even before she was born, she was just 100% our baby. When she arrived, my God, the love

was so supernatural. At the beginning I had hoped for some kind of neutrality, but now I have something so much better, something beyond neutrality. I have an extraordinary gratitude, which makes me feel like it's even better that I used a donor. It's an extra part of the love story I have. This was our way of having a baby, this is my angel, there was no other baby for us.

Knowing your baby has died during pregnancy, or that your baby will not survive the pregnancy for medical reasons

There is huge trauma in being told your baby has died, or that your baby will not survive the pregnancy. It is often the case that this news is completely unexpected. Although you understand that your baby has died, or will not survive the pregnancy, you are still having to prepare for the birth of a baby that you know you will not be taking home. To have to make certain decisions in addition to losing your baby can cause not only extreme distress, but guilt for making these impossible choices.

When your baby has died during pregnancy

If your baby has died inside of you, it may be days before you are given an appointment for a surgical procedure to take the baby or any remaining pregnancy-related tissue from you. If you choose to wait for your baby and/or the tissue to leave you naturally, you may be carrying your baby or remaining tissue for a longer period of time. Leaving hospital knowing your baby is no longer living inside of you can be extremely traumatising. Having care, support and people to talk to can help you to live through this experience.

When it has been confirmed that your baby has died during pregnancy, one option that doctors will present are pills to induce labour, which most commonly involves taking pessaries inserted into the vagina. There is a small chance of heavy bleeding, infection, and needing surgical management such as a D&C/ERPC at a later date if pregnancy tissue remains in the uterus. You will need to be mentally prepared to see your baby leave you, which can be deeply upsetting. You will also need to prepare for considerable blood loss and the likelihood of cramping and pain.

D&C (dilation and curettage) or ERPC (evacuation of retained products of conception – a term I don't love and one that is thankfully being phased out of medical terminology) or SMM (surgical management of miscarriage) will be suggested for a pregnancy loss within the first trimester, or early stages of the second trimester. A D&C involves a doctor inserting a speculum into the vagina, ensuring the cervix is carefully dilated and cleaned before using a medical instrument called a curette to take the baby and/or pregnancy tissue from within the uterus. In the case of having an ERPC or SMM, suction will be used to remove the baby and/or pregnancy tissue instead of a curette. The suction option is often preferred by doctors due to less risk of scarring and perforation of the uterus. The procedure can be done under local anaesthetic or with you asleep under general anaesthetic. Providing there are no complications, you will be able to return home the day of your procedure.

For later pregnancy losses, a medical management option with misoprostol is often preferred, due to the larger tissues that may remain inside the womb. The medication will cause the induction of uterine cramps to allow the baby and/or pregnancy-related tissue to leave the body. Surgical management or suction curettage is done if there is retained tissue within the womb. If pregnancy-related tissue still remains after both treatments, a repeat of either a medical or surgical procedure will be required.

Along with the medical and surgical options, there is the option to wait for a loss to leave you without assistance. This is called expectant management. In earlier stages of pregnancy loss, for a missed pregnancy loss or a confirmed loss, the baby and pregnancy tissue will likely leave your body between a few days or a few weeks. Depending on how many weeks pregnant you are, you may pass tissue that looks more like a fetus, or a small baby. For later-stage pregnancy loss, it is generally not advised to wait for labour to begin naturally. There is a high chance of significant blood loss and, with a demise in the condition of the baby who has passed away, this can put the mother at risk of medical complications. It is a consideration that in waiting for the pregnancy to leave you, a baby's condition will worsen in the womb. The worsening condition can affect the appearance of the baby, and in turn can be more traumatic for the parents.

Gubby Ayida, Consultant Obstetrician and Gynaecologist MA FRCOG DM (Oxon), gave further insight into what options parents may be presented with when their baby has died in the womb:

When a mother has to give birth to the baby after the baby has died in the womb, it is very sad. I will often tell my team (doctors and midwives), so all we can give is our kindness and care. Sometimes if a mother is much further on in a pregnancy, they are often given the choice of an epidural or a PCA for good pain relief. PCA is patient-controlled analgesia. You press a button every time you want a small amount of opiate pain relief. Labour can be a long process. Mothers tolerate labour because there is a gift at the end of it, a living baby at the end, which sadly is not the case in this situation.

I spoke to brand consultant Holly Scott Lidgett about her own experience of late-term pregnancy loss and the time she spent with her baby in hospital.

When did you first think there could be something wrong during your pregnancy?
I was over halfway through my pregnancy. I saw a little blood spotting, researched it and it seemed very common, so I didn't worry. Earlier that morning, my midwife had come round. My baby had been kicking so much and I had a pain in my side. My midwife used a doppler, did her checks and all seemed fine, so she left. I was working from home that day while also looking after my two-year-old son.

I remember I couldn't get my feet flat, it was the strangest thing, I was walking the entire time almost on my tiptoes. I put my son in his cot for his usual nap. I am unsure if it's a mother's instinct to carry on, but as soon as I put my son down to sleep, I felt an intense sensation rush through me. I couldn't reach my midwife on the phone, I couldn't sit down, I was pacing around my home. Out of pure physical need, I was squatting close to the floor, holding on to the arm of my sofa. It was an animalistic instinct to crouch, hold that position and bear down.

I called the hospital. It was a Friday, and I was told my pain was likely trapped wind and to come in on the Monday. I hadn't had a natural birth before, as my first son was born via caesarean section, so I didn't know that I was experiencing the onset of labour. I had an urge to push, and I could feel a pressure within my body that I needed to release. I sat on the toilet, and immediately saw blood.

Was it just you and your son at home at this time?
Yes. I reached my midwife on the phone and explained I was bleeding. I don't remember letting her in, but she was soon with me. I was panicking and asking her to listen for my baby's heartbeat. All I kept asking was whether my baby was alive. My midwife explained she couldn't find a heartbeat. I had called my mother to be with my son, then the ambulance arrived.

At the hospital I was taken straight to A&E, where I went into full labour. I was bleeding everywhere, on all fours, writhing on the bed, screaming. I have no idea how long I was there, it could have been an hour, it could have been four.

A calm doctor arrived. She put her hand on my thigh, explained that she was from the labour ward and that she was going to examine me. She told me she could see my baby, but that she didn't know if he was alive. It was then that she told me I was going to give birth to my baby. She promised she wouldn't let me give birth on the way to the labour ward, which was on the other side of the hospital.

Do you remember much of what happened that morning?
We arrived on the labour ward and I was taken straight to a room. The nurses around me removed the cot, the birthing ball, any reminder of a birth that would give me a living baby.

I was left with my midwife to give birth to my son. As soon as it was just me and my midwife in the room, my contractions stopped. I tried looking at pictures of my elder son, who was at home. It was his second birthday the next day, and I thought the emotion of seeing him might lead to my contractions returning. I was trying to push and nothing was happening.

I kept asking if my baby was alive. My midwife kept telling me that my baby was small and my contractions were strong, but I wanted to know if he was alive. I continued bleeding through the night, but my contractions didn't return. It got to the morning and I was very weak.

The doctors had changed shifts that morning, and someone I hadn't seen before came into my room. She had a portable scanning machine with her. She told me my baby was in my birth canal, that there was no heartbeat and I was going to need to push my baby out. I just couldn't believe this was happening.

One of my biggest fears in that moment was whether I was going to feel the arms and legs of my baby. I hadn't given birth vaginally before, and I was scared of how it would feel, how the baby would feel. The sound I made when my baby was born was primitive. Even though I knew the gender of my baby, I asked if he was a boy and ironically I kept asking if he was okay.

Did you spend time with your baby when he was born?
After my midwife took my baby from me, it could have been five minutes, an hour before I saw him again, I don't know. My baby was brought back to me wrapped in a blue blanket. I held him. His tiny arms were crossed on his chest. He was beautiful. I didn't think he looked anything other than my baby. I named him Fox, a name I had given him when I had found out I was having a boy. I spent hours holding him.

I had to go to surgery to remove my placenta. I felt tiredness like I had never felt before. I was numb, totally divorced from any emotion at this point. Whether it was the trauma, the drugs I had been given, I don't know, but I just didn't care. After the surgery, when I was back in a hospital room, I asked to see Fox again. I spent time with him, studying his face, just us together. I loved holding him.

On the third day, my mum came to the hospital to sit with me. I could tell she was in so much pain as a mother herself. It's hard for anyone to find the language, so my mum brushed and plaited my hair for me. It was the closest I had ever felt to her in my entire life. It was such a maternal thing to do. My mother had terminal cancer, and I remember this as one of the closest moments I ever had with her.

How do you see your experience, now there is the space of a few years since Fox died?
I still feel embarrassed about the sadness and trauma of losing him and whether I am justified. I still can't quite believe that I physically gave birth to my son, who had died. I look at his pictures once a year, on his birthday and I sometimes think about what our life would have been like had he made it. Thank goodness for him, I feel lucky that I had him for the time I did.

When your baby will not survive the pregnancy due to medical reasons

If you have made the decision to end your pregnancy for medical reasons (TFMR, as in Termination For Medical Reasons – as previously mentioned, I don't love the word termination, but for medical accuracy I will continue to use it here), the two most common options given at the hospital will be a medical or surgical procedure.

When it has been confirmed that your baby will not survive, you can have a procedure involving two doses of medication, this is most common if you are within the first nine weeks of your pregnancy. The first will stop the pregnancy hormone progesterone being produced in your body, meaning your pregnancy will not be able to continue. You will be asked to return to the hospital between twenty-four and forty-eight hours later, where you will take the second medication. This medication causes the uterus to contract and you will give birth.

I spoke with Creative Director Marina Guergova on ending her pregnancy at five months and how she honours the memory of her baby each day.

I had to end my second pregnancy at five months. When I went to the twenty-week scan, the obstetrician asked if I had lost any waters. He was scanning quietly, so the silence and the lack of the expected 'Oh, baby is moving around a lot, isn't it?' commentary made it obvious something was not going to plan. It was explained that there was no amniotic fluid around my baby. Then silence and no follow-up. I asked if it was serious, and the obstetrician replied that yes, it was. The way he said it will for ever remain imprinted in my memory. I was told that my baby hadn't developed her kidneys and bladder, this was why there was no amniotic fluid around her.

During the inevitable full-body cataclysm and tears, the obstetrician went on to explain that this was a very rare condition called Bilateral Renal Agenesis. It means that, as he put it, the 'make-kidneys-button wasn't switched on'. Sunny didn't have either of her kidneys and, as a result, no bladder either. Even if I had carried her to full term, with life support through my umbilical cord, she wouldn't have survived without those vital organs. Sunny would have been born still at birth, or, at best, she would have only lived for a few moments. This was a 1 in 4,000 condition.

Everything I thought I knew about the next day, week, month or year of my life flew out of the window and stuck its middle finger up on the way out. I was told that terminating as soon as possible was best, as I wouldn't want the pregnancy to progress any further. I was offered the first pill to begin the process that day, but I decided to spend one more day with her. Here she was, safely cocooned, perhaps not with the usual comfort of amniotic fluid, but still she was warm and safe. I spoke to her, hugged my small bump and tried to pass love through somehow, into her heart.

How did you navigate the next day, returning to the hospital to give birth to Sunny?
Taking the pills to bring on labour felt like I was taking poison. I cried a lot throughout that time. I knew it

was free fall from there. We were placed into what the hospital called the Butterfly Wing, saved for cases like ours. The name was delicate and thoughtful.

For my birth with Leo, Sunny's older brother, I didn't want my husband in the room. Birth to me is a very special time where my baby and I work together, alone. I imagine that, if I have my husband there, I wouldn't be able to let go and have tunnel vision. I'd be thinking if he's all right, what he's up to, where is he? I wouldn't be able to connect fully to my baby. It's very unusual not to want your partner there, but I know myself so well. I block everything out, even the midwives. I just do my thing and, for me, it works. I love labour. However, with Sunny I needed my husband there. I was scared and emotionally unprepared for something like this. I needed someone to hold me through this heartbreak, while it was happening.

When my contractions began, they were just as intense as my first birth. I had made a promise that I would give birth to her with love and so I whispered, 'I love you, I love you,' especially towards the end. The feeling of giving birth to her was sad. I cried in that wailing way that you hear in movies. It was pure heartbreak and deep, deep grief. She passed away in labour and was taken away without us seeing her, while I sat with my legs shaking on the bed.

Did you choose to spend time with Sunny that day?
I knew I wanted to see her and I am so glad that I did. The wonderful midwives had put on a little knitted hat and placed her so beautifully with a blanket in a Moses basket. A little lilac toy octopus lay beside her. She was tiny, perfectly formed, beautiful to me, and everything I could have hoped for. She looked so much like my son, Leo, when he was born. She looked so peaceful, happy and forgiving. I said 'I'm sorry' over and over again. My belly felt empty and useless without the usual reward of giving birth.

How did you tell your son, Leo, that his baby sister had died?
When I was little, my parents would hide the truth about people dying around me and I would find out later that they had died. They had kept it from me at the time, so as to not upset me. I felt so lied to and so left out. This feeling has for ever stayed with me and I remember how traumatised I was, so I knew that I would tell Leo the truth. I told him that Sunny was very unwell and that we had lost her. I told him that she was the brightest star in the sky and that she will always be there for us when we need her. I told him to never forget her and gave him the little toy octopus that had been lying next to Sunny. I told him, 'Her name is Sunny.' He cried and cuddled me and told me that it was going to be all right.

Are there ways in which you keep the memory of Sunny with you as a family?
Almost two years after Sunny died, I gave birth to my second son, Kristo. He is here because of Sunny. He is what people would refer to as an easy baby and I would completely agree. He is happy, he laughs a lot. Every morning we still try to say 'Good morning, Sunny. We love you. Have a nice day!' so as to honour her and never forget her. The little toy octopus lives by Leo's bed and she is always by his side. I am so glad that he knows about Sunny, and that Kristo will too.

If your pregnancy is at an earlier stage than approximately fourteen weeks, you may also be offered surgical management in the form of a vacuum or suction aspiration procedure. This procedure involves the insertion of a tube into your womb, which uses a suction method to remove your baby and any pregnancy tissue. The procedure itself should last around fifteen minutes, and you can return home later the same day. Should your pregnancy be at a later stage than approximately fourteen weeks, and has not exceeded twenty-four weeks, a medical option will be suggested first, then a surgical procedure, if needed. Mothers are usually admitted into hospital for the medical management due to an anticipated risk of bleeding.

If you end your pregnancy after twenty-one weeks and six days (UK), you will be given the option of having an injection administered into your abdomen, which will send the baby into a sleep that they will not wake up from. This procedure is referred to medically as feticide. The injection does not cause the baby any pain and makes labour less traumatic for the parents. It will be on the doctor's advice how long you stay in hospital before being able to continue to grieve your baby at home.

Gubby Ayida, Consultant Obstetrician and Gynaecologist MA FRCOG DM (Oxon), gave this advice for parents who learn that their baby will not survive the pregnancy:

It is a decision that parents can work through. The shock is when parents find out there is an abnormality. Then they wrestle with what they are going to do about their situation. They do have a choice and can take time to really consider their options. Ending a pregnancy is awful, but having good information and understanding the abnormality and impact can allow a mother options on the next steps. There can be an opportunity once the decision is made to say goodbye mentally.

I spoke with author and journalist Katherine Ormerod on coming to terms with the grief of ending her pregnancy for medical reasons.

When did you first think there may be a concern in your second pregnancy?
As the weeks went on, I did notice that I was quite small. I just assumed I must be having a smaller baby

this time around. At my twelve-week scan, my baby was growing well and everything looked fine. Then, during the twenty-week scan, suddenly the atmosphere in the room changed. I knew something was wrong. My partner was recovering from norovirus, so he wasn't with me and I'd taken a close girlfriend instead. There hadn't been space that day in the hospital, so I was at an external scanning unit. This had quite a big impact after, as there wasn't a specialist to see. It was obvious my sonographer and those in the unit hadn't had much experience with people whose babies were not okay.

Were they able to give you any information at the time?
I was told there was something dramatically wrong with my baby's legs. I could see on the screen that my baby's skeleton was deformed. It was the worst thing I could have imagined. Before the scan, I was so chilled, so happy. But afterwards it was like stepping into a black hole. It was four excruciating days before we could see a doctor, so I had to go home and get on with life without any idea of my baby's chance of survival, or what we could do.

Psychologically that was pure torture. The worst part was the not knowing. You can't make a decision if you don't have any information. There should have been immediate mental-health care available to us at this point. The sheer panic was all-consuming.

When you returned to the hospital, were you given a diagnosis of your baby's condition?
We saw one of the leading consultants and were told that a medical diagnosis couldn't be confirmed until we had had an amniocentesis, but they suspected it was a case of dwarfism and it appeared to be at the profound end of the spectrum. We made our decision based on that diagnosis, though when we finally got the results of the amnio six weeks later, it showed our baby had a severe type of Glass Bone Syndrome and birth survival would have been highly unlikely.

It was explained to us that, even if our baby made it to term, they had no chance of a good quality of life. My boyfriend and I had already made a decision to end the pregnancy if that was the prognosis. So, immediately after the confirmation scan, I began the process to end our pregnancy.

Was everything made clear to you about what to expect, and what was happening?
A lot of the details of that day are fuzzy and there were definitely some gaps in the information we were given. I didn't realise that after I took the first of the two pills, my baby would then die. In the two days after taking the first pill and then going back to the hospital to take the second, my baby had passed away. I had gone home on the day of taking the first pill thinking my baby was still alive, that I could feel her moving, and that was dreadful. Through the process, we had to sign

so many documents and make so many decisions on the spot. We said yes to everything on the medical side and yes to all testing. We wanted to know if our baby had an inherited disease and the possibility of a future baby facing the same issues.

When we went back to the hospital at the appointed time after two days, we were kept waiting for three hours downstairs in the cafeteria, which was hideous. Finally, we were taken to a special suite for women who give birth to babies who are no longer alive or won't survive after birth and I was given the second pill to induce labour. It was on the labour ward, so we could hear other women giving birth to living babies. That was really difficult.

Everyone was so lovely to us, so incredibly understanding throughout. I completely believe everyone's heart was in the right place, even though there were some things that happened that made the experience worse than it perhaps had to be. I decided not to go for an epidural as I was told that there was an increased risk of paralysis in the second trimester (I was twenty-one weeks at this point), but I tried morphine initially, but stopped as it made me lose my sense of balance completely. The contractions were painful, but thankfully my labour was quick.

When you gave birth, did you spend time with your baby?
We knew we didn't want to see our baby. We were told we could make a memory box, that we could bring

family into the room, have keepsakes. Although we had made our intentions clear from the get-go, we were actively pushed several times to look at the baby. I feel it would have been far better to have been told that, if we changed our minds at any stage, then we always had the option to see our baby, because in the end it made me feel like there was something wrong with me because I didn't want to see our baby.

A tissue-like paper sheet was held up to conceal me from seeing anything during the birth. They rested my baby on my thigh after I had given birth and I felt the baby's skin on my skin, which is something I can recall even now. I could feel pulsating blood from the umbilical cord, so, for a second, I thought my baby was alive, which was just devastating. I had asked not to know the gender of our baby, but a nurse asked me at that point if I wanted to see her. That's when I found out we had a little girl. That's when, internally, I lost it, though I kept myself under control in front of the nurses. For what reason, I don't know. In the end, I didn't go to pieces because of giving birth to a stillborn baby, it was because I had been given that new information, which made the whole thing feel so searingly real. Knowing she was a girl gave her a pronoun and a personality. It changed everything. It would have been easier to not know the baby's gender. I still wish I didn't know.

One of the hardest things was when I was asked if I had a blanket for her to go down to the morgue. I hadn't been told to bring one. I was heartbroken that

I had sent her down there without a blanket. It made me feel as though I had left my child to go down to the morgue without any covering or love, when the reality was that I loved her so much I felt like I couldn't breathe. Even now, I have so much guilt over the thought of her uncovered. I don't think I will ever get over that.

After losing her, did that change your thoughts on a future pregnancy?
It felt very much that we were a two-child family, with only one child at home. I was a mum of two, so I *needed* to have another baby. We were told by the hospital that there was nothing genetic that caused the loss of our baby, so we started trying again as soon as we could. Following the loss of my pregnancy, I had a forty-day period and then I didn't have a cycle for two months. That first period after losing my baby was gut-wrenching. It felt like losing her all over again. That whole time we had together. Her house was gone. It's like it had never happened. We were told to wait six months or so to start trying, but I felt I didn't have that time on the runway ahead and, five months after I lost my baby, I was pregnant again.

I went for scans every fortnight. Lying there on the bed with the gel on my tummy felt like revisiting the scene of my trauma every single time. I always asked not to see the images or the scans, or hear the heartbeat, and I was so scared that I was going to see the same image as I did with our second baby. At eight weeks, I got a call from a geneticist to tell me that there had been some mistakes made with our post-birth screening and there was no clear proof that the syndrome wasn't genetically inherited, and our new baby was at risk. It was like being punched in the chest and, throughout the following tests, which took three weeks, I totally checked out mentally. Fortunately, it was found not to be hereditary, but we were told that, as the genetic mutation had happened once, there was an increased risk of it happening again – about a 1 in 20 chance, which felt like a death sentence to me at the time. We were assigned a fetal medicine specialist and we also had additional private care, so I spent my life in doctors' offices, but there was no mental-health support offered. Fortunately, at twenty weeks, both specialists confidently signed us off from additional care and I went on to have a wonderful water birth at thirty-nine weeks.

Were you able to enjoy your third pregnancy?
No. I tried to keep as calm as possible and had a lot of words with myself. I kept myself busy and off my phone. I did a lot of DIY, and knitting. Knitting was the best thing, as you can't do it with one hand, so you're kept from scrolling through your phone. Woodworking was helpful, because it took hours and hours of work where you had to concentrate on what you're doing down to the centimetre. I'm also very superstitious, so

I didn't buy anything for our baby. We got the bassinet out of storage when I hit thirty-five weeks pregnant, but there was nothing else, no pushchair. We didn't decorate his nursery until six months after he was born.

Had you prepared anything while pregnant with the baby you lost?
I had knitted socks for her. I remember unravelling all the stitches, then using the wool to knit a blanket for my third baby. There are all the things you read about as a woman who loses a baby, these ideas that your baby's spirit comes back for the next child. Even though I'm superstitious, I'm sceptical of all the spiritual, woo-woo stuff 99% of the time. But that 1% of me felt I was making a blanket with the spirit of my little girl in it. It was a nice thing to do. The continuity of her spirit, keeping my new baby warm, and that blanket made from the socks I never got to give to her is still part of our family.

How have you navigated your loss in the years that have passed?
The heat of the experience has passed, but I definitely still find it challenging as time has gone on. I think we all have to acknowledge that time doesn't just heal, healing heals. Sometimes things in your life happen that bring your grief back into such sharp focus, and it can be kneecapping. It's not something that's lessening

the quality of my life, but it's still something I grapple with, sometimes at unexpected moments.

While my loss hasn't defined me, I'm not the same person. I feel like my heart got broken in a way that there's always going to be a hairline crack. In saying that, it doesn't mean my heart can't be filled with joy, I'm full of joy all the time. If you lose a baby, it's not like you will be so sad that you can't appreciate the beauty and magic of the world again. The experience of grief is not always what you think it's going to be. It's so unique and individual. Yes, there is light at the end of the tunnel, it just doesn't mean it's going to fix you or return you to factory settings. You've added a complexity to your soul. You're different now and that is something else that takes some time to come to terms with.

While in hospital

Making Memories – While in hospital on the day of my loss, I knew I wanted to have memories of our son to take home, but having never faced this situation, or spoken to anyone who had, I didn't know what to do. There are a few things I wish I had known, or been told, in the hospital that morning. I am sure it was suggested that I make a memory box of the things my husband and I would take from the room that morning, such as a hospital tag and hand-knitted teddy that I placed under Axel's arm, but, due to the trauma,

I cannot remember. I wish I had understood the importance of having as many memories as possible of that day.

Photos – Most hospitals will have specially-made clothing to dress early and late stillborn babies in, which are often donated by charities. It will be hard to consider anything in the hours after losing a baby, but I would love to have a framed photograph of Axel dressed in baby clothing. The photos I have are precious to me, but they are of Axel unclothed, lying on a sheet with blood in places. To me he looks beautiful and absolutely perfect, but I can see that having this photo hung in our home could cause discomfort for any guests, and possibly my children. When I see articles in the press or social media with images of parents holding their babies who died, wrapped in blankets and looking peaceful, it does induce feelings of sadness. I also get cross with myself for not thinking to have a composed family photo, of Axel with his parents, taken at the time. I couldn't think of anything that morning, other than that my baby had died. A family photo is the main thing I wish I had from that morning.

Keep something that directly touched your baby's skin – I wish I had kept something that had directly touched Axel's skin. The small knitted blanket that he was wrapped in when he was brought to the hospital room, or the identification tag that was loosely around his body. I have neither, which does cause feelings of guilt. I feel guilty for not taking enough care to ensure these things were safely with me. There is an enormous amount of guilt that comes with pregnancy loss. I talk more about this emotion on page 142.

Hand and footprints – I left the hospital with two sets of Axel's hand and footprints. The midwives suggested the prints as a way to remember our baby. A couple of years after he died, knowing I wanted to have memories of Axel displayed in our home, I created two framed pictures with Axel's prints. I hung the frames, one in my son's bedroom, one in my daughter's room. These memories of our baby make me smile when I see them hanging on the wall. There is a level of sadness attached to the images of Axel's small hands and feet, but, more than anything, it allows us to have a small part of him at home.

Birth certificate – Most hospitals will give you a certificate of the birth. If your baby is below the age of stillborn recognition (currently twenty-four weeks in the UK, differing from country to country), the certificate will be a kind hand-written gesture, rather than an official birth certificate. Any gesture at this time can be a source of emotional comfort, but to know that your baby is not officially recognised may be hard to process.

In the UK, there is little official acknowledgment of a lost life if your pregnancy was less than twenty-four weeks. The hope is that the medical staff you encounter will be empathic and understanding of your trauma at any stage of pregnancy loss. There is something in the official recognition of the baby you were carrying that can mean so much to parents.

Hospital care – There are many questions we could ask about the time parents spend in a hospital following pregnancy loss. Some parents I have spoken to had exceptional care, while others didn't. There were two questions that often became part of the conversations I had with parents, which I could also relate to. I asked Gubby Ayida, Consultant Obstetrician and Gynaecologist MA FRCOG DM (Oxon), the two recurring questions relating to a mother's care while in hospital:

Many of the mothers I speak to detail the failings they feel occurred in hospital during and after their loss. I had a few moments where I felt things could have been dealt with in a more compassionate way. I know you can't speak for all hospitals, but why do you feel there can often be such disparity within the care system?

Maternity units can be quite busy at times, as the nature of service means many women can come in in spontaneous labour at any time. When maternity staff are busy, indeed when anyone is busy, there may be less time to spend with mothers and this may come across as less sensitive or compassionate than is intended. Best practice now in the maternity services, for excellence or outstanding care, is to have dedicated bereavement rooms that are soundproofed, with en-suite bathroom facilities and with a less clinical feel. There should usually be a bereavement specialist midwife or team to ensure there is follow-up arranged and to help with logistics and questions and support. All of these measures, along with ensuring there is a midwife allocated to looking after the mother's needs while in hospital, is what we wish to get right each time. We want to feel and be able to say, 'We can't bring your baby back, but we want you to leave hospital feeling as though you have been cared for like royalty.'

I was in a room on the labour ward when I held my son, who had died hours earlier. I could hear babies being born through the day, and it was torture. Are there plans in place to take women off of the labour wards and, in some situations, change the way in which women are cared for?

Most new maternity services have a soundproofed bereavement suite that is usually in a corner on the labour suite separated, if physically possible, from the busy central area. Mothers can birth in there, and remain there after delivery. Suites have a separate private bathroom and toilet, so mothers don't have to walk through a labour ward and hear other mothers giving birth, or see them with newborn babies.

From an obstetrician's point of view, we want to concentrate on what we *can* do. What we can't do is change what has happened. There are things we can do to make sure we limit future trauma, such as offer women medication to stop breast milk that will come in on about day three after late pregnancy loss. Milk coming in can often be the undoing for women. We will hear of people breaking down then, as it's such a symbolic sign that they should have their baby with them and they do not.

It's about the detail of making sure that, when women come back to the hospital after loss, for a follow-up appointment, that they are not seen in an antenatal clinic setting. The ideal situation is that women come back to a gynaecology clinic where there are no other pregnant women in the waiting room. That's best practice. If you are being seen privately, it's making sure appointments for those who have lost a pregnancy are at the beginning of the clinic, or at the very end. This reduces the chance of women sitting in a waiting room, surrounded by pregnant mothers.

I spoke to Dr Shema Tariq about her experience in hospital after losing her son late in pregnancy and how she keeps his memory alive.

Our eldest son, Altair, was stillborn at twenty-one weeks. My waters broke on the train as I was coming back from work. My husband met me at the station and took me to hospital.

There are lots of gaps in my memory about that time – it was so traumatic. When we reached the hospital, we were told to go straight to the delivery suite, the same place where women checked in during labour. The receptionists took my name and said we'd be called when it was our turn. My clothes were soaked through with amniotic fluid and, when I mentioned this, they handed me an incontinence mat to put on the chair. I felt so exposed. So stigmatised. So vulnerable.

After an hour or so, one of the doctors called me in. I was really distressed; she told me to calm down, that there was no reason to panic. As she scanned me, we could see our little boy bobbing around and moving, oblivious to what was happening. The doctor then examined me and confirmed what I already knew, that my waters had broken. At this stage of pregnancy, the chances of our son surviving would be very low and, if left without treatment, I'd be at risk of a serious infection. I needed to be induced.

There were no beds available on the ward, so I decided to go home, have a shower and pack a bag. Throughout this time, fluid was slowly leaking from me, but I just pushed on. It seems hard to believe now. I was numb and on autopilot.

We returned to hospital and finally, at 10 p.m., I was given a room, seven hours since my waters had broken. My room was in the labour ward; throughout the next three days of my induction, we could hear mums giving birth to babies they would take home.

What was your experience in the hospital leading up to Altair's birth?
Before I took the tablet to start the induction, I asked the doctors if they would scan me again. They dismissed me, as they didn't understand that I wanted to see him alive one last time so I could say goodbye. They were looking at things very clinically. But, for us, this was our son, who was still very much alive. The decision to be induced was gut-wrenching. After two days, I'd still not gone into labour and had started to become very unwell with an infection (caused by my

waters breaking). I was also scared of giving birth. I'd always been advised to have a caesarean section, so hadn't prepared for a vaginal birth. I didn't know what to expect or how to cope and that made everything even more frightening.

When Altair was born, in the early hours of 10 June 2017, he was too small, too early, and too fragile to survive. I can't remember much of that morning, except the silence in the room.

How long did you spend in the hospital after you lost your son?

We were discharged on the day he was born. I was torn – I needed to be out of there and to be in my own space, but of course I felt the absolute desolation of leaving my baby behind. My entire body ached for him. Before we left, we both spent time with him, holding him, trying to take in as much of him as we could.

The next day I needed to be with Altair again. The thought of him being alone, as he waited to be taken to the mortuary, was overwhelming. We'd bought him a little teddy a few weeks earlier, so I placed that in his cot, along with a photo of us. Altair was cremated with the photo of us, so we'd be with him.

How did you learn to live alongside the loss of Altair?

Like most people who've experienced bereavement, time splintered in an instant for us. There would only be our lives before Altair, and our lives after. I now embrace the changes his short time with us have brought. We're all changed by our children, whether they live or die. Altair has shaped me, just as his younger brother and sister continue to do.

I have needed to find meaning in Altair's death. His is a life that was never unfolded, so it's up to me to keep his name and memory alive. The longer he is gone, the more important that feels. I speak openly about our experiences and hope, in a small way, I have normalised conversations about baby loss, especially within racially-minoritised communities. Black and Asian women are the most likely to lose babies, but until recently our stories weren't heard.

Our grief for our son has become more gentle over the years. It is woven into the fabric of our family life. His ashes sit on our mantelpiece and within a ring I wear on my right hand. We have a painting of his name (Arabic for eagle, and also the brightest star in the Aquila constellation) in our dining room. We celebrate his birthday with a cake every year. His younger brother and sister will always know they have an older brother in the stars.

Leaving hospital without your baby

Although desperate to return to the familiar surroundings of my home, the thought of leaving Axel at the hospital caused me extreme anxiety. The guilt of leaving my baby behind was overwhelming. It felt as though I was abandoning him. A midwife had explained that, as we had requested a post-mortem, Axel would be taken to the morgue to await transfer to another hospital. I couldn't stop thinking of how he would be alone without anybody there to hug him. I wanted to know that someone would be checking on him and telling him I didn't just leave him there. In my mind, I knew this wasn't going to happen, so I tried to divert my thoughts whenever a vision of Axel in the hospital came to mind.

When the doctors were satisfied with my condition, the release paperwork was signed and my IV drip removed. My husband had left the hospital for a short while earlier that morning in order to collect a change of clothes for me. I changed and sat on the bed. I was desperate to leave the room that held such intense emotions, but longed to stay in order to be closer to my son. I stroked the bed where I had held him, the place where I had said a final goodbye.

When it came time to go home, I momentarily forgot we had been given a room on the labour ward. As we left the room, I was confronted with the sight of pregnant women and happy faces moving about the ward. Babies were coming, preparations were being made, nobody could hear the screams inside of me telling them that my baby had just died.

There were a few knowing smiles from parents as we walked through the ward, only I knew that they were smiling in a way to say: it's soon your turn. There were no expressions that said I know your baby just died. I still looked pregnant. I was on a labour ward. They thought I was one of them, but I was now one of the others. One of the ones you have to handle with care.

What Now?

Walking out of the hospital doors and on to the street brought a huge sense of reality to my situation. Only minutes before, I had been holding on to a thought that the doctors may have made a mistake. Such was the intensity of my grief over the following weeks, this would not be the only time I would believe that Axel was still alive.

And here we were. Two people, who thirty-six hours before had been expecting a child. Now my husband had a very pregnant-looking wife, only no baby. We walked to the car. There was no thinking 'What happens from here?', there was only what happens right now, right this moment. I strapped the seatbelt under my empty pregnant bump and we drove home.

With the intense level of grief I was experiencing, I didn't have the mental capacity to ask questions about where my baby was and what would happen once I had left the hospital. I agreed to a post-mortem, without really considering why. It was only later that it became clear that it would be not only helpful to know possible reasons for my baby's death, but also to be aware of these potential challenges in a future pregnancy.

Post-mortem

It is the decision of the parents whether their baby has a post-mortem, which is most commonly offered from sixteen weeks gestation onwards. It may not be made clear why a post-mortem can be helpful, or it may be overwhelming for the parents to make this decision while grieving the loss of their baby. I asked Gubby Ayida, Consultant Obstetrician and Gynaecologist MA FRCOG DM (Oxon), if she could better explain why post-mortems can help parents following a pregnancy loss:

> The length of time a hospital will keep a baby depends on whether the hospital is going to do a post-mortem, which usually happens with pregnancies from sixteen weeks onwards. First trimester losses are approximately 15% of all pregnancies, so often there is not a post-mortem done on these babies. Mid-trimester losses are more unusual, so it can be helpful to find out why the baby died. Was it an abnormality, was it the cervix, or perhaps an intrauterine infection? There can be many reasons. Some parents feel their baby has been through enough, or they simply don't want one. It's really important, as there could be something that can be done differently in the next pregnancy, or we know what to monitor a mother for. A negative post-mortem can still be very useful. So although one may not find the cause, we can still rule out many things that it is not. Coming to the next pregnancy, you know what it wasn't and that is helpful.

Naming your baby

Months before our baby was born, we had chosen his name and began referring to him as Axel. The hospital registered his name on an unofficial birth certificate (he was twenty weeks, therefore not recognised as a stillborn in the UK) and whenever we spoke of our baby going forward, he was

Axel. For me, it was comforting and a simple way for me to include him in our family. I felt it would be a way for people to better understand our grief, to understand that we had lost a baby. More often than you would imagine, those who have not experienced a pregnancy are unaware of the growth stages of a baby in pregnancy. It can be assumed that, until quite late, the baby is simply an unrecognisable figure. When we met Axel, he was 20cm and resembled our older son. A small, but beautifully formed, little boy.

Whether you choose to give a living baby a name before their birth, or choose not to name them until after they have been born, there is an understandable divide in whether to name a baby at any stage in pregnancy. When a baby dies, the divide in choosing to name them, or not, takes on different meanings.

Some parents feel that by leaving their baby without a name, it allows for the distance they need from the trauma of losing them. Some feel that their baby needs a name, to further include them in the family. Since losing Axel, I have connected with hundreds of parents who have experienced pregnancy loss. Approximately a third of those I have spoken to made the decision not to name their baby. Some parents who lose babies in the later stages of pregnancy choose not to know the gender. Some don't wish to hold their baby due to the intensity of the trauma. There are no definitive answers as to what is right and what is wrong in any situation during or after pregnancy loss. The three things that helped me on a personal level were trusting my own instincts, guidance from doctors, and speaking with those who had previously experienced pregnancy loss.

Holding your baby

I knew I wanted to hold my baby, but when a midwife asked whether my husband and I wanted to unwrap the blanket he was concealed in, I hesitated. I was nervous that I may find his appearance too distressing. My husband knew he wanted to see Axel, so I agreed. Seeing our baby was the best personal decision I could have made. For me, having that time with our baby was a connection I needed, something I may have regretted had I not spent that time holding him.

If you choose to spend time with your baby after they have died, the best practice in hospital is for midwives to clean your baby, wrap them in a small blanket and bring your baby to you when you are ready to be with them. Not everyone will choose to spend time with their baby, and that is to be respected.

Gubby Ayida, Consultant Obstetrician Gynaecologist MA FRCOG DM (Oxon), explains why it is often suggested that parents hold their baby, while fully respecting why some parents feel it is not the right decision for them.

> I always ask parents if they want to hold their baby, and if they don't, I wait and ask again a while later. It is not unusual for women to change their mind during the time spent in hospital. Some women who choose not to can have deep regret later for not seeing or holding their baby. The choice to say goodbye to one's baby is a personal one and should be respected. It's okay if the parents don't want to see or hold the baby, but at least we have started the conversation. Emotions are different

at different times. It can be a fear of what they are going to see. The conversation has to be led by how much curiosity or willingness there is for the parents to see the baby. The mother may not want to see their baby, but the partner may want to, so we have to consider this. Once a partner sees the baby and can describe them, then the mother may change her mind. There is an element of fear in some women of how the baby will look. We have occasionally heard from parents months after their loss expressing regret that they didn't get to see or hold their baby and say goodbye. I think in many ways seeing your baby brings closure. In not seeing the baby, women's imagination can be dramatic. I feel it's better to see the reality. We will always bring the baby all clean and dressed and perhaps wrapped in a little shawl, no matter the age. The parents then see the baby treated as it would be if it were alive. Handled with the same sense of dignity. It can change something in the parents' thought process. To see a baby treated in this respectful way, you're not seeing it as just a dead baby. It helps to humanise the baby in this way.

What to do with everything you have bought for your baby

You may have decorated a nursery, or have items in your home that you bought ahead of your baby's arrival. With good intentions, friends may rally around you and clear anything from your home that reminds you of your baby. These actions have the potential to cause feelings that those around you are trying to erase any memory of your baby. Most friends and family members will be thinking of what they feel is best for you, so be honest about how you would like to take care of anything concerning your baby. How you leave a nursery, or pack items away, needs to be your choice. The smallest of decisions concerning the loss of a baby can be extremely emotional.

If you choose to keep the nursery as it is, there is no time limit on when to redecorate, or move anything from that space. Holding on to anything that reminds you of your baby will be incredibly important. A nursery can be a particularly painful reminder of your loss, as this is the room you have lovingly renovated for the arrival of a baby you were expecting to bring home.

If you know you would like to try for another baby in the future, redecorating at a time that feels right for you can bring hope for the future. A newly decorated nursery can bring feelings of optimism and form part of your journey through the deep pain you feel. A sense of a new life somewhere in your future. It can be comforting to keep a teddy that was meant for your baby in the newly decorated room. An image of their antenatal scan, or footprints in a frame on the wall, as we did with Axel, can also be a way to hold their memory close. These items can be a way to see a future baby sharing this space with the baby you lost.

A nursery can be left as it is for years, or packed up and repainted soon after loss. Items for your baby can be packed away, given to friends, or a charity. Everything depends on the wishes and emotions of those who have lost a baby and this is to be respected. There should be no expectations and no pressure to make decisions in any set timeframe.

Emotional and Physical Effects of Pregnancy Loss

Dealing with the often overwhelming emotions of loss was like trying to dodge tennis balls being hurled at me by a defective ball shooter. Every time I ducked, or jumped to one side to avoid an extreme feeling, another would come at me with full force. I would overcome one emotion for a moment, only to be faced with another. It was relentless. I would stop being angry only to be overcome with guilt, which would in turn be replaced by fear, then envy. These emotions would go round in my head on a loop, with little mental respite. I can see that a trained grief counsellor could have helped to minimise and manage the intensity of these feelings, but as I didn't have this help during the crucial first weeks following my loss, my mental state spiralled and I had little control of my thoughts.

Within this section, I wanted to highlight the main emotions you will likely encounter, along with help and guidance as to how to manage and rethink the mental challenges you may face.

Emotional effects of pregnancy loss

Depression

The feelings of depression after pregnancy loss can be varied, and at different levels of intensity depending on how traumatised you are by what has happened. Feelings of anger, guilt, confusion and loneliness can be tied in with anxiety, feeling worthless and, in severe cases, suicidal thoughts. There are so many factors relating to depression and it may be difficult to place one particular emotion as a main focus.

Feeling depressed after your loss is completely natural, but you may feel fraudulent in just how deep your feelings are due to the often misunderstood grief. The inability to function as you did before you lost your baby can compound your feelings of hopelessness. Most mothers who have experienced pregnancy loss will acknowledge just how difficult they find it for others to understand the severity of their feelings towards their loss.

I asked doula and author Latham Thomas how she advises mothers who are experiencing depression following pregnancy loss.

Community meetings in person are really effective. I think it's really helpful to be in a space with people physically, as the experience of loss is visceral. It's not a heady experience. One of the things I feel is lost in our discourse around healing is this idea that you can use the western framework of psychology or psycho-therapy to heal yourself from traumatic experiences. Therapy is an amazing mind tool, a processing tool, but healing has to happen through the body, because the things that are lodged in our tissues as trauma, how it stores in the body and shows up in our nervous system, is completely impacted, influenced and informed by the body. You have to move your body, you have to move stuff through your body. The best spaces to be in are spaces where you're in a community with people where there's movement. Sometimes people will go to church, and they will clap and sing and sway their bodies. Suddenly they're crying and moving energy. It's different than being in a therapy chair, where we talk our way through issues. We often feel better after therapy, but we haven't moved the issues out of our tissues. Movement is key. I recommend finding a dance class, or a forum where there's going to be interactive touch, or something connective where you're with people. Mindfulness or somatic healing allows you to use mind and body tools to connect with the feelings you have inside and helps release some of the trauma. Resilience practices build us up. You can fully be in a dialogue with someone online and doing healing work virtually, but I think the real benefits are when someone lays hands on you, it feels really good when someone places their hand on your shoulder and you lean into them. You can feel the warmth, their heartbeat. That does something different to you rather than sitting in front of a screen. I think that impact and the science of connection cannot be underplayed, especially in times when we're really vulnerable and have endured painful events. We need to feel connection at that time.

Post-partum depression coupled with grief

To be faced with the combination of both grief and depression can intensify your emotional state. It can be hard to differentiate between the two, making the healing process a confusing one. Often, you will be counselled for grief, with the factor of natural post-partum depression put aside, or not considered, during the initial weeks or months after your loss. The treatments for grief and post-partum depression differ, so it's important to ensure you, or someone close to you, raises this point with your doctor and/or counsellor. The grieving process can be a long one. You may experience feelings of shock, numbness and, in many cases, overwhelming sadness. Our minds can cause us to have one particular thought on a continuous loop, focusing on why we lost a pregnancy, whether it was our fault, or any number of other scenarios connected to our experience. Sleep patterns can often be affected, with too much or too little sleep disrupting our natural cycle. Anger, confusion, anxiety and emptiness can all cause us to feel as though we are losing control.

The guidance from a grief counsellor and the ongoing support of medical staff can be crucial to long-term recovery from pregnancy loss. From a personal experience, I feel that had I seen a counsellor specifically trained in grief therapy, and had further support from the medical staff I met with following my pregnancy loss, this would have allowed for a smoother period of recovery.

Anger

Anger can often be a difficult emotion to work through. There are many elements of anger following loss. Anger at others for being pregnant. Anger at yourself for thinking you caused your pregnancy loss. Anger at doctors for not noticing issues you feel could have saved your baby. Anger at those around you for not being sympathetic. Anger at those around you for not coming to see you, or for not saying the right thing. Anger at the injustice that this happened to you. Anger at a partner for not seeming to grieve as long as you.

With the anger that presented itself through my grief, I wanted to find ways to channel this emotion so as not to take it out on those who I now realise did not deserve it. Well, perhaps one or two people did deserve it, but mostly they really didn't. This is not to say it was easy, but being angry was not going to help me grieve my baby, or begin to navigate my journey out of the intense grief I was faced with. I felt comfortable being sad; I did not feel comfortable being angry. This emotion was preventing me from finding the mental peace I desperately needed. On top of everything else I was going through, the anger was causing more guilt, as I directed my negative feelings towards others, then felt awful for doing so. Feelings of anger, then guilt, became a negative cycle that I wanted to break.

Therapist Claire Bidwell Smith feels anger can sometimes be a positive when working through grief. I love the way she reframes an emotion that I thought could only be a negative.

It can be very satisfying to be angry at other people for not understanding. Anger can be a useful emotion in grief in that it has a lot of energy. Grief is very draining, it's tiring and exhausting. In these moments where we can feel anger, it's powerful and energising. Sometimes we can get a little extra activated when we feel anger towards someone who doesn't understand our experience. Rather than focusing on that person and stewing on it, sometimes anger can be a great distraction. It can be satisfying and a relief. Obviously, you don't want to take it to places where you're seeking revenge or taking things out on people, but just feeling a little anger at people can feel good.

Whenever I was angry with someone for words I felt were insensitive, I would try to communicate in a calm way and explain just why I was angry with them. This certainly helped in releasing my anger towards them. Ordinarily, it can be hard to face situations like this, particularly if you hate confrontation. Where possible (I did not always have contact information for people), I sent a message via email or text to explain why I was feeling the way I was. I am sure some people who received my messages may not have understood my reasoning, but I had to do this for *me*. This was not a time to consider what others thought of me. I knew that, as long as I was polite and kept my messages as brief as possible, this was going to be the right thing to do for my mental state.

One way I was able to channel, and temporarily release, my anger was to write everything I was feeling down in a book. Alternatively, you may want to type a document, whichever you feel is best for you. I found the act of writing my feelings to be more effective in releasing my anger, to see the words coming from the pen in my hand was some-how a greater way to release my emotions.

Talking was by far the best way to release any anger I was feeling. It can be hard talking to someone close to you about your anger, as this can cause them to take on a great deal of weight from the conversation. Friends and family will often gladly be there to listen on some occasions, but it is worth considering that you could cause those around you to distance themselves a little if you can only talk of anger and negative situations. This is just human nature and not a true reflection of how they feel about you. Finding a neutral person to talk to, a counsellor or healer, can be a good way to be able to get everything you are feeling off of your mind. Not only are these people trained and can help guide your emotions, they know why you are there and it is their job to listen. I loved talking to the healer I saw for a year after Axel had died, as I could do just that: talk. Finding someone to talk to without fear of judgement is one of the best things I did for myself during my intense grieving stage and I would highly recommend this route.

Denial

I was in a state of denial about many things after Axel died. I vividly remember having delusional thoughts that he was still alive. One of the most intense and painful moments was following a call from the hospital where I had held Axel in my arms only days before. It had been a few days since I returned home and I received a routine call from a midwife to check on my progress and answer any questions I had. I clearly remember seeing the hospital's number on my phone and feeling somehow hopeful. I believed they were calling to say they had managed to revive our baby and that we would be able to bring him home soon. My mind created this belief in response to the extreme longing and denial of what had happened. To know that I was able to believe Axel was alive, when I had held his sweet body while he was no longer breathing, made me feel completely crazy. When we are experiencing mental-health challenges, for any reason, to be called crazy is deeply insulting. But I can only describe the way I felt as utterly crazy. I called myself crazy out loud. But I wasn't crazy, I was simply traumatised to a point where I hoped the unbelievable was possible.

I hadn't begun to decorate a room for Axel's nursery. I knew that he would be in a cot in the bedroom I shared with my husband for some months, so had decided not to arrange anything in any room for a while. I had expected to bring him home at full term, so had made very few arrangements for his arrival. I thought I had a few months ahead to buy the things we would need, never expecting to give birth to him at five months into my pregnancy. For those who had decorated a nursery, however, it can be a place where the denial of your loss can be heightened. It is not uncommon for parents, particularly mothers, to spend time in a nursery in a dream-like state. Such is the state of grief after losing a baby in pregnancy, it is completely understandable that there will be a magnified level of denial that your baby will not be coming home to that room.

Fear

Having lost one baby, there was no longer the stability in my mind that my body would be able to carry another, or even get pregnant again. My first IVF cycle had resulted in a pregnancy, which I lost, but with the years it took to get pregnant after our first son, there was nothing to say that IVF would work for us a second time. The thought of going through IVF again, which wasn't an entirely positive experience, and not having another baby, led to a fear of my husband leaving me. There was no indication that my husband loved me any less, or thought of me as a failure, but I was leading my thoughts in the belief that I could lose him too.

I also became overly fearful of my elder son dying, or that my husband would be involved in a fatal road accident. Experiencing a death that was so sudden and unexpected left me feeling incredibly vulnerable and anxious that another traumatic event was moments away from happening. Rather than accepting the death of my baby was trauma enough, I was expecting more pain to follow soon after.

With all the thoughts that continued to swirl around my mind and create newly embellished fearful scenarios, I then became fearful that I might never mentally recover from the trauma. It was a very natural, but utterly draining, cycle of fear.

I spoke to Courtney and Sabrina on their challenges to conceive, fear after pregnancy loss and how they welcomed triplets into their family.

Did you always plan to have children together?
C: I never had a desire to carry children. When I was younger, I would tell my mom that, if I don't have kids, I will adopt. Sabrina, on the other hand, always had

the desire to become pregnant. It was very important to her, so very early on we knew she would be the one to carry our children. We wanted to conceive in the most natural way, so that's when we decided we would try IUI.

S: We were successful on the second attempt, but the pregnancy ended in a loss. We were seven weeks pregnant, so in some ways we felt lucky the pregnancy was not later. We did have to take some time after that for our wellbeing. We took some time off before starting another round of IUI.

How did this affect you?
C: We knew we were pregnant from two weeks, so had told our family and close friends. We were extremely excited as we had dreamed of becoming pregnant, of being parents. It was an early loss, but that still doesn't take away from the fact we were planning a life with this child.

Did you then continue with IUI?
S: We tried IUI multiple times after that, following my natural cycle and not using medication. We were not getting pregnant, so on the sixth attempt we started to incorporate some of the more aggressive medical treatments to increase our likelihood of getting pregnant. Thankfully, we were successful at our eighth attempt.

I remember at times being concerned that I was letting my husband down by not being able to get pregnant. Sabrina, did you feel this pressure with Courtney?
S: I was really fortunate to build this support with Courtney, I never felt alone in the journey. Courtney was at every insemination appointment with me, every exam, ultrasound. I very much felt supported through the times when I wasn't pregnant. I never felt like I was failing her or us. It made our relationship even stronger to have Courtney uplifting me when I felt like my body was failing me at those moments.

On your eighth IUI attempt, you became pregnant with your three incredible children. Did you begin telling people, or did you keep your news private?
S: We knew we were pregnant at week two, but didn't want to share anything with anyone in case things didn't work out. Every moment I felt like I was stepping on eggshells. We were so excited, but didn't want to have another pregnancy loss, so kept it to ourselves. Other than our parents and close friends, we didn't share our news until we were in the second trimester.

How did you feel through this pregnancy?
S: The first seventeen weeks were really hard. I was constantly nauseous, my hCG levels were really high. Quite early, around seven weeks, I began to experience a lot of pain and bleeding. I had my blood work done at the hospital and that's when we found out we

were having triplets. With the pain and blood, it was terrifying. I thought we were going to have another pregnancy loss.

C: We both felt the worry, but I didn't want to mention it. I didn't want to put Sabrina under any more stress. We didn't really talk about it until after we found out we were still pregnant and having triplets. It was a quiet ride to the hospital. Waiting for the ultrasound. It felt like the same steps, the same motions we were taking at the same week we found out we had experienced our previous pregnancy loss. It was very familiar territory and we didn't really talk about it.

S: Then, at the hospital, we had quite a shock. During the ultrasound we had a surprise.

C: In our whole journey, I had always said I thought we were going to have twins. During the ultrasound, the doctor told us he had found one heartbeat. Then another, so I knew we were having twins. Then he found another heartbeat. We were having triplets. It was the first time we heard their heartbeats, it was beautiful.

Following pregnancy loss, when fearful thoughts can lead to further fearful thoughts, it can be helpful to practise mindfulness in addition to writing down fearful feelings in a notebook. To calm your mind and see your projected fears written down in front of you can be effective in reframing your thoughts and minimising the opportunity to catastrophise unlikely situations.

Through previous Cognitive Behavioural Therapy I had for another reason, I located a questionnaire template I had saved from my counselling sessions, printed many copies and, most mornings, would complete one of forms. Along with beginning to heal in other ways, the guidance from the CBT questions worked to stop the continual loop of fearful thoughts that seemed unstoppable.

I have copied the link to the CBT questionnaire on page 334 so you are able to access it. I hope that it can help you to reframe any negative scenarios from playing in your mind and calm your own fearful thoughts.

Envy

To be told that a friend, family member or colleague is pregnant can cause feelings of envy. You may also feel guilty for having those feelings of envy towards those you are ultimately happy for.

As I was often on social media, or saw pregnant women while out, at one point my envy became consuming. I was unable to see pregnancy posts on Instagram, or look at any pregnant person in the street, without feeling overwhelmed. When trying to conceive after my first son, my envious thoughts had been light and controlled. After Axel died, the thoughts were deeper and more prolonged. I never wished the women I saw were not pregnant, it was simply that I longed to be pregnant myself.

It's quite natural for pregnant mothers to complain, even jokingly, about how difficult pregnancy can be. When encountering these comments, it's quite natural for your envy to be coupled with resentment. Feeling resentful when others have something you want is entirely normal. It is often about accepting the resentment and understanding when you may need help to control these feelings.

From someone who struggled with envy, I know that trying to focus on the positives in life is easier said than done. Some great advice I had, from somebody who had experienced their own pregnancy loss, was to do just this. If possible (and trust me, it took me a while to grasp how to do this), each morning write down five things that you are grateful for and read them out loud. I know this sounds like an unlikely mood lifter, but it often worked for me, even in my darkest of times. The key was to not only read what I had written previously, but to write the positives down again. The act of writing down the things I was grateful for – my husband, home, job, even my bicycle – helped me to see the things I was taking for granted more clearly. The five things would change frequently. My enhanced mood was often short-lived, but it did allow me to break the loop of feelings I wanted to escape from for a while.

Envy and resentment of others were two emotions I disliked throughout my grief. I could accept anxiety, guilt, denial, as these were about me. Envy and resentment involved others, so I wanted to find a way to release these emotions. After I began writing this book, I spoke to therapist Claire Bidwell Smith, who gave me this advice on overcoming those feelings:

These emotions are hard to avoid completely; they will come. It's difficult. It comes with any kind of hardship, loss and grief. To see other people thriving, other people having what you lost. These are emotions we hate to feel, especially towards people we care about, family members or friends. It can be difficult to suddenly feel resentment towards them. One of the ways to move through this is loving kindness meditations. Again, it's that self-compassion piece. Another way is group support, being with other women who are going through the same grief and loss. When you find a community of support you stop feeling as though you are alone and the only one experiencing this type of loss. You have people to talk to after you encounter situations that may upset you, and it helps you move through that pain – having someone who understands what you are experiencing. If you can't say that to someone who understands, it's going to sit with you.

The guilt and trauma of flushing a pregnancy loss down the toilet

There is another form of guilt that is often highlighted in conversations I have with those who have experienced pregnancy loss. The guilt of pressing flush when they have felt the loss of their baby while on the toilet. These conversations are not easy for the mother to be immediately open about, such is the guilt and shame they feel. It is a natural reaction to a shocking event and there is nothing to feel shame or guilt for. Many parents have been through this experience, as, at the time, it feels like the only thing they can do. Only later are there considerations of how else they may have reacted in that moment. The majority of mothers will press flush as an immediate reaction to what they have just experienced.

From speaking to hundreds of women, this situation is not uncommon. Most have felt the only thing to do is to quickly flush, to clear the toilet, then face the reality of their pregnancy loss. The bathroom is the first place most mothers go when they feel fluid release between their legs. When you are pregnant, it is a practical thought in a moment of panic. There is usually a tiled floor, a toilet to hold further fluid that you suspect may follow. But what happens when the fluid becomes a pregnancy loss? There is often pressure and cramping when experiencing a pregnancy loss, so it is instinctive to head to the toilet. While in shock or distress, many mothers flush the toilet without thinking. It is a natural reaction. This happens in so many situations, at home, at work, while out. You may only consider recovering what you see as your baby if you have experienced pregnancy loss before. What may follow losing a pregnancy and saying goodbye in this way is guilt for the unconscious reaction of pressing the flush.

With the shock of this experience, there is seldom time to consider picking up your baby, no matter how small, from the water in the toilet. It's often the case that the mother won't call someone else to the bathroom, not even their partner. The guilt, shock and shame mothers feel is not justified, but can be a huge weight on top of an already traumatic experience. Internal questions are asked of whether this should be a shared experience, or something to do silently and alone. And many mothers do go through this alone.

Therapist Claire Bidwell Smith gave me the following advice about the ways in which you may be able to release the guilt and pain of seeing your baby leave in this way:

There's no way to change what's happened and it's never going to feel okay for the mother. Accepting those facts is the first step. But the mother also has to have self-forgiveness and self-compassion, I can't emphasise it enough. Meditations and exercises for self-forgiveness are so important. One of the things that can be helpful is creating a spiritual and internal relationship with your baby, really connecting with your baby. The physical form of your baby did go into the toilet, but you're still holding that spiritual relationship with your baby close and taking care of it. Try doing visualisations where you are holding your baby close. Every time a woman has that image in her mind where she is flushing the toilet, she can pivot from there and imagine holding her baby close and knowing that she will energetically and spiritually always be with her baby. It's about finding a way to create this other relationship with your baby. The work is to forgive yourself for being human and doing this thing, and let yourself have this beautiful spiritual relationship with your baby.

Claire practises meditation and suggested this form of mindfulness when creating a new memory of how you see your baby. She wrote the following meditation, which she suggests practising often, while sitting in a peaceful, comfortable setting. Reframing the experience of flushing after your pregnancy loss and visualising your baby in your arms can help to release any guilt and sadness you feel. You can see yourself holding your baby, creating a new memory as you move forward.

Meditation for Pregnancy Loss

Find a comfortable and quiet space in which to meditate. Once you are settled, close your eyes and take slow even breaths for several minutes, allowing your body to relax. Once you are fully relaxed, imagine your heart opening. Let yourself feel safe and held by the world around you. Then bring your baby into your mind's eye. Maybe the baby is an image. Maybe the baby is a feeling. No matter what form the baby takes, imagine yourself cradling it. Reassure yourself and your baby that part of you will always be together and that you will always be its mother. Let yourself bond and feel the love between you. And when you are ready, open your eyes, knowing that you can always connect with your baby in this way.

Guilt

Guilt can come in many forms. From speaking with hundreds of mothers who have experienced pregnancy loss, the two main focal points of guilt seem to be centred around assuming they caused the death of their baby, and of moving on. I agree that these were the two main areas that I felt most difficult to navigate.

Guilt played a huge part in the months after losing Axel. Firstly, I could not shake the thought that something *I* did must have caused his death. I questioned the acts of working, exercising, sleeping and even eating. What did *I* do. It was clearly my fault. I was carrying my baby and I didn't look after him in the way I should have. These are all thoughts that went through my mind often.

In almost every case of pregnancy loss, the baby's death is not caused by the mother. There is nothing most of us can do to prevent it happening. Yes, you can have more regular scans to monitor the baby's progress, not smoke, drink alcohol or consume excessive caffeine. You can be more aware of your baby's movements in the later stages of pregnancy. But, mostly, pregnancy loss will occur for reasons that are hard to detect early enough, or indeed prevent (see page 57 for possible causes).

There is also the guilt that you are moving on from your baby. One of the things I found most upsetting was the thought that I may be forgetting my baby, that I was living my life without considering a space for him in it. I am often apprehensive to speak of Axel when a conversation hasn't been naturally led in the direction of pregnancy loss. Sometimes he is strongly in my thoughts and I want to talk about him. When this happens, I either call my husband or a close friend. I don't want to conceal conversations that include him, but I am also aware that it may not be something others wish to talk about when it feels out of the blue. It can be conflicting. You want to speak of your baby, but so often you feel as though it is not socially comfortable to speak of pregnancy loss.

Therapist Claire Bidwell Smith gave this advice:

It's always different. Sometimes you have to take a break socially when you're in that place. It becomes impossible to have surface conversations when you're grieving and to go to social events where you're talking about things that are so meaningless in the face of this kind of grief. At a certain point, you need to take a break from it all as it's going to make you insane to try to do that. This antidote of having a support group, or friends, you can speak about this with, it relieves that part for you, where you can eventually go to parties and be social again. You can get everything out to a group of trusted people, then you have the capacity to face the more meaningless conversations. It's a loss that goes through your life with you, constantly coming back up. For those women, they can feel resentment and envy that they can't talk about regular things, but when they have the support of women who are going through the same thing, it takes that weight off needing others to understand all the time.

When having another baby, there can be enormous guilt that you are somehow trying to replace your baby who died. I was longing to be pregnant again, but felt the familiar pull of guilt that I was trying to move on from Axel. Knowing I was actively trying to get pregnant brought on conflicting and confusing thoughts. I questioned whether I was expecting a new baby to fix my emotional state and be the thing that allowed me to move forward from my overwhelming grief. In the end, I understood that it came down to wanting another baby in our lives, but it was almost a year before I could accept that it really was that simple.

Memory loss

Like a wave washing over you to erase blocks of time, grief took away so many moments that I may never get back. Perhaps grief does that to help you, to stop some of the pain of remembering. There are a lot of memory gaps from the first months after losing Axel. Things I did, things I said, things other people said and did. When I am reminded of certain events or conversations, I tell people I have no memory of these things happening. But not in a vague way, like it may come back to me soon, but in a way that I know I will never remember. I have felt frustrated at times, a little foolish too. Sometimes it feels as though people think I am being difficult. 'Oh, you remember!' The truth is, I really don't. The intensity of grief, in its many forms, can affect your brain in ways you would never imagine. Memory loss after a traumatic event is often directly connected to PTSD. Dissociative amnesia, which occurs after your mind experiences a great level of stress, is one condition that has been linked to pregnancy loss. This form of amnesia can be short-lived, or in extreme cases it can have a prolonged effect. Avoidance of memories can also be tied in to memory loss, where you try to avoid anything relating to the traumatic experience, keep constantly busy and feel unable to express emotion or affection. When encountering noticeable mental or physical challenges after loss, it is advisable to explore the possibility that you may have Post-Traumatic Stress Disorder (PTSD).

PTSD

As I moved forward in my grief, it became apparent that the mental effects I was experiencing were directly connected to Post-Traumatic Stress Disorder (PTSD). The feeling that my mental state was out of control and with a constant fear that those around me would die was frightening, but without the diagnosis of PTSD, my internal conversation was that I was 'crazy' and clearly unable to pull myself together. PTSD can have an immediate effect, or, as in my case, it was a delayed condition of my mental state. Flashbacks of losing my baby would wake me in the night, or cause me to be rooted in anxiety in the middle of the street. I would see vivid images of my baby and the blood on the floor of our bathroom. I was unusually fearful of places and situations, and experienced prolonged headaches that medicine wouldn't lift. There can be many symptoms of PTSD, including irritability, anger, avoidance, fear and physical pain. Following loss, we can put any and all of these challenges down to the shock and upset of our experience, but if you recognise (or somebody close to you recognises) that you have a number of the issues connected to PTSD, it's advisable to seek specialised counselling and get support through this time.

Suicidal thoughts

I felt I was stuck in a cycle of anxiety, sadness and hope-lessness. I couldn't find a way to break the loop of these emotions and became mentally exhausted trying to escape my own thoughts. I relived my experience daily, with flashbacks and nightmares, until there was a turning point three months after my baby died. That turning point was a night when I contemplated ways to take my own life. Such was the mental torture of being unable to escape my grief, I could no longer face the intense anxiety that hit me each morning when I woke. I felt I couldn't continue in this cycle, but didn't know how to break it. My husband sat up with me through my suicidal night. We talked for hours, trying to find ways in which I could begin to navigate my way out of my grief. I never had another night as severe, although it took months to manage the level of anxiety I was faced with each morning.

Therapist Claire Bidwell Smith gives this advice:

It's the idea of bearing the unbearable and waking up to it every day. This fear that you cannot do this for the rest of your life. For most people, that feeling will change, but, in the moment, you can't know that. Doing things such as meditation can be really helpful, just to take a break from those thoughts. It's cognitive thought, that you can't do this for the rest of your life. Pivoting from that and doing a meditation where you're stepping away from that thought is helpful. Doing breathing exercises where you're calming yourself and bringing yourself into your body in those moments is also helpful. Mindfulness and being present is so important as well. When you are acutely grieving, you're thinking of the enormity of your pain and the longevity of it, so doing things to bring yourself to the present gets you through that moment. It's about getting through that day. When we're grieving, we're doing two things constantly. We're either in the past, thinking about what has happened, or we are in the future, thinking of how we are going to live the rest of our life with this loss. So any time we can bring ourselves to the present moment is helpful. We won't be able to do this all day, but short periods, even ten minutes a day can be a reminder to give ourselves breaks.

The importance of talking to someone about suicidal thoughts is paramount in working through these intense feelings. Having support from a friend, family member, doctor or organisation can be the difference in life or death when you cannot see a way past your grief. I have listed UK-based organisations that can help with counselling and guidance on pages 333–4.

There are many ways in which grief can affect your life. I asked leading doula and mental-health advocate Latham Thomas for her advice on a pathway to guide a grieving mother through extreme thoughts following loss.

A key person in guiding a grieving mother is a licensed mental-health provider. There are things that are even outside of my scope, and I refer a trusted practitioner to help support the journey. I can identify that I'm seeing what looks like depression, anxiety. What I would always suggest is talking to a therapist, for them to locate what is happening, give a name to it, and start processing the trauma. In addition to the therapeutic tools, there are mind–body tools that can be integrated.

Healing for me always incorporates touch and movement. Doing womb work, massage, acupuncture, reiki. It's the body tools in addition to the mental health and therapy tools that I would bring in early on. I would have these things in place even before the mother is ready to talk about her experience and have a protocol in place as a response for what's happening right then.

Grief

The grief after losing a pregnancy can be overwhelming. Thinking a day ahead can often feel as though it's too much. After I had lived with my grief for some weeks, I found that I would give myself the task of getting to the next hour. Then the hour after that. This released the pressure I placed on myself to 'pull myself together'. There was no pulling myself together, there was just living.

I remember an almost unbearable level of emotional pain caused by the intense feeling of hope that my baby was still alive. Although I had held his body for hours in the hospital, there were occasions where my longing for him became so intense that, for brief moments, I believed he was still alive. My intense grief continued for close to six months, where waking each morning to once again be faced with the reality of Axel's death was an unbearable Groundhog-Day experience. It took six months until I could feel the grief easing.

There can be occasions both in person and online where grief hierarchy can become apparent. We cannot know who is experiencing a greater level of trauma, but those who have experienced earlier-stage pregnancy loss are frequently categorised as having a less serious, possibly temporary, state of grief. If they are recognised as grieving at all. For those who do not understand the experience of loss, at any stage in pregnancy, it can appear that those who lose a pregnancy in the first trimester have less of a right to be upset than those experiencing later loss. This is where it is necessary to consider the circumstances of a fertility journey, rather than the gestational week of a pregnancy loss.

I spoke to Grace Mortimer, author and children's chef, about her eleven pregnancy losses and how she finally allowed herself to grieve.

How have you coped with eleven pregnancy losses and the culminated grief following each experience?
I didn't deal with my grief at all. It wasn't until my eleventh loss that I began to understand my grief. I was constantly told you're more fertile after pregnancy loss, and I couldn't forget that. I didn't allow myself to grieve. Instead, each time I experienced a loss, I would try to get pregnant again straightaway. Mentally it was exhausting. I had hope and disappointment on a constant loop.

After the trauma of my eleventh loss, a consultant strongly advised me to give myself a three-to-six-month break before trying to get pregnant again. This break gave me permission to stop and grieve. I really regret not grieving previously. I wouldn't have had so many losses if I had taken things slower.

Why was the eleventh such a turning point in your fertility journey?
For the first time in three years, I was safely over the twelve-week mark. I was awake in the early hours of the morning researching missed miscarriages. There was no suggestion anything was wrong in my pregnancy, but I was overwhelmed with anxiety. I rang the early-pregnancy unit at my local hospital the following morning and, a few hours later, I was lying in a dark room hearing the words 'I'm sorry, but there's no heartbeat.' In that moment, I let go of three years of silent screaming. I howled like a child. Sobbing and shaking, I had to walk past a waiting room full of pregnant women making apologetic smiles at me. I honestly debated walking in front of a bus once I got outside.

How did you navigate the trauma of this particular pregnancy loss?
I bled for three months after I left hospital. Every trip to the toilet was a crushing reminder of what should have been. I couldn't shake the darkness, the sadness and the unbelievable anger. I kept having this flashback, one that I think I'll always struggle to push out of my mind. I'd seen my dead baby. It was little and whole and perfectly formed and it was lying in a pool of blood in a cardboard toilet bowl and I wasn't good

enough for it. My body should have loved it and cared for it, but instead my body was just a tomb and I hated every inch of it.

I think there's another side of pregnancy loss that simply isn't understood or talked about. It's the bit afterwards, the bit where you feel worthless, useless and a failure. It's usually triggered when you see a pregnancy announcement or a newborn baby. It isn't envy, I don't think. It's self-loathing. I failed, I let my baby down and, worst of all, I don't even know what I could have done differently to stop it.

Was there a point where you became able to manage the intense grief of your losses?
I have found a way to manage the vault of feelings. Talk. Tell everyone. I find the more you talk, the more you make it okay for others to talk. We realise we are not alone and the dark cloud isn't just following us around.

Talking about our babies is an important part of healing. For those who go on to have children after pregnancy loss, those women are still grieving for the babies they lost, but they often feel as though they cannot vocalise it. There's something almost ritualistic in talking of the babies who couldn't stay.

What has given you the strength to carry on trying for another baby?
There is an acceptance of the past. Unlike the death of a family member, where you know they are gone for

ever, there is hope that you may get pregnant again. Hearing others' stories of having children after multiple losses give me hope.

Having now allowed myself to grieve after my last traumatic loss, I am in a better place than I was. I had to ask myself what can I do to make things better. I had to take back my control. I now ensure I am doing all I can to control what I can. If a healthy body is the best place to grow a baby, then that is what I can do. I have always been healthy, but now I am really considering what I eat and my overall health, both mentally and physically.

I am terrified to go through a similar experience as my last loss. I look at my son and think that, if we never had any more, I would be okay, but I would love another child.

As I immersed myself further into research and interviews for this book, something unexpected happened. As I spoke to more and more people who had experienced pregnancy loss, I began to feel as though I had no right to feel as traumatised by my experience as I do. I am the first to say we should all be able to speak of our grief with conviction, to be open and honest and raw if we wish. But, suddenly, my single experience of pregnancy loss didn't seem as extreme as those who had gone through multiple losses at different stages. I was experiencing what I call 'pregnancy loss imposter syndrome'.

Those who had experienced loss spoke to me throughout my process of writing this book. I was often asked if Axel had been my only loss, or if I had experienced earlier pregnancy losses too. I found myself in the same position as those I tell not to apologise for any loss at any stage. When explaining I had not experienced multiple losses, I found myself apologising, the words 'I'm sorry, but I only . . .' preceding my explanation of not understanding early losses. I felt guilty for not having gone through the trauma of loss many times over a period of years.

We will never be able to understand the level of grief that another person is feeling, we can only navigate our own way through the personal experience of loss. One loss, or multiple losses, are all significant in our lives and there is no greater, or lesser, grief. There are no imposters, there are only those who understand the pain of knowing they were carrying a life that left them too soon.

I spoke to Elizabeth Day, author, journalist and host of the podcast How To Fail, on her ten-year fertility journey and experiencing loss at different stages of pregnancy.

Was there a point when you began to question that your fertility path may not be straightforward?
I was thirty-two when I came off the pill. You hear all of the stories that, when you come off the pill, there's a surge in your fertility and suddenly you're pregnant. I did have a little voice of caution in the back of my mind wondering if maybe it's not going to be that easy. As it turned out, it wasn't, and I didn't get pregnant.

After trying for about a year and a half and not conceiving, I had all the investigations and was told it
was unexplained infertility. The only thing the investigations revealed was that I had a bicornuate uterus.
Which, as ever in fertility medicine, could mean something, but it could also mean nothing. Everything that
you're told is so ambiguous.

*Did you have a clear idea of how you would move forward
after doctors couldn't ascertain why you were not getting
pregnant?*
Having had all my fertility levels measured, I was
told IVF would be the best course of action. I found
the process of IVF incredibly lonely. I had completely
underestimated the enormous pressure that you're
under when you're doing IVF, which is essentially like
taking on another job. There are scans at the clinic
every other day, you inject yourself, you have to be
somewhere specific for egg collection. I remember
injecting myself in restaurant toilets and trying to fit
IVF around everything else that was going on in my
life, absolutely denying the fact that the hormones
were going to affect me, the emotional resonance was
going to affect me. Also the fact that it was a lot of
medical intervention. It was a lot to handle.

How did the process of IVF affect your emotional state?
Looking back now, I was very disconnected from
myself. I became like an automaton, I just got through

it. That's when the numbness started, I think. During the first cycle I was constantly told I was 'failing to respond' to the drugs. I got one egg and the clinic asked if I wanted to call the cycle off, but I wanted to see it through to the end. The egg fertilised and we did get an embryo. It didn't make it to blastocyst, so I had it transferred at the three-day stage and had the two-week wait. It didn't work. That was crushing. Because I had that alpha female 'I'm in control of my life, I need to get this done', I went straight into a second IVF cycle. It was a longer cycle, it was exhausting, but we got four embryos that time. Two were transferred, then the two-week wait. They didn't stick. I was thirty-four and was left feeling like I was at a stage where I was contemplating a life without children.

Did you consider another IVF cycle at that time, or did you feel as though you needed a break from it all?
My second IVF cycle ended in June. In August I got pregnant naturally, which was a massive shock to the system. I had come to the conclusion that it wasn't going to happen this way. For women like us who have had fertility issues, there is no such thing as a joyful, anxiety-free pregnancy. There's so much that goes through your head and that's what was happening then. I felt even more disconnected from myself and anxious and worried. I felt very lonely. I felt like I was observing the world through a fog.

I never felt fully at peace with that pregnancy. That could be explained by all the anxiety I had around fertility. Maybe it's also explained by a level of intuition. I started spotting a week before my twelve-week scan. Everyone told me not to worry about the blood spotting, that it was very common in pregnancy. I went in for an emergency scan. The sonographer explained my baby had no heartbeat. She was so lovely and so compassionate. I remember crying and making immediate conversation with her, as a way to make the situation less awkward.

I was booked in for a D&C and, because I had a bicornuate uterus, they needed to do it with video equipment. I had my scan on the Friday and I had to wait until Tuesday.

How is it possible, mentally, to leave the hospital knowing your baby has died?
It's a head-fuck! I was told I may experience the loss naturally and, if that happened, I should go straight to A&E, because there can be a lot of blood. There was a level of necessary detachment for me. I wasn't allowing myself to think of my pregnancy as The Baby. I wasn't even letting myself think of it as a pregnancy at that stage, I was cut off from myself. A friend came to collect me from the hospital, she was amazing. The situation was awful, and yet I was like 'That's it then'. I was almost like 'Well, that's shown you. You didn't really think you were going to have a baby, did you?

You're not really worth that.' There was almost . . . a relief? I've only recently been able to talk about this, as I felt so bad about feeling it. It was as if the worst thing that I had thought about myself was true. There was almost a feeling of expecting it. I think I had a lot of self-hatred. I turned the grief inwards and attacked myself.

How did you manage emotionally while waiting for the D&C?
I didn't have to wait until Tuesday, as the next day my loss began to happen naturally. I had gone to meet a friend for lunch and remember going to the loo and it starting to happen. I went back to the table and told my friend, who took me to A&E. I spent the weekend in hospital, losing my pregnancy. It was extremely painful in both senses. It was very lonely. I don't know what I would have done without my mother and my best friend, who talked to me through the night. I had the D&C in hospital on the Sunday.

You have spoken openly about having three pregnancy losses. Have you found the experiences to be similar, or were there considerable differences in each loss?
I experienced two later losses with my now husband, who was extremely loving throughout. I had a natural pregnancy loss just before Christmas in 2019, where we had been to see an obstetrician at six weeks and were told there was a gestational sac, but no embryo.

We were told I could start losing my pregnancy naturally, or I could go back for another scan and maybe we would find the pregnancy was underdeveloped. You're just left hanging, and nobody can do anything. The day I would have been seven weeks pregnant was the day I started to lose that pregnancy.

Because this was the first natural pregnancy loss I had experienced (my first had been surgically concluded), I was really taken aback by how much blood there was. How are you meant to handle that on a practical level? I remember going to record a podcast and I was still bleeding heavily. During the recording, the host asked me about fertility, the medicine and the language of fertility medicine and whether there's a patriarchal constraint around it. I was losing my pregnancy while answering his questions and, looking back at it, I don't think I've ever been so passionate or eloquent. I didn't know what I was saying. But I was living it.

I remember you speaking publicly about your third pregnancy loss during the first pandemic lockdown. Was your experience heightened due to what the world was experiencing at that time?
A couple of days into the 2020 lockdown, I found out I was pregnant again. I had just had an operation to remove the septum in my uterus, which in and of itself was quite traumatic. You have to walk around afterwards with a balloon inside you to ensure your

uterus doesn't scar over. The balloon has these plastic tubes that sit outside of your vagina. You have to walk around like this for five days. It was awful. I subsequently had the heaviest period of my life, then I became pregnant naturally the following month.

I was highly anxious, because we were living through Covid and I had had a pregnancy loss a few months earlier. I was being monitored and my progesterone levels were going up. We had a scan at seven weeks; our baby had a healthy heartbeat, so we began to relax a bit. As our baby was measuring a little small for seven weeks, I was advised to have a scan a week later. I went back and was told there was no heartbeat. This loss was medically managed, where I had to take pills. That was the worst one of all. The experience was compounded by the lockdown. It was a really scary time.

How was your partner coping with all that was happening?
It's really hard seeing someone you love go through it. I had experienced losses before, so knew how it would feel, but my other half hadn't, so I felt a real sense that I had let him down. He doesn't make me feel like that at all; it's how I made myself feel.

It was our second pregnancy loss together, where my partner really understood what it meant to lose a baby. I hate having been the gateway for him to have that knowledge. I know it's not my fault. I know it sounds cliché, but it has brought us even closer together. It's something really precious to share together. It helped me access my own sadness and validate my feelings.

You didn't let anybody down. How did this pregnancy loss, in lockdown, affect you?
My third pregnancy loss was the worst one. I was given the option of waiting to lose my pregnancy naturally, or to take pills. Because it was Covid and the hospital staff were overstretched, a D&C wasn't presented as an option at the time. I decided to take the pills. Now, knowing what I know, I would have insisted on a D&C. You take the pills and it is such intense pain. Surges of it. I was throwing up with the pain. I was in bed, in lockdown, it was horrible. Not only do you have the pain, but you have the bleeding. You have it all at once. It was also my third pregnancy loss, and I was like, this is going to take some recovering from, which it did. It took a good few months to recover, until we were ready to try again.

How have you processed your grief through the experience of three pregnancy losses?
The most important part of this journey has been real-ising that my grief is valid. For a really long time, not only did I feel that it wasn't, but I didn't connect with it being an emotion. I didn't think I felt grief. I now realise that was self-protection and I think what hap-pened with me – and maybe other women can relate to this – is that I went to a place of numbness in order

to cope with it. A place of numbness and continuing as normal, but I now realise that was just a slow-motion stalling of the inevitable process of grief.

The grief is difficult to calculate, because you're mourning an absence rather than a presence, but the moment you get pregnant you start to think about having your baby and the name you will give them. You're also grieving the person who didn't come into existence. I think it's only with my third pregnancy loss that I have been able to admit to myself that I feel really sad about it. Some days I feel sadder than others, and that's all part of the process. I am also a real believer in the fact that a massive part of living life as it must be lived is that you can feel sadness and it can last a lifetime and you can choose to be at peace with that sadness. That's been what I've really been looking at this last year or so.

How do you feel about your fertility journey now? About your losses and the future.
I've had a full experience of the fertility world. I feel like a veteran. I'm still in it and I am absolutely determined that I will be a mother. It's been ten years of trying and that can be really tiring.

I firmly believe that a really important staging post in the grieving process for my pregnancy losses was getting a physical object that could represent their existence. A therapist I had at the time suggested some kind of object and it took me a while to come round to the idea. I found a beautiful stone carving, which is now in our garden. Every time I see it there, I get a sense of peace and joy because I firmly believe that the stone carving represents those three spirits who were sent to me as teachers, as guides to life and to the universe. Another thing I have come to believe is that the experience of pregnancy loss or infertility or struggle on your path to motherhood is simply preparing you to become the best mother you can be. In whatever form that may take. It's the struggle that makes you. I find that immensely comforting, to think of myself as a mother already, because of the parenting I have already had to do to get through those times.

During our time of grief, we should not need to consider how we speak of our loss, or have to acknowledge others' opinions on the level of trauma we feel inside. It can be helpful to remember that others' opinions are not ones we need to absorb and respond to, or spend time thinking about.

Following Axel's death, I allowed comments I perceived as negative to affect me. I wish I had a magic rule for not allowing others' comments to get under our skin, but having experienced pregnancy loss, this is absolutely the time to tell yourself you will not allow anybody to negatively affect your mood. I found talking to myself in the mirror helped. I told myself not to allow anybody to affect my feelings, that I was hurting enough already and their opinions were not important. These verbal moments were incredibly helpful, as they released the internal conversations that looped over in my mind. At this time, more than any other, do all you can to release any external factors that add to your grief.

Therapist Claire Bidwell Smith explains more about why hierarchy and comparisons arise through grief and loss:

> We need to give people permission to grieve. For some reason we are constantly comparing ourselves to other people's losses. It's irrational and yet we do it all the time. It can be a way of understanding grief, this constant shame we feel, apologising for our loss, or wanting to diminish our own loss. It's part cultural, part internal, that irrational shame we feel. The shame feeds into the comparisons. It's very human and part of it is that our loss feels so enormous that we cannot imagine anybody else has ever had a loss as big as ours. We can't imagine that anyone has felt a loss the way we feel it. It's beautiful in some ways, there's something about love there. Nobody has ever had to love something as much as this and lose it. But grief is grief. I think we need to be grief curious, to find out what it's like for others in their grief. We have to recognise that everyone's grief is so big, even if it's not what we would understand it is.

We can acknowledge the different experiences parents may have in varying stages of loss during pregnancy, but we cannot grade pregnancy loss in levels of trauma, validity and grief.

Grief can be a consuming emotion, one that doesn't allow you to feel as though there is any way forward, or that there is life outside of that grief. To be a support to someone who has experienced a great level of trauma requires compassion, time and understanding. To the person grieving, there will be little else in their life, a blinkered view of the outside world as their experience envelops them.

My grief in the first months following Axel's death caused me to focus on little else. Unable to find any peace or mental escapism, my mind would constantly relive the night I lost my baby. I cannot remember many conversations during that time, but I am certain most were centred around Axel. I am sure I was repetitive and I am sure there were not many occasions where I asked about others' lives at that time. I don't feel uncomfortable about these things, as, if it were someone else who was grieving, I hope I would give them the time they needed to talk about their experience.

I spoke with Gubby Ayida, Consultant Obstetrician and Gynaecologist MA FRCOG DM (Oxon), about being able to talk of little other than my baby dying, and feeling that I was becoming a burden to those around me. Gubby gave this advice:

You have to be authentic to yourself and what you need. There are some people who don't want to talk about it. Those who do want to talk can find the hardest part is the people around them. People don't quite know what to say, they don't know whether to try and cheer the mother up, or put on a sorry face. There are those who haven't had children, or those who have never experienced loss.

When you lose an early pregnancy, all of this is happening, but you may not have even announced your pregnancy yet, so you have to deal with your loss privately. Then there's the situation in later pregnancy where everybody knows and you are having to deal with family, friends and colleagues. Both situations can be very difficult.

For those who are very open about their loss, it can be easier for others to know how to communicate. For those who keep everything in and feel they have to keep a stiff upper lip, people around them can feel very awkward. They can feel as though the best thing is to try and cheer the parents up, when that's the last thing they want.

There are patients I have had where I just sit, hug them and let the deep sobbing come out. Some women need information to help them process. Asking 1,000 questions can be their way of processing what has happened, even if there are no definitive answers. There are some women who want to make it okay for other people by pretending they are okay. Some women may benefit from seeing a perinatal psychologist. Perinatal psychologists or psychiatrists are specialists in dealing with mental wellbeing during pregnancy, birth and the postnatal period. They are skilled in supporting women struggling after pregnancy loss.

It can be helpful to identify the type of grief you are experiencing, to enable yourself and those around you to be there for you in the most effective way. The grieving process is not always clear and you may identify with a combination of grieving experiences, finding that varying forms of grief may be present in different situations. In social situations I often masked my grief, while at home there was a feeling of prolonged grief for the baby I couldn't bring home. With the help of a counsellor, I found that once I was able to identify the combinations of grief I was experiencing, I was able to better understand the route through that grief.

Remember that your grief is unique to you and there is no time limit on how long it will take for you to feel any positive changes in your emotional state. I felt stuck in an ongoing state of heaviness and hopelessness for months. I contemplated suicide, such was the weight that hung over me every day. Then, one day, I felt a shift. A very slight change in how I was feeling, but I knew there had been movement in just how dark everything seemed.

I spoke to Sarah Gwonyoma, creator of What Sarah Read Next, on the grief of losing her twins twelve weeks into pregnancy and the death of her husband during their final IVF cycle.

My first loss was an ectopic pregnancy, although at the time, I didn't know I was pregnant. I remember waking up feeling dizzy. As I got up, I felt a warmth between my legs and noticed a mass of blood on my friend's sofa. I didn't think to call an ambulance, instead I decided to head to the tube. I collapsed somewhere between my home and the station. I woke up in my bed, with a tall stranger watching over me. This kind stranger had found my ID and carried me home.

Did you know at the time how serious your situation was?
No, I didn't. I called a friend, who then took me to the hospital. We were taken to the labour ward. A sonographer called me into a room and I was instructed to lie on a bed and await a scan. During the scan, the sonographer confirmed that I was indeed pregnant.

The sonographer had concerns, and called a consultant into the room. It was explained to me that I had experienced an ectopic pregnancy, that it was serious and I would have to go to theatre immediately. I woke up from the general anaesthetic to see the face of the man whose baby I had been carrying. That day I lost him, our baby and my left fallopian tube.

How did you process all that had happened in this short space of time?
I was in total shock initially. I knew I wanted babies one day, but to suddenly have my chances halved was brutal. After the shock came the grief. I had to learn to accept my loss. I had to stay positive and believe I would meet the right man and eventually we would have our own baby, even with my one fallopian tube.

I did meet the right man. Tim. He was kind, funny, supportive. A year after getting married, we were equally surprised when we conceived naturally with my one fallopian tube. Seeing those two lines on the pregnancy test was utterly surreal. Isaiah arrived nine months later at 7:35 a.m., in Suva, Fiji. A healthy 7 lbs ball of magic. The best day of my life.

My husband was working for the UN. He was asked to transfer to Samoa, so we packed up our life in Fiji and made the move. Soon after settling in our new home, I discovered I was pregnant again. From the beginning, the pregnancy didn't feel right. I had debilitating nausea, blood spotting and almost constant stomach cramps. At the six-week scan, I was told there was no heartbeat.

A week later, I returned to the clinic for a follow-up scan, only for the sonographer to find not one embryonic sac, but two. Both with strong beating hearts. Twins. What are the chances? With one fallopian tube. I felt untouchable. At the twelve-week scan, I was told one of my twin's heartbeats had stopped. The following week, there was no heartbeat on my remaining twin. My babies had died.

What happened after you had been told this news?
I was given tablets to encourage the babies to leave me naturally, but the tablets didn't work. After a week I was advised to have a D&C. I was admitted to a labour ward, where mothers cradled newborn babies. The lady next to me had just delivered her baby. She was in pain and asked me to hold her baby. My twins were dead inside my womb while I held this new life. It was torturous.

How did you cope with all that happened after knowing you had lost your twins?

I mourned the loss of my babies deeply. As a woman, those two lines mean so much more than a pregnancy. I saw a whole lifetime ahead of me with these children.

Immediately after losing my twins, I went on a frenzied mission to get pregnant again. My periods hadn't stabilised, but it seemed more than just natural irregularity. Each time I typed in my symptoms online, the term Asherman's Syndrome came up. My symptoms matched the diagnoses. Lack of blood, but extreme pain when menstruating. Intrauterine surgery tied to pregnancy, including D&Cs for early pregnancy losses. Two expensive trips and two invasive surgeries resulted in the removal of scar tissue in my uterus. After the surgeries, I was then told my one remaining fallopian tube was damaged. My only chance of conception was through IVF.

Knowing all that was ahead, did you choose to do IVF?

Yes, immediately. My husband and I returned to live in Fiji, but the closest IVF clinic at that time was in Melbourne. I travelled back and forth for appointments, injecting myself daily with the necessary drugs. The first four cycles failed. We decided to try one last time. The day before my last embryo was due to be transferred in Australia, I received a call from a friend in Fiji to say my husband had died.

How did you get through that time? Did you make the decision to transfer the embryo?
I didn't transfer the embryo. I immediately returned to Fiji to be with my son and my mother. It was one of the hardest decisions I have ever had to make, knowing I would not have another child with my husband, Isaiah's father. But I knew Isaiah needed me more than anything.

How did you process your grief, not only for Tim, but for the baby you may have had with him?
I gave myself time; I saw a therapist and a healer. I had to be okay for my son. My energy healer recently told me that in a past life I lost three children in Uganda, my Motherland. Our village was ambushed. She told me that, as a result of this, I closed myself off from the world. That it hardened me beyond recognition. So, you see, grief has been part of my journey. And while in a past life grief owned me, in this life I have chosen to own grief.

Live through the grief in your own way. You may believe you have to put on a brave face, or mask how overwhelmed you are, but I believe the best way to navigate the first few months is to be honest about how you are feeling.

Physical effects of pregnancy loss

Your body

I remember looking in the bedroom mirror as I sat naked on my bed. I hated my body. I wanted to cut away the bump, such was the torment of seeing the place where Axel had happily lived until his premature birth. This was a part of the journey that I found particularly difficult. I looked pregnant, but I had no baby inside of me. I wore the expandable jeans and loose-fitting tops that had been my staples through the months when it had become clear that I was pregnant. After losing Axel, with the pregnancy weight still on my body, my pre-pregnancy clothes didn't fit. With no desire to shop, I wore the clothing that had grown with my bump. Wearing these clothes was like a strange torture, reminding me of just why I had bought them in the first place. With my mind so clouded, I couldn't find a solution for this situation. Looking back, it could have been helpful to ask a friend to kindly loan me clothing, or give them my bank card to buy some pieces to replace the pregnancy clothing. To wear clothing that wasn't a constant reminder of pregnancy would have been one less thing to cope with.

Along with the emotional benefit of time alone and a much needed endorphin release, cycling each morning was also a way for me to lose some of the pregnancy weight that was affecting my mood. Losing weight for vanity reasons is the last thing on someone's mind after losing a baby, but in finding ways to move forward, seeing your body return to its pre-pregnancy shape can be helpful. It would be a while before my uterus would return to its pre-expanded size, but it did help to see my body change in other areas over time. I didn't care how I looked, but I did want to erase the daily reminders of a body that had carried my baby. It took months, but when I began wearing my pre-pregnancy clothing once more, I could feel a shift in my mood. I felt more in control. I hadn't realised it would be such a momentous moment, but packing my pregnancy clothing away turned out to be a significant step in the journey of slowly piecing myself back together.

At whatever stage of pregnancy, seeing your body after you have experienced loss can cause a strong emotional reaction. It can be painful to look at the space where you knew your baby was growing inside of you. In early pregnancy, your body may not have changed noticeably to those around you, but you likely felt the changes as the pregnancy progressed. You will have felt the waistband tighten on your jeans, or already be wearing a larger bra size. These are all reminders of a body that was preparing for your baby. A body that now has to readjust, far earlier than expected.

Exercise

As with any workout, pre- or post-pregnancy, it is always advisable to consult a doctor before returning to any form of exercise. Exercise can prove effective in lifting your mood after a pregnancy loss, helping to relieve some of the anxiety and depression you may be feeling. The release of endorphins and the feeling you are doing something for yourself are positives, but take it slow and don't push yourself too hard.

I found that, along with cycling, walking helped me immensely. To get up and leave home without any set schedule, or the need to talk to anyone, took the pressure off of exercising. I didn't need to be anywhere on time. I didn't need to interact with strangers. I could do everything in my own time and at my own pace. I listened to podcasts while I walked, as it helped to take my mind off of Axel for a short while. I chose to listen to uplifting content that was unrelated to pregnancy loss. The lighter tone of conversation took me away from my own, heavier, thoughts.

The standard rule, with some exceptions, is that after early pregnancy loss, you can return to your usual exercise routine when any bleeding has stopped, which should be no more than a couple of weeks. You need to feel ready and to not exert yourself in the first weeks after your loss. Not only have you experienced physical pain, but, in most cases, you will also feel emotionally affected. Take it slow.

Experiencing loss later in pregnancy tends to come with slightly different advice. Wait for your body to recover and monitor your blood loss. Following a loss in the later stages of pregnancy, it is expected that you will bleed for weeks, possibly months, afterwards. Continuous blood loss is likely to affect your physical state, along with your energy levels, and can lead to serious illness. Depending on how late you were in your pregnancy, your lower back and core abdominal muscles may be weaker than before. You may also have to consider how the natural movement of your joints and ligaments have been affected, so only exercise when you have been given the all-clear by your doctor.

Providing your doctor has confirmed you can return to exercise, swimming can prove to be a calming and gentle way to move. There's little pressure on your body and the water can prove meditative for some. I had never meditated before Axel died, and haven't since, but there was a brief period of time where I would go to a pool close to my home and slowly swim lengths. I felt the release of the anxiety within my body and was able to calm my mind for the periods of time I spent in the water.

Not a yogi at all, I did find that gentle yoga sessions helped to take my mind off of all that had happened. I knew I had to be in an environment with little mental expectation. The slightest thing would make me tearful, so I couldn't have an instructor barking at me, or a high-energy class. I joined a beginners' yoga class at a local studio. I had a job that allowed me to choose my hours, so I would attend a mid-morning session, which was mostly filled with older participants. The pace and calming energy was the perfect match for my mood. I was always at the back of the room. I needed to feel invisible. Due to the level of the class, there were no expectations to contort or create the perfect angles with my body. I did what I could and there were no judgements on my ability. It was the perfect environment in which to exercise on my own terms.

I found that leaving the house improved my mood a little too. However, getting to the point of walking out of the door was never easy. If you simply cannot face the outside world for a while, taking time most days to do a gentle online workout may help to lift your mood. In the midst of grief and depression, it can be hard to even get dressed, but, if any form of movement, or the feeling of completing a task, can make you feel the slightest bit more positive, that can only be a good thing.

Breasts and breast milk

In early pregnancy, I had joked with my husband that my A-cups growing to C-cups was something I had longed for since my teens. Now here they were, those Cs that were proving to be another source of discomfort I had with my body. At the hospital, it had been explained that, as I had given birth, my body would assume I had a baby to feed. My milk would soon come in. I could either express the milk for as long as my body continued to produce it, or take pills to prevent my body from producing milk at all. I chose the pills. I knew that, emotionally, I would not be able to cope with seeing the milk that was meant for my son.

Some mothers choose to express their milk, donating it to new mothers who were unable to produce their own. Some express milk as a way to feel closer to their baby and then simply pour the milk away. The act of expressing milk can be a huge comfort to a mother, a way to stay close to the baby they lost. I knew I didn't want to see the milk that was meant for Axel, but as with any decision that is made about your baby and your body, you will choose the right one for you.

Pain

Along with emotional pain, in most cases there will be physical pain throughout and following your loss. Cramping, pelvic and back pain are common symptoms. Further effects can include headaches, feeling faint, diarrhoea and vomiting. You may experience one or more of these effects in the days and possibly weeks following your loss.

Procedures and operations such as D&C and, in later pregnancies, a caesarean section or vaginal birth, can cause pain. There is nothing to say your pain will not be mild, but prepare for the possibility of more intense pain as you experience the physical effects of pregnancy loss. I explain the most common procedures following pregnancy loss on page 89.

Your period

I had mixed emotions when my first period came after Axel had died. My initial thought when seeing the blood coming from me was that I was definitely no longer pregnant. I knew I was no longer pregnant, but with a level of grief that so often distorted a rational way of thinking, there were times when I convinced myself that what had happened wasn't my reality. This part connects in some way to the denial I had that I was no longer carrying a baby. To see my period was, in many ways, the first step in encouraging me to try to lift myself out of the deep state of grief that had engulfed me. I could see the blood. There was definitely no denying that this was my reality.

I wasn't prepared for the level of blood that came with the first period after losing my baby. It's common for women to experience a greater loss of blood in the first few periods after a loss, but nobody warned me. As your body didn't ovulate through the previous cycle, the endometrial lining in your uterus may become thicker and results in heavier or longer periods. I thought there was something wrong, that my uterus had been damaged and the blood loss was a side effect. It is certainly worth keeping in mind that you will likely lose more blood in your first period/s and to be prepared with high-absorbency sanitary pads and pain relief.

Parts of my mourning process were reignited when my period came. But the grief took hold in an unexpectedly firm way with the periods that came for months after too. I was taken back to the night my waters broke, the blood that followed and lying on a hospital bed with the IV drip in the back of my hand. I had lost litres of blood on the day Axel died and worn medical sanitary towels in my underwear for what felt like weeks. My body had to come to terms with me no longer being pregnant. I was navigating my way out of a deep state of grief, but my periods signified my loss each time they came. Axel died in June. It wasn't until early the following year that I no longer felt the weight of my loss return each time I saw the arrival of my period.

Along with the negative mental reminders of pregnancy loss, there was also something hopeful about the return of my period. Hope that my body was working in a way that could, potentially, lead to another pregnancy. Seeing my period meant that my cycle was returning to its pre-pregnancy state. I had experienced years of unexplained infertility before Axel was conceived through IVF, so there was nothing to indicate that I would now be miraculously fertile, but there was definitely a sense of renewed hope.

Counselling/Healers

Counselling/Therapy

I can see from my personal experience where improvements in both the immediate care and aftercare concerning my mental health could have been made. Some parents will receive satisfying and compassionate care, while others won't be so fortunate. The way you will be guided after your loss depends a great deal on the medical professionals you encounter while navigating your grief.

A few days after Axel had died, I explained to my doctor that I needed help. I requested that I be referred for counselling. I didn't have the mental capacity to ask friends to recommend grief counsellors, and was unsure they would even know of any. My doctor said she would refer me to the local counselling service and listed me as a priority patient.

Weeks after Axel died, I received a call from the counselling service the doctor had mentioned. I was grateful that this help was being offered and that it was through the NHS, but I had needed the most help during the first weeks of my grief. Had there been an immediate point of contact for mental-health support, I believe I would have fared better in navigating the loss of my baby. It hadn't been made obvious to me when I lost my son that there were various charity helplines I could contact. Having spoken to many parents about the helplines, it's clear that they are a great resource for initial help and guidance if you are unable to access counselling in the first weeks following your loss. The details for the leading UK-based pregnancy loss charities are listed on pages 333–4.

Although grateful to be granted counselling sessions, it soon became apparent that my counsellor couldn't fully grasp my level of trauma. She was in her mid-twenties, her lack of life experience obvious from the questions she asked that were outside of her textbook training. I continued to attend the appointments, but ultimately I didn't find the sessions helpful.

The only time I felt comfortable with the sessions was in the waiting room of the clinic. Looking around, we all slotted into the same category. We needed help to make sense of something beyond our mental capabilities. Outside of the waiting room, I felt exposed. Even though strangers I passed on the street had no idea of my recent loss, I somehow felt my grief was obvious. I found it hard to smile when someone made a comment, or kindly held a door open for me. I was so sad that I couldn't even force myself to look happy.

If at all possible, mentally and financially, finding your own counsellor who is specifically trained in grief will be beneficial in most cases. Hopefully a friend or family member can help you find a grief counsellor, as you may be too emotionally overwhelmed to do this yourself. If you seek counselling via a government system, you are generally assigned a counsellor who is trained in therapy, but specialises in no particular area. With a counsellor whose expertise is grief therapy, the level of help and understanding will be that much more effective in navigating you through the most intense and traumatic period of loss.

Healers

A few months after Axel died, and with the counselling service my doctor had recommended not proving effective, a friend suggested I see a healer. At first, this suggestion seemed a little woo-woo. I imagined a softly spoken woman in a flowing silk robe, wafting around a room and insisting she could feel the spirit of my son from above. Although sceptical, I wrote the healer's number on a piece of paper and placed it in the drawer of my desk.

A few weeks passed, and desperate to lift out of a deep state of grief, I called the number. I was willing to try anything. I made an appointment and set off on what I assumed would be a wasted journey.

The healer opened the door. A kind, but forthright woman invited me in and made me a cup of tea as I waited on her sofa. I felt a little uncomfortable. I wasn't sure I believed in healers, but here I was, wondering if she could tap into my thoughts and know that I was questioning her healing abilities. I tried to redirect my thoughts to more positive ones.

I told her the story of Axel, and was surprised that she cried. I thought this seemed kind and very human of her, to be with me in my sadness. We talked for a while on the sofa, before moving to a pretty room overlooking her garden. There were oils and crystals, soft music playing. I assumed we were now getting to the woo-woo part.

As I lay on the bed, the healer relayed some of what I had told her, while encouraging me to connect with Axel. I allowed myself to try and connect with him. A short while into the session, something happened. I felt him brush my hand with what I assumed was his. Now, as a non-believer at that time, I did get home and question whether I had imagined his touch. I still don't know for sure, but I decided I wanted to believe it. What started as scepticism turned into a form of belief.

I enjoyed many sessions with the healer over the first year following Axel's death. I loved speaking of him and believing he was in the room. The healer reassured me he wasn't lonely, that he had lots of friends. I clung to this thought more than any other. I really didn't want Axel to be alone, wherever his space in the world might be.

I look back at my time with the healer with fond memories. Those hours were special. I spoke about Axel, I spoke to Axel and I often felt he was in the room with me. To be able to talk to someone about Axel without feeling I was a burden was incredibly helpful. For each 90-minute session, it was all about Axel and me. I could say anything and there would be someone there to listen. No interruptions, no fear that I was boring someone, no insensitive comments coming my way. I would highly recommend finding a healer, or accessing free online mental-health resources, such as YouTube videos. Some months on from my loss, I spent time viewing various healers and certified therapists on YouTube who offered advice on grief and I found their guidance incredibly helpful.

Spiritual signs

Before Axel died, if anyone had asked if I believed in spiritual signs from those who had died, I would have said no. My thoughts would have been that such signs were as woo-woo as healers (see above). Then I had an experience in a bar that changed my thinking completely.

I was working on a project that involved a number of women. It was a panel discussion on relationships, dating and love. I was on the panel with six incredible women and found myself drawn to one particular guest that evening, a highly respected astrologer and psychic named Michelle Knight. I was fairly sceptical of whether anybody was able to predict futures, or connect with the past, but from all Michelle had said during the talk, it was clear she knew what she was talking about.

After the panel discussion, those involved in the evening went to a bar for a drink. I began speaking with Michelle and the conversation turned to Axel. I told her my fears. That I worried he thought I was moving on, that I was forgetting him. As we continued our conversation, we were interrupted by a woman who had walked from the other side of the bar to greet us. She commented on Michelle's hat, which was wide-brimmed and as striking as the rest of her outfit. Out of nowhere and without prompt, this woman shared her birth date with us. The 6th of June. The 6th June is Axel's birthday. The day he was born in our home. As the woman walked away, I explained the significance of the date to Michelle. She simply smiled and gave me one of her warm embraces, seeming unsurprised this had happened. In that moment, it had been proven to me that, woo-woo or not, signs are there if we are lucky enough to receive them.

Protecting yourself from reminders and triggers

Social Media

It was once the case of only knowing friends, family and colleagues who were pregnant. Avoiding them would likely be uncomfortable, but it was possible. With honesty regarding your reasons for staying away, or a string of carefully considered excuses, you could avoid seeing them until their baby was in the world and the initial attention of their newborn had subsided. Social media and online content is less easy to avoid. The pregnancy announcements, growing bumps and those welcoming a newborn can be constant reminders of what you no longer have. The reminders can be torture, but social accounts can also be helpful in connecting to others and allowing for a little escapism when your grief and longing become too much. Social media can be a double-edged sword, a place where you need to assess whether it is helping you through your loss, or becoming a hindrance in how you cope.

I promised myself I would stay off of social media, but, after Axel died, I initially enjoyed getting lost in beautiful images. The only issue was, along with travel and interior accounts (personal favourites), unavoidable pregnancy posts would frequently be staring back at me. Due to algorithms and my recent search history, I was a prime target for all things pregnancy related. On the one hand, I found reading of others' pregnancy loss experiences made me feel less alone. I also loved how scrolling through beautiful images distracted me from my grief, even briefly, in the first weeks after Axel died. On the other hand, the continual damage to my mental health in seeing pregnancy announcements and newborn posts needed to be addressed.

Social media, particularly Instagram, often gets high-lighted in discussions relating to mental health. The app is attributed to causing unhealthy addictions, comparisons and the need to compete with others for a seemingly perfect existence. I agree with these points entirely, but there are also the benefits of community, support and knowledge. During the first weeks after my loss, my Instagram account did become an undeniable source of support. When I announced on my account that Axel had died, I received unexpectedly compassionate messages from those I knew and those I didn't. Those messages helped me through some of the most traumatic times soon after my loss. Some of the messages were so honest and kind that I felt I was being cared for, sometimes by those I had never even met.

Writer Leandra Medine Cohen was one of the first high-profile people on social media to write openly about her pregnancy loss. I asked Leandra how she navigated the attention surrounding her loss and the effect it had on her.

I had become so accustomed to processing in public, I had been doing it for such a long time. When you're depressed, even when you're impacting people in the most positive way, you can't help but be depressed.

Intellectually I was very happy people felt connected to the writing. In an embodied sense, I was still so lonely. Nothing anyone said made me feel less lonely.

In the time after your loss, how did you cope personally?
I dived head-first into commodified self-care. I can see it now in that way. I tried everything, a mood-lifting eating plan, hypnosis, acupuncture. Anything that would zen my body out and put my head in the right space. I was thinking you could put a Band-Aid on some psychological wiring that actually just needs to be detangled. I wanted to feel as though I was doing something.

Did any of this self-care have an impact on your mood?
Maybe it made me more anxious, more stressed out, because I applied the same lens as I had to get this done, check this task off my To Do list. In some ways I look back and I was such a relic of the moment. I couldn't step back and observe the experience that I was having, because I was too caught up in trying to change it.

Did you go back to work immediately after your loss?
I had just lost my pregnancy, and went on a TV show where they wanted to talk to me about consumer trends in fashion. I was so sad, because I had just had this life-altering experience. I didn't want to talk about fashion trends and what people were going to buy. I remember going on air and the people on the show

were put off by me. I don't blame them. I felt so much self-hatred at that time. I put myself into these situations that I'm usually very comfortable in when I'm in a good headspace, but when you're in a darkness, to put yourself into these places, it just perpetuates a sense of self-disgust and hatred that it's hard to recover from.

Did you feel obligated to continue working?
My relationship with myself took a really tremendous toll after those experiences. I didn't let myself heal. I was so caught up with distracting myself and also getting better. It threw me into this vortex of . . . I don't know what better words than 'self-disgust' are.

How did you communicate with friends and family in the time after your loss?
My best friend and sister-in-law were both pregnant at the same time as I had been, which I didn't know until after my pregnancy had ended. Both were due on the same day that I was. It felt very biblical, it felt like I had this anger and resentment and jealousy inside of me. It was difficult for me to be around anyone, frankly.

Were you able to spend time with your best friend and sister-in-law through their pregnancies?
Not for a little bit, no. When my sister-in-law gave birth to her son, I think that was the peak darkness for me. The following summer I went to their house to see

the baby and collapsed on to the floor. I was a ghost. I had to leave. It was extremely dramatic. I look back and I wish I had been able to embody what I knew intellectually. That none of these other babies were my babies, and I didn't want them to be my babies, I wanted my own. I have apologised to my sister-in-law multiple times, but we've never quite spoken about it candidly. She's extremely respectful of what I had gone through, but I would be surprised if she wasn't hurt. I understand, I would be hurt too.

Would you be as open now, as you were when you shared your experience a few years ago?
On the one hand, I've already gone through the motion of sharing the loss and I think contributed to starting a conversation that has been meaningful and healing for a lot of people. I think if it were to happen again, I would probably just want to grieve in private. There's an intimacy and beauty about grieving with loved ones, that I didn't actually experience as I was so caught up with the public performance of the grieving. I connected more with the commenters, many of whom were faceless strangers, than I did with my own family. That could be because none of my family had experienced it to the degree that I did. I felt very alone, and I think I perpetuated that sense of loneliness, when I could have found some really deep and intimate togetherness from the people I needed it from most. I wouldn't want to sacrifice that again.

Real life happens when your online life is closed. I know everyone says that and it sounds so trite, until you experience it deep in your bones, the intimacy of human connection, sitting in a room on a couch with your friends, empty wine glasses all around you and no phone anywhere near you.

It's been five years. How do you look back at your experience now?
I see it as time that I stole from myself, if I'm being quite honest. I had an opportunity to really slow down and start to evaluate some of the decisions I was making in the broader scope of my life, and whether they were aligned or misaligned with my integrity. I didn't take that opportunity. It almost felt like I was being given this godly chance to course-correct, if that is what I'd wished. I'm extremely grateful I've been able to help other women feel less self-conscious and alone in their own loss, but I didn't prioritise healing myself. I don't regret anything. It is how it is and the only way I know how I stole time from myself is because in the past two years I have done just the opposite. I have been very patient with myself and have given myself time, so I see that disparity, that difference. I think of how much more meaningful the sharing could have been if I were going a little slower.

It can be hard to make any decisions following loss, but the one area where I would advise paying close attention to how your mental health is being affected is on social media. I can see that during the deepest state of my depression after losing Axel, even though I found a lot of kindness from others, it would have been advisable for me to not be on social media. I was finding the simplest of daily tasks challenging, so to have the constant swirl of pregnancy loss information I sought added to my thoughts became a mental overload. My mind was extremely fragile and, looking back, I can see that social media wasn't a place where I would be able to rebuild my mental state with any clarity. The continuing lives of those on social media made me feel hopeless. The beautiful images of those with toned bodies made me feel hatred for my body that was carrying weight, with no baby to make me feel it was all worth it. I began to feel jealous of those who were pregnant, or had recently given birth. Somehow, in the depths of grief and confusion, I knew that the negatives were far outweighing the positives and I made the decision to no longer scroll through the daily feed of images. I posted images to my account and responded to messages, but, for months after my loss, I didn't look at another account. Ultimately, this was a positive move to protect my mental health.

I asked doula and wellness advocate Latham Thomas for her views on how to use social media in the immediate period following pregnancy loss.

> I think it can be both positive and negative. Social media can be a powerful tool, but a cruel master. It can help people find community and friendship, and people they

want to be friends with for ever. You may also encounter places where you leave feeling angry, or anxious. I recommend all of us take some time to practise 'phone fasting'. Tuning out social chatter and being present with yourself and your feelings is helpful as we navigate challenging times. Sometimes reading other people's stories online doesn't feel good, and also reading the comments about it can be worse. In the attention economy that we're in right now, where everything's about 'likes', it can be extremely harmful to engage when you are emotionally vulnerable. There are some people who have found ways to commodify their loss in ways that don't feel good. On the other hand, social media has been a wonderful way for people to share their personal experiences with loss and create a virtual family and find that much needed village online. It's been life-saving for people to find the professional resources and content needed to advance their healing.

With social media being a hard habit for me to break, I replaced scrolling through images with manual tasks. I read books, getting lost in memoirs and accounts of political scandals. I cleared drawers and organised wardrobes and cupboards. I spent time writing about my feelings and experiences of loss. I created physical photo albums that I had been meaning to do for years and mended clothing that had lost buttons or pulled fabric. Anything to keep my hands and mind busy. It was at this time that I realised how addictive social media had become in general, which was positive to note for a time when I would return to a more active relationship with the apps in the future.

Although it can be difficult to remove ourselves from social media, we have a choice. I personally found the activity of pregnancy loss posts too conflicting. Although some accounts were straightforward and informative, other accounts were highlighting and encouraging negative feelings towards those who were announcing their pregnancies or enjoying posting beautiful images of their newborns. I did not want to be angry. Quite the opposite. I wanted to feel uplifted, not join in the berating of those who were right to proudly show their scans, pregnancy bumps and newborn babies. My loss should not mean that others needed to hide their baby joy.

If, like me, social media caused unhealthy triggers, then it could be more beneficial to remove yourself from the apps for a while. Knowing what I know now, if I were to go back to when I lost my son, I would have an immediate go-to activity to minimise that self-inflicted pain. Write in a journal, continue with a DIY project, bake a cake, anything! Just have something that you have already decided you will turn to when unhelpful urges arise. For me, there was no pre-arranged agreement with myself that I would do something to avert my attention from baby news, so I continued to scroll social media and websites that made me feel infinitely worse.

Pregnancy apps

I had registered my account using an email address I use for apps, mailing lists and anything connected to paying bills. I seldom checked the email account, so when I deleted a pregnancy app from my phone, I didn't think to unsubscribe my email at the same time. My mind was overwhelmed, so to think of these actions was the last thing I would have considered. When opening that email account, I saw the email headers alerting me to the growing stages of my baby. Rather than deleting them, I opened one and clicked a link to the main site. I spent what must have been an hour reading how big my baby would be that week had he lived, how big he would have been the following week, the week after that. It wasn't helpful. It can be incredibly difficult to not click links and read information, but if you can walk away from the phone or computer and find a distraction, that's going to help your mental state greatly.

A shared pregnancy journey

One of the most isolating times after pregnancy loss is knowing you are no longer part of an in-person or online pregnancy group. The friends you made in these groups will be continuing their pregnancies without you. It would likely be too painful for you, and too uncomfortable for them, to have you remain connected to the group. Hearing of the pregnancy milestones and eventual births would be too upsetting. In these instances, it is important to consider that you are mourning lost friends, as well as mourning your baby. This friendship group will not be a considerable loss in all you have experienced, but it will be an additional hurdle you may encounter.

I didn't join a physical parenting group or online space, but did meet a lady in the local park who was a week ahead of me in her pregnancy. We would frequently see one another and conversations would revolve around our pregnancies and how we were feeling. Part way through the expected nine-month pregnancy, my stomach began to decrease in size, hers continued to grow.

Although my local park is close by, I began walking to a park a mile from our home with my son so as not to see her. I largely managed to avoid her, averting my eyes if I happened to see her in the neighbourhood. I am unsure if she realised that I had lost my baby in pregnancy. I sometimes see her, back in the playground across the street. We no longer say hello, so I assume she must have worked out what happened to me and my baby. It became a little uncomfortable for a while.

I see her son with her at the park and think that's how big Axel would be too. I see him climbing the stairs to the slide and imagine my son at his age. I try not to stare. I don't want to get a reputation as the strange lady in the park who stares at children. Imagine, I could be known as the neighbourhood witch causing nightmares amongst the under-fives. But I do catch myself staring sometimes, as my reality hits me. Until one of us moves away from the neighbourhood, I think I will always look over and see what could have been.

Parenting forums

Parenting forums can be excellent. They can guide, advise and encourage. They can also cause anxiety, fear and accentuate depression in those who are feeling vulnerable. There can be a fine line between having online forums act as a form of self-help, or exacerbating existing grief and anxiety.

What Now?

After Axel died, I needed help. I needed information, comfort, guidance and the hope that somehow everything was going to be okay. I did what most of us do and spent hours online each day searching for websites and forums that may offer some answers. There were helpful moments, where I found a blog post or site that I connected with, places where I found practical advice and gentle support. There were also moments where my grief was compounded by information and comments that were not at all helpful to my mental state.

The pregnancy loss community as a whole is a supportive one. A community that understands this shared experience and wants each and every person touched by loss to find their way out of a state of grief. Unhelpful scenarios occur when anger, fear and competitiveness arise. There can be a hierarchy in stages of loss, levels of grief and in planning future pregnancies. This negative tone in forums isn't something that presents itself too often, but if you find yourself consuming this unhelpful content, it can result in the prolonged effect, or worsening, of your mental health.

Therapist Claire Bidwell Smith has her own views on how forums may, or may not, be helpful following pregnancy loss.

Online can sometimes get tricky. People can feel they have licence to say things that may not be helpful. In-person support groups that are held by a therapist or counsellor are terrific because they are moderated by someone who has training, but I think you can hurt yourself or get hurt by reading some of the forums that are out there. I feel you have to be careful, you can be traumatising yourself by reading the content, taking in all of the information, comparing your own experience to others'. It often doesn't serve you. I think when you're in acute grief it can do more harm than good. In the long run, social media has a lot of positives that can come with grieving and community, but in the beginning throes of grief, it can really hurt. Nobody's really showing the full picture online, so you may feel others are doing better than you are, or even that you should be grieving more. But eventually, when you've come to understand your grief and you're more settled with it, you can hold it in a different way – in that realm you can feel more confident in your experience of loss so the forums are no longer as dangerous in their potential impact.

I found the vast amount of information overwhelming and, a few weeks after losing Axel, I stopped myself from reading any sites or forums. I found it difficult to cut myself off in this way. I now realise that the habit of reading, and rereading, certain sites and forums acted as triggers for my pain. I already felt terrible, and reading this content had the capacity to make me feel worse. If you feel that online forums may help you to make sense of your loss or offer much needed support, my advice would be to find one space that makes you feel comfortable and stay right there. Ask questions in the space you have found, find your answers that way. Going from forum to forum can sometimes prove unhelpful. Changing of opinions, unfamiliar names and a great deal of shared pain may prove overwhelming. It can be helpful to have a friend recommend a forum, or help you search for one that feels right for you.

The day you lost your baby

The first year after Axel died was the hardest. I could feel my emotions building in the week of his birthday and felt understandably teary. I wanted to tell everyone that it was Axel's birthday that week, to let them know I wasn't forgetting him. There was nobody to invite to his birthday, nobody knew him. My husband, my son and I walked around the cemetery that day and ate cake underneath the tree where Axel's ashes were scattered. We sang happy birthday and told him how much we loved and missed him. That night, my husband and I went out for dinner and marked the one-year birthday of our baby. The toast to Axel was sad, I was sad, but it was helpful to get dressed up, leave the house and be surrounded by an atmosphere that wasn't sad at all.

Doing something ceremonial, such as a gathering of family and friends, or dinner with your partner, can mark the day in a simple yet meaningful way. You may not wish to do or say anything, but instead light a candle and watch a film on the sofa. Walking in a forest, or along a beach, can be a way to clear your mind and spend time in nature, which usually allows for a mental reset, no matter how brief. This also works as a way to take a temporary break from your usual surroundings, where memories of your loss are likely to be more vivid.

The five years since Axel died have become easier. I can still feel a deep level of sadness as Axel's June birthday approaches, but I notice the difference in how I feel each year. There is the distance of time, which causes mixed feelings of peace in acceptance and guilt in moving on. I keep busy in the week of Axel's birthday, which allows for welcome distractions. I see friends, or ensure that's the week I clear paperwork and reorganise cupboards and wardrobes at home. There is no guarantee that time will heal your trauma, but the hope is that you feel your grief lessen with each year that passes.

Your due date

The days leading up to Axel's due date were not as emotional as I had expected. Perhaps because I had lived with his loss for a few months and the reality that he would not be born on this date was heavily ingrained in my mind. I was still struggling with the grief and depression of his loss, along with going through another cycle of IVF, so his due date became one part of a bigger picture. I felt I should have been more connected to his due date, but in some way I was thankful that I was not facing another highly emotional challenge. The day was peaceful, and I didn't remind friends or family of the significance of this date. It was lovely for my husband and I to keep Axel's due date quiet and to celebrate simply by ourselves.

Like me, your baby's due date may not cause further trauma, or you may be heavily triggered by the date you were planning to bring your baby into the world. For many, planning a future with your baby begins after you see a positive pregnancy test. Predicting the due date, then having it confirmed at your first scan can mean months of planning ahead in your mind. What was meant to be the day you met your baby can then become the biggest reminder of your loss.

Ahead of your due date, it can be advisable to schedule a few days' holiday leave from work during that time, or plan to do something with your partner or friends on the day. Be mindful of previously highlighted due-date reminders, such as in your personal calendar, or pregnancy apps that you may have inadvertently forgotten to delete. Staying off of social media as a way to avoid further pregnancy triggers can be helpful. Doing something to honour your baby, such as arranging a small dinner at home, can be a gentle way to occupy part of your day and be with close friends or family. Spending the day with your partner doing things you love can be a way to make the day special, rather than feeling overwhelmed at home. I have always found distractions helpful, not as a way to forget, but as a way to lessen the intensity of unavoidable pain.

Burial, memorial and rituals

Having a funeral or memorial, in whatever form, will be a personal choice for parents following pregnancy loss. A few hours after Axel had died, a midwife brought a folder of information into our hospital room, placing it gently to the side of the bed. The information detailed the options for funerals, should we wish to have one for our baby. There was no question in my mind that I wanted a ceremony for my son. I didn't want to leave the decision of what to do with his body in the hands of others.

Funeral

Different ways to bury or cremate your baby will be available to you. It is always best to be clear on how you wish for your baby's body to be cared for when they have died at any stage in pregnancy. Some parents choose to arrange a burial in their own garden, or have a private funeral director take care of the funeral. My husband and I chose to follow the guidance from a midwife who looked after us on the day of our loss. She suggested we contact a local funeral director to help us with the cremation plans, which we did without considering other options.

A few days after Axel died, my husband and I walked to a funeral director's close to our home. Arranging any kind of funeral was not something that had ever crossed my mind, and I didn't know what to expect. The lady we met was kind and explained the types of services that would be available for our son. We looked through a catalogue of coffins. I remember staring at the pages, trying to make a considered decision from the options we had in front of us. Everything felt so utterly surreal. The coffins were sized for dolls, but our son would be placed in one on the day we would say a final goodbye to his body. We chose a simple, beautiful white wooden coffin with silver accents.

Axel's funeral was scheduled for weeks after his death. We had to await his post-mortem results, and for his body to be taken from the hospital to the funeral director. The waiting was unbearable. I wanted my baby with me, to know where he was. Although I knew his body was now naturally cold, I wanted him to be wrapped in a blanket for warmth.

I knew he couldn't hear anything, but I wanted someone to read him books in the evening. I needed the funeral to happen. I needed to have my baby back.

Weeks after Axel's death came the morning of his funeral. A hearse had been arranged to carry Axel's coffin for the fifteen-minute drive to the cemetery. My husband and I were asked if we wanted to travel in the hearse, but we decided to cycle our bikes directly from home. The hours ahead already felt overwhelming, so cycling to the cemetery relieved some of the emotional weight of the morning. We cycled slowly through the cemetery, commenting on gravestone tributes as we passed. We could see a hearse slowly driving to the entrance of the crematorium ahead and knew the car was for us, that Axel was inside. We locked our bikes and stood for a moment just looking at the car beyond the manicured gardens. We were at our baby's funeral.

We had chosen the Beatles song 'Here Comes the Sun' for the service. It was playing as my husband walked with our son's coffin in his arms from the car and into the main building. Without having been in this particular cemetery before that morning, I hadn't known what to expect. I imagined the crematorium setting to be a simple room, similar to a stark-looking corporate office. But it was lovely, with carved wooden pews and stained-glass windows reflecting on the walls from the bright July sun. It was just my husband and I there that morning. We wanted the final goodbye to be simple, to be between us and our baby. I found the day very calm, peaceful even. My husband cried much of the morning, but this was the one time that I didn't. To me, the day was a chance to have my son back with me. I hadn't been close to him in person for weeks. It seemed as though he had been on a trip and was coming home. I am not religious, but I felt that this was finally the end of the journey for his body. It was comforting to know he could now rest and I would know where his body would be. The final verse of 'Here Comes the Sun' played, and we could see Axel's coffin begin to move away from us. As Paul McCartney's last line told us it was going to be all right, my husband tightly gripped my hand, and we knew Axel's body had gone.

I hadn't considered that there may be varying ways in which to hold a burial or memorial service. There can be questions around just how to mark the loss of a baby you may only see in person as you say goodbye. After Axel's death, my mind had taken me straight to the two funerals I had attended at that point, seeing them as the order in which things were done. I loved Axel's cremation ceremony, it was exactly as it should be, peaceful and kind. Only months afterwards did I start to think of the different ways in which we could have said goodbye.

It can be hard in the weeks after a pregnancy loss to take control of anything around you. I found I followed the guidance of others, rather than having to think of anything myself. Medical appointments, nursery drop-offs, funeral arrangements. I went with whatever schedule I was given. My husband and I arranged to see a local funeral director, were given information on burials and cremations, and that all seemed fine. It *was* fine. Only now, with research and a clear mind, can I see other ways in which we may have said goodbye to our baby.

Religion

As someone who does not follow any religious or spiritual belief, it was difficult for me to ask a god, or a spiritual power outside of myself, for help. Through the most intense grieving period, I often prayed at night, although to which god I was unsure. I just knew I needed the help I wasn't finding in my daily life. For the first time, I understood the power of belief and finding another source to ask for guidance and clarity. Those moments alone in my bedroom were private, and I found a level of power in taking control of my situation in this way. I found comfort in the ritual of asking, begging almost, for someone to help me through a grief I did not believe I could ever move beyond. It felt as though, for these moments, I was taking charge of my thoughts, rather than have my thoughts overwhelm me.

As I read more about certain faiths and the religious beliefs concerning pregnancy loss, I found there was unexpected empathy surrounding pregnancy loss in many cultures. I had wrongly assumed that, in many faiths, a pregnancy loss would be seen as a failure. I have no doubt my assumptions stemmed from the failure I felt in myself as a mother due to my own loss.

There are faiths where deep consideration must be made in certain situations concerning pregnancy loss. Choosing to end a pregnancy in certain religions brings another level of grief, judgement and mental conflict. When speaking of pregnancy loss, we can often forget that ending a pregnancy for medical reasons is a huge part of the conversation. When parents know a longed-for baby will not survive, their faith will affect not only their decision, but the long-term mental effects of going against what they may believe is right.

In writing and researching this book, I spent time speaking with mothers who had differing religious beliefs. Mothers who generously gave their time to speak of their pregnancy loss and explain how faith played a part in their healing. I heard how communities often rallied round the mother and how, in many instances, there was an honouring of the life the parents had seen as part of their future. There were times when pregnancy loss was kept private, only spoken of between the couple who had lived through the experience. There were mothers who had not spoken of their loss to anyone, not a partner or doctor, deciding to live the experience alone. As I went further on my journey to understand how others navigated the journey of pregnancy loss, it became apparent early on in my conversations that there is no set or standard way to experience loss, grief and eventual acceptance.

Memorial and rituals

A memorial service or ritual can help parents and those close to them acknowledge their loss in a meaningful way. Being present for any form of ceremony is something that can be spoken of as you remember the loss through the years. It can be a way to honour a baby that was seen as part of your future.

There is no time limit on memorial services or performing rituals. You may wish to hold a memorial service soon after your loss, it may take years, or you may not wish to do anything at all. Many parents choose to keep the memories in their mind, instead of speaking of their experience at any time in the future. Others find that, in time, they want to commemorate the baby they lost privately, or with friends and family. There are many ways in which you can create a memorial or ritual, I have detailed popular ways, but a memorial or ritual can come in any form.

Something many parents choose to do is plant a tree in memory of their baby. It can symbolise growth, hope and new life. Having a tree in your private garden is often the favoured option, but in the future you may choose to move, leaving you without access to the tree. Unless you are certain you will not move from your current home, planting the tree (with council consent) in a public space means the tree will always be accessible to you. If you do not have a private space or public permission to plant a tree, there are many environmental organisations that will plant one in your baby's honour for a small donation. To know a tree that symbolises your baby is within a protected forest can feel both comforting and meaningful.

A naming ceremony is an occasion to bring family and friends together to remember your baby. Any ceremony where those close to you are present forms a memory and acknowledgement of the life you lost. If you don't know, or chose not to know, the gender of your baby, a neutral gender name can be chosen. Or a nickname you called your baby through pregnancy.

There is a tradition in Buddhist culture where small statues that represent babies and children who die are placed in a meaningful space. Many cultures have adopted this tradition, using interpretations of the original Japanese figures, which are called Jizo statues. Jizo is often described as the Buddhist guardian of lost children. Those who place a Jizo in their chosen space, such as in a garden or in their home, can find focus and peace in a statue that represents and honours their own loss. Placing your own Jizo publicly or privately can be a comforting representation of a future you envisaged with the baby you lost. It is said that Jizo also protects any future pregnancy you may have, which is another way to focus on something hopeful when your mind may be overwhelmed with negatives.

Having a tattoo to symbolise your baby can also be a way to feel they are with you. I have often considered having a small A tattooed somewhere on my body. It is only my fear of needles that is preventing me. Ironic that I should be so afraid of needles, having injected myself hundreds of times through six rounds of IVF. I do love the idea of a small tattoo and think there is something beautiful in looking at a part of your body and seeing something that symbolises the baby, or babies, that couldn't stay.

There are many ways in which to honour a lost life. Reading a tribute, or poem, at a gathering of family and friends. Releasing balloons and watching them until they can no longer be seen can symbolise the beginning of letting go of pain and grief. Laying flowers on open water and seeing them float away is another way that can signify the start of a journey to releasing painful emotions.

THREE

What Next?

Facing the world after loss can be incredibly hard. You may have announced your pregnancy to friends and family, so will have to explain that you are no longer pregnant. It's possible you will face potentially difficult questions and experience unintentionally hurtful comments from those who are unsure what to say or do. Returning to work may be a challenge, as in many cases women feel they have to hide their physical and emotional pain so as not to make others uncomfortable. Most losses are unexpected, so it's unlikely you will know how to navigate life soon after losing your baby. Through the first months following loss, it can be helpful to find ways in which you can release expectations from yourself and from those around you. I hope you will find this section particularly helpful in guiding you, and those supporting you, with life after pregnancy loss.

Through the first year – a personal experience

When the story of the night my baby died was published in British *Vogue*, I thought I would receive a few kind words from friends. I hadn't anticipated the reaction and the numerous familiar stories of shared grief that reached my inbox.

When I wrote my story in early September of 2017, two months before it was published, I was feeling more optimistic, with a renewed sense of hope. By the end of that month my emotional state had drastically altered, I was sinking and couldn't find a way to pull myself out of what had become a state of deep depression. The experience of watching my baby die had taken me from shock to trauma, to cruise control. Only now I was really living it in a way that I hadn't before.

I didn't make the understanding I craved easy for anyone. I went out, I masked how I felt and tried my hardest not to talk about what had happened. It had been months. Life moves on. But for me it wasn't moving, I was reliving my pain every single day.

I continued working, not believing I could stop at any point due to running my own business. Each night after returning home from a day of interaction with the outside world, I broke. I cried hard the minute I walked through the door. I had returned to work five days after my baby had passed away. I hadn't taken the time to grieve. I desperately needed to find a way to lift myself out of what was becoming an endless, exhausting cycle.

I had read that you are incredibly fertile following the loss of a pregnancy. Not emotionally ready at all, I had my first IVF embryo transfer a couple of months after I had lost my five-month pregnancy. I desperately needed to be fixed. I assumed this was my answer. The pregnancy test was, unsurprisingly, negative. A second IVF cycle followed. Another negative result.

Soon after the second failed IVF, I reached a point that I hope never to experience again. Facing another day waking with a feeling of overwhelming grief and trauma was something I couldn't face any longer. As I lay awake in the middle of the night next to my husband, an intense fear overcame me as I contemplated how to end what had become a Groundhog-Day reality. The physical and mental pain of waking each morning with a tight chest and extreme anxiety had become unbearable.

Although I had no means to make this a reality, and had not attempted to search for anything that may have aided my darkest thoughts, I could feel how dangerous these thoughts were and woke my husband. We sat talking for hours. The talking kept me just above desperation level, where I could begin to understand that I had reached my lowest point.

Ordinarily days turned into months with exasperating speed, but I hadn't known a year could be so long. The depression didn't ease until spring, when I felt things were finally getting lighter. Having not been successful in our natural attempts to get pregnant, the conversation returned to IVF and my husband and I decided that, as things were improving on an emotional level, we were ready to embark on another round of IVF.

Certain that now was our time, the prospect of another baby and my renewed energy for the next IVF cycle made life feel positive. The transfer was successful and the two-week wait to see if this third attempt had worked was both consuming and exciting. Another negative. Not to be beaten, IVF round four was placed in our diaries and, yes, like all the others, I thought this would be the one. With what felt to be sure signs of pregnancy, I was both surprised and hugely disappointed to see only one line appear when taking the first of many home pregnancy tests.

Early nights, no alcohol, limited exercise and a strict diet that becomes wholly monotonous may seem like small sacrifices, but a continual stop-start existence coupled with loss and hope for another child became intensely draining.

In the year following the loss of my baby I experienced trauma, depression, heartache and unexplained reasons for not getting pregnant. Although that year remains a dark period in my life, in many ways I had been given a sense of freedom that I didn't have before. There's a lightness that cannot be explained when you can let go of anything that doesn't have true meaning in your life. And that is what Axel gave to me the night he couldn't stay.

I spoke to Rhiannon and Nico about losing their daughter during childbirth and how they navigated the first year without her.

R: Our pregnancy was really straightforward. I was content, managed to stay relaxed and did loads of yoga and hypnobirthing. We happened to be put on a community midwife programme, where we were assigned the home-birthing team, who do all their appointments at home, so our fantastic midwife turned up at our house at the eight-week booking appointment and was with us through the rest of our pregnancy. With everything that happened for us, some things do feel like fate, like there were certain people who were gifted to us because we would need them, and she is one of them.

At forty-one-plus weeks, after a few sweeps, my waters broke at home. I was getting a few aches, but nothing was happening, so I knew we would have to go to hospital. We'd been planning for a home birth if possible, but I'd always been relaxed about having to go into hospital if we needed to.

It was in September 2020, during the Covid pandemic. One positive was that two days before I was admitted to hospital, the rules had changed, allowing partners to be with the mother giving birth. Before this, until the mother was in active labour, the partner wasn't allowed to be in the hospital.

N: Had Rhiannon gone into labour the week before, I would have missed everything. I think I would have been so angry. I wouldn't have believed it had happened in a way. Everything had been fine when we went to the hospital.

Did you feel any reason for concern during your labour?
R: The midwives explained that our baby didn't want to come out and I would need to be induced, which made me feel wobbly. I was mentally preparing for a caesarean section, which I didn't want to have. As my waters had broken, I was on antibiotics from when I arrived and was being monitored continuously. In our situation, nothing more could have been done in terms of monitoring. They started the induction and I slept a bit through the night, and the next morning Catrin still wasn't showing any signs of coming. The midwives

upped the induction medication and I tried to stay as active as possible to encourage my baby to come.

I was attached to machines monitoring Catrin's heartbeat and movement. There was a slight concern due to her heart rate slowing, then the monitor lost her heartbeat. The emergency cord was pulled and I was being asked if I could feel any movement from my baby. I didn't know, I was in a panic, I had just been focusing on my contractions until this point. When they pulled the cord, that was the moment when I was truly scared.

Close to fifteen people came into the room at once. It was like a military operation. I was laid on my side, the induction drugs that were being administered through tubes were stopped. The team of doctors and midwives were clearly working through each scenario, if one thing didn't work, they would move to the next thing.

I had an emergency caesarean under general anaesthetic. Everyone was amazing. I remember being wheeled down to theatre, terrified and sobbing. One of the midwives I went past looked at me, her eyes looked so sad. It was then that I thought, oh no, I knew what was happening wasn't good.

In theatre, the lovely anaesthetist told me he was going to put me to sleep and when I woke up I was going to meet my beautiful baby. As I was going under, I called for Nico, who told me he loved me and that everything was going to be fine. One of the hardest things was that Nico then had to wait outside the room.

N: A midwife gave me some scrubs for theatre, but I was told I couldn't go in because of the surgery Rhiannon was having.

R: I had an acute infection, which my baby couldn't cope with. When they opened me up in theatre, my entire womb was filled with meconium. Catrin was overwhelmed by it. The doctors tried to resuscitate her, but it was too late. I had been on antibiotics, but it was a fluke that the infection took hold. Catrin wasn't able to make it.

Nico, how were you feeling throughout this experience? With all that was happening, and you not being allowed into the operating theatre with Rhiannon.
N: I went back to the room we had been in before Rhiannon was taken to theatre. I was told Rhiannon wanted to see me, so I ran back to the operating room and was able to see her for a very short time. Rhiannon was just going under. All I remember is seeing Rhiannon's face and about twenty people standing around her. I was told to pack our bag in the other room. Although it was unclear to any of us at this point what was going to happen, I was told we wouldn't be going back to the room we had been in. Adrenaline was pumping as I packed our things into bags. A porter, or perhaps receptionist, came into the room and I said, You're just going to have to talk to me. I was feeling

manic, my whole body was shaking. I just needed someone to talk to me. I wasn't considering what the outcome could be.

Nico, were you there for Catrin's birth?
N: No, I was still in the room we had been in. A doctor came in and told me Catrin had been born, but that she wasn't doing well. He said they were working on her. I later found out they had tried to resuscitate her for about twenty minutes. I was feeling dazed, partly because we were convinced we were having a boy. I thought it was a nice surprise that we were having a girl, as I had been so prepared to have a boy. I was reassured Rhiannon was fine, that she was recovering.

About fifteen minutes later, which felt like for ever and no time at all, a doctor and three midwives came into my room, shutting a curtain behind them. The doctor knelt by me. It was then I was told Catrin had died.

I was asked if I wanted to see Catrin, which I didn't want to do without Rhiannon. I was terrified to see my baby. I didn't want to believe what had happened was real.

R: At this time, I was still unconscious. I didn't come round from the anaesthetic for forty minutes. Nico had to live through it, knowing Catrin had died and waiting for me to come round to tell me. That's the part that hurts so much, that Nico knew and had to wait.

N: I was so in shock at that point. I sat down and didn't know if I could stand back up. My legs were jelly. At some point I was told I could see Rhiannon, but I don't remember getting from my room to her in the recovery room. It was all very hazy.

R: When I came round from the anaesthetic, I just knew. It very quickly became the process of living with the knowledge that Catrin had died. I had been given a lot of morphine, and I remember repeatedly saying, 'Oh dear, oh no.' It slowly came to me, the enormity of what had happened. Even a month after, I could only look at the situation in little bits. I could only look at the tiniest part of it, as if I looked at the whole of it, it was overwhelming.

How long were you able to be with Catrin at the hospital?
R: Our midwife, who had been with us the night before as I was being induced, came to see us an hour after Catrin had been born. Catrin was with us, and our midwife held her. She immediately placed Catrin on me so we could experience skin to skin. We hadn't had a baby before, so hadn't thought to do this. We held her. She was so cute. She was 8lbs 4oz and long, she was a big baby. She was perfect.

We spent a day and night with her. We knew she couldn't stay with us, we knew she couldn't come home. We had photos with her, and the hospital gave us a lilac blanket. It's not a colour I would ever go to, but that is now the colour I associate with Catrin.

Even though it was the Covid pandemic and visitors were not allowed, because Catrin had died, they let my mum into the hospital to meet her.

The morning after she died, I was stroking her back and knew Nico hadn't truly bonded with her at this point. I understood it was more difficult for him, he hadn't carried her, he hadn't given birth to her. I called him to Catrin while I was stroking her back and saw him realise she was his. That she was ours. It was at this time I knew we had both bonded with her. We spent that day preparing to say goodbye. We knew one day was the right amount of time for us to be with her.

We spent our time holding Catrin, telling her how much we loved her. I had knitted her an elephant before she was born, which we gave her to take with her. Knowing Catrin and the elephant were together made me feel safe. I kept checking with the hospital that the elephant was still with her. We could give her so little, but we could give her that.

We knew she couldn't stay with us for ever. I felt so terrified of saying goodbye to her, but when she was gone, I felt utter peace.

How did you navigate telling those around you that Catrin had died?
R: One thing we found really important was to tell Catrin's story. We told the story so many times, we wanted to put our experience with other people. We

needed to cement it in our minds. Anyone we could tell the story to we did, so they could know Catrin. This is all we have of her. I was pregnant through the lockdown, so nobody really saw me. She felt very much ours throughout.

N: Because of lockdown, she felt almost like a secret. We were the only people who knew her.

R: We had to extricate ourselves from our bump and baby group. We had a message thread where they were all having their babies and would post pictures, so we started a separate thread to let them all know why we would be leaving the group. They were basically strangers, but were all so lovely when they read the news.

You're trying to claim you're a parent, but in the traditional sense, you're not a parent. I would overthink how people were reacting to us. I spent time trying to work out whether we call ourselves parents. Of course we're parents, but we did no active parenting.

When you lose your child in the way we lost Catrin, nobody says congratulations. I did all the work, but we didn't quite get there.

How have you found pregnancy announcements from friends and those close to you?
R: A lot of our friends have had children in the past year. Finding out they were pregnant was quite difficult, and once they have had the baby, their reaction can also be difficult. They have the best intentions,

not wanting to make you cry or hurt you, but it's happened, it's not going to hurt me any more than I'm hurting already. I cry whenever and wherever, although it happens far less now. There have been a few occasions when things have been said by friends where I can see they have no idea how much a casual comment can hurt.

N: I sometimes find it difficult to hear of others talking about their new-parent experiences. You don't want to get in the way of anybody's happiness, or remind people of our loss. It stings when you think, I should be in that situation.

R: I don't want anybody else's baby, I want my baby. I want Catrin here. The only thing I find hard now is when I see people actively parent, like getting their baby ready for bedtime. That's the bit of parenting I haven't done and I have nowhere to put all that care I was preparing to give.

Your whole life has been derailed. In that moment after Catrin died especially. The grief of losing a baby isn't like losing another family member. The grief is that your life hasn't changed. When my dad died, my whole life changed. When Catrin died, we were preparing for our lives to change, but they didn't. We could sleep through the night, we could go out for a drink.

N: The future with Catrin was all imagined. It hadn't happened yet. We had all this time as non-parents back.

Did you sit alone with your grief, or did you want to get out and amongst people?

R: I threw the doors open. Anyone was allowed in. I wanted to be with people. I had to keep moving. There were times I went over my limit, and had to be quiet in the house for a while. I was learning how to exist and sit with myself and be with myself.

Shortly after Catrin died, my mother and brother came to stay with us. We were watching a comedy programme one evening and I was doubled over with laughter. Obviously there's everything in the middle of your grief, but if you can find moments of humour, then you know you're going to survive it. If you can find a reason to just smile, see humour and understand it, then you know you will be okay.

I hated the idea of people thinking of us being here and it being a house of sorrow. There was sorrow, but, for us, before this happened we had chosen to build a house of joy so that was still there too. We were still ourselves, we were just coping with what we had been through.

N: My biggest fear was that I would become a different person. I'm optimistic, I like to be positive and I was scared of losing that. I realised you don't lose it, you just add to it. I still laugh at the same things I did two years ago, but you just have this element of grief you never knew existed.

R: If you protect yourself too much, how will you ever emerge into the world after it? Somehow the days do get easier and your mind does switch back into things. Sometimes the next day is not okay, but you know you have a good day in the bank, you know there will be good days again. You're able to contain anything after something like this happens.

I draw a lot of strength from Catrin. From the knowledge of her. During my pregnancy, I often listened to a Women of Rock playlist, with artists like Stevie Nicks and Janis Joplin. A month after she was born, I clearly remember walking home in the dark, listening to the playlist, feeling the power in the music. I had a little girl and she was mine. She's my daughter. I needed to learn to say those words, My Daughter, when she wasn't present. That's so important. It's empowering.

Did you choose to have a funeral for Catrin?
R: We held Catrin's funeral in the December of that year. The cemetery had Christmas trees up, with really pretty twinkling lights on them, it was so lovely. I sobbed through the entire ceremony, but I found the day really healing. My mum had sent a single rose and a card for Catrin, but it was just Nico and I who went to her funeral. We questioned ourselves on what to wear to our baby's funeral. It wasn't something we ever thought we would have to consider. I made myself a dress in a lilac colour, to match the blanket Catrin had been wrapped in at the hospital. Nico wore the blue suit from our wedding and I made him a matching

lilac pocket square. It felt like we had dressed for the wedding she was never going to have.

N: It was a beautiful, freezing sunny day. That day went back to Catrin being just ours.

R: When I was pregnant, I had woken up one morning with the Billy Joel song 'Always a Woman to Me' in my head. We thought we were having a boy, so the song had no relevance at the time. When we knew our baby was a girl, it became Catrin's song. We told everyone the time of the funeral and if they wanted to think of her, play that song, or light a candle; it could be a collective thing. After the ceremony, we walked around the cemetery and I just felt at peace. I didn't cry for the rest of the day.

Birthdays can be hard. How did you mark Catrin's first birthday?
R: We cried that morning, took a walk to get coffee and talked about Catrin. That afternoon we had arranged a gathering of friends in the park. I needed a focus for the day, so made plans, bought wine and cake and told friends where we would be. I laid out a large quilt and people came. There was no toast, no ceremony. A friend texted me after to say that's exactly what a first birthday party should be. Her birthday felt like this really brilliant day of healing, and since then I have felt a lot of peace.

What to expect from those around you

Talking to your children

If you have children at home, it can be helpful to assure them that the loss was not connected to anything they may have done. More children than we realise can have thoughts that something they did may have caused the loss of the baby. Even if you have not said or done anything to make them feel this way, it can be a huge positive to explain that pregnancy loss happens to many people and was in no way connected to them.

I felt it was best to tell my son what had happened immediately. As soon as he arrived at the hospital with my husband, I told him his baby brother had died, but that everything would be fine. I thought it might be confusing to tell him the baby was sleeping, or was unwell. He may have expected to see the baby alive at a later stage, causing further disappointment and possible distress. I also felt not telling him the complete truth may cause him to mistrust me in the future.

Accept that your child may ask insensitive questions. My son asked me on a few occasions why I kept crying. He asked me when things would get back to normal and why I was so upset all the time. We need to give children the space to ask these questions without getting upset or frustrated with them. My son had a way of repeating questions often, but I just had to give him the same response each time he asked and not let it upset me. I had to remind myself that it was impossible for him not to have been affected by what had happened and to be patient.

If possible, have friends or family take your other children for play dates, or do activities with them. Anything to get them out of the house. It's going to be unsettling for them to see their parents upset, or to sense a change in mood at home, so being distracted and out of the house can be hugely beneficial for their wellbeing.

Having a child's routine maintained as much as possible can help greatly. Although you may be deeply affected by your loss and may not want to do anything other than stay indoors, it can be a huge positive to focus on your children and keep their routine as normal as possible.

Often there can be a feeling of guilt that you are not paying your child or children enough attention. Or taking out feelings of sadness and anger on them. I know I could be snappy when my son, by then six, did nothing more than want me to play, or talk to me about something I would ordinarily have found endearing. My grief consumed me to the point that I could not hide it, even when I wanted to.

Sometimes a thought will come to mind that I have caused my son long-term psychological damage. That we will not see the effects of his experience until he reaches his teens. Or perhaps even later. I think about this often, and wonder if he has been deeply affected by his presence in the house on the night Axel died and by my depression that followed.

I spoke to therapist Claire Bidwell Smith about the effects loss and grief can have on the children of parents who lose a baby in pregnancy.

I think we have to make space for children to have their own questions, their own grief. And we also have to remember that it's okay for them to see us grieve. It's healthy to model grief for children – it will help them understand how to move through it for themselves. I also think it's important to include them in ways of honouring the baby that was lost, recognising that baby as part of the family, and including their memory.

Explaining you are no longer pregnant

Telling those around me who knew of my pregnancy, but were not close enough for me to call directly, was something I wanted to do soon after my loss. Sending a group email seemed a little too stark. I also wanted to tell those who had seen my pregnant images on social media and were kindly following my journey, many of whom I didn't know personally. I was apprehensive to share my deeply personal news via an online platform, but decided to write a post on my Instagram account a week after losing Axel. Alongside an image of his footprints surrounded by flowers, I explained that I had delivered Axel five months into my pregnancy and that he had passed away. I knew this would be the quickest way to let everyone know that I was no longer pregnant. I felt uneasy exposing myself and my baby in this way, but it prevented the well-meaning pregnancy comments that were unintentionally causing more pain. This post closed the door on needing to explain what had happened. Even if people were not connected to me on Instagram, I was sure those I knew would be told at some point that I had lost my baby. This felt like the first step of a long journey ahead, but it was a significant starting point.

Taking your time to let people know you are no longer pregnant is your privilege. If there is a time to feel absolutely no obligation to others, it's now. Should you wish to make your news known, asking a close friend or family member to do this for you can take the weight off of finding the right words to say. Spending hours on your phone telling people of your loss, along with responding to kind replies via messages, will require energy you are unlikely to have. I seldom used my phone in the weeks following my loss, I mostly just wanted to ignore the world around me.

I spoke to Kraig Wiedenfeld on his experience of surrogacy and how those around him reacted to his pregnancy loss.

Did you always know you wanted to be a father?
I am from a big family and always wanted to be a father. I spoke to my doctor, who was able to recommend a surrogacy agency for my husband and me. A surrogacy match doesn't happen immediately, so we waited for months before we heard anything. Then, one morning, I got the call. We had been matched with a surrogate who would carry our baby. We didn't want making a baby to be a business relationship, we wanted whoever would be our surrogate to play a part in our baby's life, to be an auntie.

The next part of the journey was finding an egg donor through an agency. After many meetings and lots of research, we decided on our donor. Then it was the process of moving forward and hoping we may get embryos for our surrogate to carry. We were lucky and did get a number of embryos. One embryo was implanted and we were fortunate that our surrogate became pregnant.

How were those first weeks of pregnancy?
I felt everything was going well. A few weeks into the pregnancy, our surrogate called. She wasn't feeling positive. We were told that at a scan there had been no fetal heartbeat. I had made so many plans for the baby. I wish I hadn't included so many people in the process. There was so much love thrown at me and I was so excited to have a baby that I couldn't stop telling people. Then when we found out we were no longer pregnant, I was devastated. I asked everybody who knew about our pregnancy not to contact me for a while. Both my husband and I were hit hard.

Were those who knew about your pregnancy supportive when your surrogate experienced pregnancy loss?
As a man, people treat you differently. I was told 'You got this.' I was expected to be fine immediately. It's not as soft as it is for females. The treatment I received was a little more encouraging, that I would be fine and to just try again. A lot of people expected me to

be fine. There's no way anybody would say to a female 'You've got more eggs, you've got more embryos,' but that's what it was like for me. I guarantee straight men get the same treatment when their wives or girlfriends lose a pregnancy, or their IVF doesn't work. It's a pat on the back and then we're expected to move on. I believe people had the best intentions, they were just quick to dismiss my concerns and tell me it was going to happen.

Did you want to try and get pregnant again immediately?
It took some time in between losing our pregnancy and for our surrogate to have another embryo implanted. When we tried to get pregnant a second time, I was worried. Other than family, I didn't tell anybody that we were trying again. After the second transfer, I was counting the days. I was anxious every day. This time our embryo didn't implant. It was now that I thought maybe we would never have a baby.

Did you begin to question whether you should try again?
I was unsure whether we should try again, but a great friend encouraged us to keep trying for our baby. She said we had embryos and that in the future we may regret not trying to have a baby when it was possible. We knew she was right, so we tried again. I remember at the IVF clinic, our third frozen embryo had been thawed, but the doctors had concerns. We were advised to wait and thaw our fourth embryo, which we

did. This embryo implanted and our surrogate carried our baby to full term.

Were you able to relax and believe that this time your baby was coming?
I counted down every day. Having experienced a pregnancy loss the first time, I knew that at any time things could go wrong. At the beginning, I only told a couple of close friends and family, then as the pregnancy progressed, I became more confident that our baby was going to make it. My husband and I also knew this was our last pregnancy, that we wouldn't go through it again. There was an additional pressure this time.

Did everything go well through this pregnancy?
Everything was great. Our surrogate carried our son to full term. I vividly remember the call that our surrogate was going into labour. I ran around our apartment getting everything we would need. My biggest fear leading up to the birth was missing it. When I knew our son was past the thirty-four-week mark, I stopped worrying that we were going to lose him, instead I began worrying that I would miss the birth. Everybody at the hospital was so kind to us. My husband and I were there for the birth, we cut the umbilical cord, it was beautiful.

What Next?

The world around you can be a very different place after pregnancy loss. I found I became overly aware of people walking close to me, noise levels seemed heightened and I was generally more nervous when leaving the house. Extreme scenarios such as being seriously injured while out often came to mind, caused by the anxiety of having something taken from me that I simply couldn't replace. I have always been very outgoing and generally unconscious of any potential danger, but I became introverted for a period of time and suffered from intense anxiety for many months following the loss of my baby. I was fearing my own death and the death of those I loved. Fearing death after loss is completely natural, but it can give you the sense that you are slowly losing control of reality.

Talking to friends helped immensely. I chose not to call friends, instead I let those around me choose their own time when they would check in on me. There were a few friends who really showed how much they cared, contacting me often and letting me know that I could talk for as long as I wanted about my loss. I felt I was a burden much of the time, as I was unable to talk of little else, but friends allowed me the time and space to talk about my experience. I talked about my baby for much of the time spent with others, but also reminded myself to ask questions about my friends' lives too. It was difficult to change the subject, but asking about others' lives was actually a much needed distraction. It made me feel part of a more normal world than the one I was living in at that time.

Returning to work

If you are returning to a workplace where nobody knew you were pregnant, you will be hiding your physical pain and grief. There may be occasions at work where you feel challenged and need additional help with tasks while your mind is occupied with your loss, but are unable to ask without explaining to colleagues why. It is your decision whether or not to share your reasons for seeming distracted or vague in the workplace, but, in most instances, it can be helpful to explain that you have experienced a loss. With hope, your employer will be compassionate. It is not unheard of to be given a couple of days' paid leave, but as leave for pregnancy loss is not legally recognised in most countries, this will be at the discretion of your boss. If you do share your reasons for wanting time away from the office, you will need to be prepared that not all employers will understand the level of pain you are going through. You may be expected to continue working as you had before your loss, which due to this lack of compassion can prove hurtful. This is when a support system outside of your workplace will be particularly helpful. If you have also chosen to stay silent with friends and family, this may be the time to confide in at least one person, so you can discuss any challenges you may be facing at work. In almost all cases, being able to talk openly about a pregnancy loss can prove effective in working through any challenges that arise as a result of your grief.

I went back to work five days after Axel died, which was too soon. To the outside world it looked as though life was normal. My Instagram posts went up as usual and at work I greeted customers in my loose-fitting clothes. As I had just opened my new clothing store, I felt I had no choice but to be there. The additional anxiety of having a failed business, along with a failed pregnancy, was too much to bear. I painfully thanked clients who had seen my proud pregnancy posts on social media for their well wishes on my pregnancy. Most didn't know I was no longer pregnant. My world was broken and every minute of pretending everything was fine was surreal.

In some ways I enjoyed carrying on as if everything was normal. It was the mental escape I needed, although pretending I was fine was challenging. Crying was an emotional release, so through the day I would lock myself in the bathroom and sob. The hum of activity outside the door masked the sound. This release allowed me to return to the shop for a few hours, before heading back to the bathroom to perform what became something of a ritual. I was in pain both mentally and physically, but crying for these short periods through the day was the key to keeping things as controlled as possible at work.

I had opened a women's fashion boutique, so naturally there would be clients who were pregnant or new mothers. Ordinarily, I loved speaking to those who came to the store, but I froze whenever I was faced with a bump or pram coming through the door. I couldn't simply ignore them, but neither was I able to show interest in their pregnancies or babies.

There were some particularly challenging moments. On one occasion, a new mother came into the store. Her newborn baby was in its pram. The mother began trying on clothes, concealed behind the dressing room curtain, while the pram was left in the middle of the store. Her baby began crying, but the mother stayed behind the curtain. I can only assume she thought I would go to the pram and comfort her baby, as any decent person would do. I couldn't go. The crying alone was causing me distress, so I knew I couldn't see or hold the baby. The mother must have thought I was awful, that I was callous not to try to comfort her baby. Thankfully I was never faced with another situation like this. I learned to live with the pregnant figures who would frequent my store, somehow finding a way to disconnect my feelings from their presence.

Although taxing to be in an environment that triggered my grief, one small consolation was that I was self-employed. I had the option to walk away from my store whenever I felt overwhelmed, and for however long I needed. Unfortunately, those who are not self-employed don't have these choices. It is often the case that there is a financial necessity to being in the office immediately after a loss. Most companies do not offer paid leave for this type of bereavement, so the parents feel they have little choice but to return to work the day after their loss. Another possible challenge is for your performance at work to be questioned while you grieve. To be away from a desk for extended periods, or to be seen as not pulling your weight in the office can create anxiety and worry for those experiencing the loss. Suppressing emotions in order to mask your emotional state, to not run the risk of being reprimanded for underperforming, will simply add to this traumatic experience.

I spoke to two mothers who returned to work soon after their loss. One mother felt she needed to go to the office the same day. Due to the lack of understanding relating to the trauma of early pregnancy loss, she felt she must carry on as normal immediately after. There are so many women who feel they will be judged for expressing their sadness and trauma after a pregnancy loss in the earlier stages of pregnancy that they simply carry on and hide any emotion from those around them.

I spoke to Michelle Kennedy, founder and CEO of parenting app PEANUT, on returning to work the day of her pregnancy loss.

I was clearly semi-conscious, as it was the morning, and I could feel this warmth between my legs. As I began to wake up, I realised what the warmth was. Then the pain came. I pulled back the duvet and looked down at the bedsheets. They were covered in blood. My first reaction was to stop my son, who was four at the time, coming in. I asked my husband if he would go and be with him.

I went to the toilet, where there was more blood loss. Then the blood stopped. As I had stopped bleeding, I thought to myself that you never know, I might not have lost my baby. I was eight weeks pregnant, we had heard the heartbeat; I held on to a little bit of hope. It was awful.

I showered, took my bedsheets off and put them in the wash. I got ready for work and dropped my son to school as usual. After dropping him off, I called a friend's mother, who's a midwife. She asked me what colour the blood was, whether it was bright red, or more of a brown tone. I wondered what would be the best response to achieve the answer I wanted. She told me it could be an implantation bleed. Instinctively, I knew mine wasn't that. There was too much blood.

Did you then continue with your plans to go to the office?
I did. I arrived at my office, said hi to everyone and went straight to the bathroom. There was more blood and it was then that I knew I really had lost my pregnancy. I walked back into the office and said to one of the girls who works with me, 'I had a little miscarriage this morning.' I don't even know what that means. I told her it was fine and that it was early. I got a little teary and I carried on with the day. How strange. What a strange thing.

It's not as strange as you think. So many women do this. We carry on as though it's not significant, because we don't feel validated in our experience of pregnancy loss.
I was playing that weird jeopardy game. I thought if I carried on and left it long enough, then it wouldn't really have happened. If I sit here long enough, it will maybe be okay. In my head I was rationalising everything. I told myself that it could be an implantation bleed, even though I knew it wasn't.

How did you get through that day in the office?
I went through the motions of meetings and emails. At lunchtime, I went and bought pregnancy tests. I don't know why I thought that would be the thing I needed to do. Due to my hCG levels, the tests obviously still said I was pregnant, so once again that element of hope returned. Hope that I may not have lost my baby. The next day I went for a scan, and it was confirmed that my baby was gone. Because nothing happened at the hospital, no D&C, no pills, I was left feeling even more like 'Well, that's that then'. I also felt embarrassed to talk about what had happened, as it wasn't treated as a big deal. I told myself not to overthink my loss, to treat it as just a really late period, as I didn't know how to process it.

Looking back now, would you still have gone to the office the day you lost your pregnancy?
When I think back now, I would have been more open about being pregnant in the first place. I was eight weeks when I lost my baby, so I would have told people by then. The morning at home, I wouldn't have just taken my bedsheets off and gone into the office. At the time I felt as though I was being self-indulgent to be so upset that I was losing an early pregnancy.

I would have stayed with my husband. We should have stayed together that day. We should have gone out for the day, gone for breakfast. We should have done something nice together. What neither of us should have done is felt we needed to go to the office. When I told the girl in my office of my pregnancy loss, what did she take from that? God forbid anything happens to her in the future. She saw me come in, so she would feel she had to do the same. I don't think I would have portrayed my experience so flippantly, because I certainly didn't feel flippant about it. I just felt that I had to be.

What advice would you give to others who find themselves in the same position? Those that feel they should dismiss the severity of their loss and go to work?
You'll have another day of doing everything normally very soon. It doesn't have to be the day you're trying to process everything. The day I lost my pregnancy was also the day I told people that I was pregnant. I had felt I should wait until I was three months pregnant before telling anyone, because that rule has been drummed into all of us for so long.

Not going to the office might not have changed how I felt about what happened, but it would have changed how I remembered the day I lost my baby. I would have still felt angry and robbed and guilty, but it would have changed my memory of that day. I would have remembered the day I spent with my partner, rather than memories of a day where I tried to keep it together at the office.

I spoke to Aimee Baron MD, FAAP, on returning to work as a paediatrician on three occasions after experiencing late-term pregnancy loss. Following her multiple pregnancy losses, Aimee founded the non-profit organisation I Was Supposed To Have A Baby.

After my first child, my husband and I had three and a half years of unexplained secondary infertility. In that time period, after our first round of IUI, I did get pregnant, but experienced a pregnancy loss at eight weeks due to a blighted ovum. I also had a lot of medical complications after that loss, which were devastating, but they were nothing in comparison to what I would go through afterwards.

I had just finished training as a paediatric doctor and was about to start a job in a hospital. My husband and I continued trying to get pregnant, and we eventually had another baby. It was really strange, but once I had that second child, secondary infertility was no longer a problem. I would nurse my baby, get my period and get pregnant. I was pregnant with my fourth child, working at a neonatal unit at a hospital, when I experienced my second pregnancy loss. This time I was much further on in my pregnancy. I was sixteen weeks, well into the second trimester.

How soon did you return to work at the hospital?
I went back after about two months. I had this incredible education, I had an incredible job, and I loved taking care of infants. I would speak to new parents, and coach them through all their worries and anxieties. I would give them space and really nurture them to the point where they felt comfortable going home with their newborn baby. I really loved that part of my job and didn't want to give it up.

What was your thought process? To think I have lost a baby, but I am going back to work with newborns.
I knew it was going to be hard, but I knew that I could do it.

You see, I had already lost a baby, albeit it was one that was in the first trimester. I knew that I would be sad, I knew that I would need to grieve and be a mess for a while, but I knew after a while I would be okay. I knew that I would come out of it, because I had already done it once. Obviously this was a later loss, but I knew that given enough time, I would come out of it too, and I would get back to some semblance of normality. I felt like I just needed to get through the grieving period. I knew that work was going to be hard (taking care of other people's babies), but I knew that I would be able to surmount that hurdle and could do it. I just had to get there and get it done.

It was the love of my work that really pushed me back, knowing I would be okay eventually. Those were the things that gave me the strength to walk back into the hospital and start taking care of babies again.

Can you take me back to the moment when you returned to work and first walked through the hospital doors?
It was like an out-of-body experience. I remember it like it was yesterday. I did this three times, so I can't tell you if I am sharing what happened the first time, or one of the later losses, but each time it was the same experience. I felt like I was just going through the motions. My feet were moving, I was parking my car, walking to the hospital. Getting in the elevator, swiping my ID card, putting my stethoscope around my neck, walking through the hospital and into the nursery ward. But I was not emotionally processing any of it. It was work.

How did you cope emotionally with seeing the babies each time?
It felt like I was watching myself go through an experience that I wasn't really living. Because I couldn't.

And then, the experience of holding the babies.
They weren't mine, so on some level it was easier. At first it was very clinical, I had to examine the babies, make sure they were okay. Check their eyes, their ears, listen to their heart. Everything needed for a newborn exam. But the end of the day, it was someone else's baby, not my baby.

But on another level, it was harder. Because every-body else got to have a baby and I didn't.

Were you always able to look at things clinically, to see that it was their baby and not yours?
Sometimes. Most of the time. There were definitely occasions where I would sneak off into the bathroom to sob my eyes out. Sometimes I was able to hold it in until I came home.

But when there were clear signs of a mother not looking after herself, or when the parents were unfit, I was particularly a mess. I just couldn't understand why there are thousands of people in the world who are desperate to have children, who would pay any amount of money and go to extraordinary lengths, but these parents didn't care about their baby. The injust-ice of it was unfathomable. Those days were the worst.

Were you able to remain hopeful after experiencing preg-nancy loss?
For me, it was knowing that I wasn't finished, that we were going to try again. That there would be another chance for a baby, or at least I hoped there would be.

My doctors thought the first second-trimester loss was a fluke. I eventually moved through the grief, thinking that, while it was terrible, it would surely not happen again. I knew from the experience of having a blighted ovum, that it was going to take time, but that I would eventually be in a space where I would be ready to try again.

But that second second-trimester loss was the worst. It was the confirmation that my first loss was not a fluke; there was something wrong. It was at that point that we started to do medical investigations. Then there was hope that, if we did what the doctors said, it might work. So I got pregnant, but I still lost a third baby in the second trimester. There was clearly something wrong. Nobody knew how to fix it and I thought this really could be the end. And because all hope was gone, I just couldn't see babies at work any more. I quit my job. I was done.

How did you move through your grief after each loss? Was there anything that led you to know you would eventually be okay?

If you have one loss, you have absolutely no idea you will be fine.

But I knew. I had climbed my way out of the first early loss, so I knew that I would be able to climb my way out of this too. With each loss, it took longer. Much longer. But I knew what I needed to do. I needed my chocolate-chip cookies, my rom-com novels with happy endings, sappy movies about people in foreign lands with stories totally dissimilar to mine, and for people to leave me alone. I needed the time and space to grieve as I wanted, to disconnect from the world, until I felt ready to face it again. But, I would be able to face it again someday. I knew that.

Speaking with you, I think you are one of the most mentally strong people I have ever met. Through your experiences, one first-trimester loss and four second-trimester losses, how did you survive that level of trauma?

I had three kids who needed me as a mother. Who needed me to show up. Who needed me to be there for them. I had to be there when they woke up in the morning, I had to be there when they came home from school. In the evening, after they went to bed, I could fall apart. While my kids were awake, I had to play act. I didn't have the opportunity to fully grieve. They needed me. We could talk about the days I didn't leave my bedroom and the weeks I refused to go anywhere. The months where my husband begged me to take the children out and do something, and I did none of that. I yelled and screamed and said don't make me do anything I am not ready for. I wasn't leaving until I was ready. There were all of those things that were happening in the outside world, but, during the grief process, I only showed up for my kids. I believe the fact that I had to do that was what really helped. There are still two or three times a year where things bubble up and I need a day to cry, to hike in nature or find a beach and disconnect. But I got my chance to grieve properly, and that helped.

I'm just grateful. I don't have a biological disposition to depression. I knew, given a certain amount of space, time and self-care, I knew that each time I would be fine. That knowledge was what helped me to survive.

Encountering hurtful comments

You will likely encounter situations where people say things that you find incredibly hurtful. In these instances, I am certain these comments will be unintentional, but may affect you nonetheless. As with most negative comments directly relating to us, we tend to focus on those words rather than the majority of positive comments. I wish this wasn't a natural human reaction, but it does seem that most of us let perceived negative comments become the focal point of our thoughts.

I found myself focusing on hurtful comments that others made towards my experience, which was extremely unhelpful in the first year after my loss. I also spent too much time considering events and encounters that I found hurtful. The examples I have given below are two of the most triggering situations that occurred after my loss, examples which you may be faced with. With any situation that arises, it can be helpful to immediately consider how your decisions and actions will benefit your own mental health. Take time to think about what is best for you, and how best to release any negative thoughts or emotions relating to what has happened.

Situation One – Being surprised by a pregnant guest

There are going to be times when you encounter pregnant people in social situations. It's inevitable and often unavoidable. One option is to ask whoever is arranging the social gathering if there are any pregnant women attending, at which point you have the choice to stay home, or attend if you feel comfortable doing so. If you are in a large group where you may not know everyone attending – a wedding perhaps – it may be helpful to explain your anxieties to a fellow guest you know well and ask for their support through the day.

My husband and I were invited to a friend's house for dinner. They knew the whole story of how Axel had died and had been incredibly supportive. We arrived, bottle in hand, to find they had invited another couple at the last minute. This would usually be a welcome chance to meet friends of those we loved spending time with, only the other couple were expecting a baby in less than a month. Although not an intentional act of insensitivity, I had just been led into a kind of hell. I should have politely excused myself. Instead, I faked a smile and asked for a large glass of wine. It was torture to be in the company of the heavily pregnant guest, constantly trying to avert my eyes from her bump. I did all I could not to cry throughout the dinner.

When you have lost a pregnancy, you can excuse yourself from any social situations that make you uncomfortable. There are a few times in your life when you can look after yourself without fear of upsetting others, or being perceived as rude. This is one of those times.

Situation Two – Ghosted by a friend

Discovering that friends are not there for you when you need them most can be particularly hard to deal with.

Unlike the friends you see at work, or those you don't see often, to have close friends pull away from you following a traumatic event is often unexpected and painful.

I experienced another type of loss while grieving. The loss of one of my closest friends. I felt this friend was someone I could tell anything to, and who would be in my life for ever. After Axel died, my messages and calls began to take days to receive a response. Then they began to go unreturned. I wasn't communicating more often than I had before my loss and there were no anxious calls in the middle of the night (and even if there were, I would hope these would have been understood and forgiven). I realised that I was simply being frozen out. Two years passed before I heard from my friend. An apology came in the form of a detailed text. Each time I tried to write a message, I went blank. In the end, I didn't respond at all.

I asked therapist Claire Bidwell Smith for her advice in handling situations when those around you are not sympathetic to your emotional state.

One of the interesting things about grief is that it really shows us what's important in our life, who's important, who shows up for us. It's very revealing and when people don't show up for us, it can be hard. When someone you expected to be there for you isn't sympathetic, that's painful. Workplaces can feel especially isolating – to be in that environment and not feel as though you can live your experience. It's about really making sure you have outside support, so you don't need that friend, or those colleagues to understand. It's important to have a supportive place where you can feel

understood and sympathised with so you don't necessarily need anybody else to understand.

Unless you have the ability to brush hurtful comments
aside with ease, you will be faced with situations that leave
you surprised and hurt. Choosing to gently address those
who inadvertently hurt me with their comments was by
far the best thing I did to help me release any anger I felt
towards them.

There is also the possibility that those around you will
not understand the level of grief you are experiencing. It
can be hurtful to be told that you can always try again, or
that this clearly wasn't the right time for you to have a baby.

What to say and what not to say to someone who has experienced pregnancy loss

After the loss of my baby, I found that some people knew
exactly what to say to comfort me through my grief. Others
said things that were unintentionally hurtful, speaking without considering how their comments may be interpreted.
Grief is tricky territory, particularly if you have limited or
no experience of dealing with loss personally. Grief causes
our emotional reactions to be heightened and allows for
possible misunderstandings and misinterpretation of others'
words and actions. The following pages will hopefully give
some guidance to both the grieving parents and those
around them, as you navigate the trauma of pregnancy loss.

What not to say when someone has experienced early pregnancy loss

1. You can try again soon

The mother didn't want to think of another pregnancy, she wanted *this* pregnancy. Whether getting pregnant was straightforward or a struggle, they were still pregnant. They knew the age of their growing baby to the day. Whether they had just taken a test or were a few months along, a pregnancy is a pregnancy and losing that pregnancy can be hugely traumatic. Yes, they can try to get pregnant again soon after pregnancy loss, but they are grieving the loss of a baby they wanted.

2. Technically it wasn't a baby

Unless you are trying to conceive, are pregnant, or have children, there can be a lack of understanding relating to the growth stages of a baby. There can be genuine surprise from some about how advanced an early pregnancy can look. This can be a particularly insensitive comment, as most parents consider they are carrying a baby after a test confirms they are pregnant.

3. It's better it happened now than later

There is no best or worst time to lose a pregnancy. If the mother has been trying to conceive for some time, they may find the loss of a pregnancy within the first few weeks as traumatic as someone who loses a baby at a later stage. As it's such a personal experience, there is no way of knowing the extent of the trauma another person is dealing with. The loss of a three-week pregnancy may be the only time the mother has been pregnant, or is ever going to be pregnant. There are many factors to consider when a loss happens, so the effect of an early loss shouldn't be deemed any less significant than a later loss.

4. *I'm happy to see you're feeling better*
Smiling and laughing following a loss doesn't mean the person has healed. There will be times when they laugh, or smile when something or someone makes them happy, and that's okay. They are not bound to their sadness. In fact it can be a welcome relief when their spirits are lifted, even for just a moment.

5. *You're so strong, you will be fine*
Most who have experienced pregnancy loss are not fine when it happens. They have lost a pregnancy that they longed for, a baby they couldn't wait to meet. The strength people have shown previously can be reduced to nothing in the initial period following a pregnancy loss. The emotional effect of pregnancy loss differs, but even those who you believe to have cores of steel can be left utterly broken. We cannot assume 'strong' friends, colleagues, neighbours will just handle this. There is often the pressure to be back to your old self soon after pregnancy loss, particularly an early loss. We need to find a way to reduce those expectations and offer emotional support instead.

6. *At least you can get pregnant*
Getting pregnant is certainly a positive sign, but losing one or multiple pregnancies lessens the confidence in any future pregnancy. The anxiety to get pregnant, or stay pregnant, after loss can be all-consuming. The mother who experi-

enced loss may never have another pregnancy. If there is a future pregnancy, it can be difficult to enjoy the early months, such is the fear of losing another baby.

7. I know how you feel (try not to make the conversation about you)

While it can certainly be helpful to share stories of personal loss with those who have just lost a pregnancy themselves, try not to make the conversation about you at this time. The majority of those who have recently experienced loss will want to talk about how they feel, their pregnancy and all they hoped for with their future baby. Allow them this time.

8. There was obviously something wrong with the baby

In some cases, there will be medical reasons with an unborn baby that cause a pregnancy loss. It can be upsetting for parents who experience pregnancy loss if those around them make assumptions. There are many possibly reasons for pregnancy loss, so it doesn't always mean there was something wrong with the baby.

9. It just wasn't the right time

To the person who was carrying the baby, it was the right time. Nothing will take away the fact that once they see a positive pregnancy test, they were expecting a baby. Although many parents say they don't want to plan ahead until after they have reached a certain number of weeks in the pregnancy, most minds start to envisage a future with the baby almost immediately.

10. Perhaps you've been working too hard

It's unlikely that any workload, stress level or reasonable lack of sleep would cause the loss of a pregnancy. As with any scenario, there are cases when a doctor may consider the likelihood of extreme lifting, or severe lack of sleep in a patient, but it's a minute percentage where the cause of pregnancy loss can be attributed to any work-related issues.

What to say/do when someone has experienced early pregnancy loss

1. Say something rather than nothing at all
If you think the words 'I'm sorry' are not enough, they are. Anybody who has experienced loss will hear these words many times, but in most cases, people would rather hear the same words than to hear nothing at all. Pregnancy loss can be a difficult subject to broach, but staying silent and saying nothing can be more hurtful than a few simple words to acknowledge the loss.

2. Acknowledge that the parents were expecting a baby
Often in the early stages of pregnancy, people dismiss the fact that the mother was expecting a baby, treating the loss as less significant. Many people play down their excitement in the very early stages of pregnancy, but most are beginning to plan their future with their child. It can be devastating to discover that you are no longer pregnant, at any stage. To say 'I know you were expecting a baby, and I am very sorry' will be appreciated by the parents.

3. Communicate
We can never know how someone is truly feeling, unless they make it very clear. Desperation and depression can set

in soon after pregnancy loss and kind words from friends and family can help. Even if you don't receive a response, send a message to let them know you are thinking of them. For those you know well, it can be appreciated to receive several messages over a period of time, so they don't feel as though their experience has been forgotten.

4. Send a note, or flowers
Honouring a loss in the early stages of pregnancy with flowers or a note will let the parents know you understand that their loss is significant. People often assume an early loss is not as traumatic as a later-stage loss. For someone to know you are recognising their experience with this gesture can mean a great deal. There are further suggestions of what could be meaningful for parents following pregnancy loss on page 261.

5. Never assume anything
We can never assume how much an early pregnancy loss has affected someone. Perhaps the person has been trying to conceive for some time and this was their only pregnancy in years? Perhaps the person has experienced multiple pregnancy losses in succession? Or they were told they would never be able to conceive, and this was an exceptional situation. There are so many factors in most pregnancies that we simply cannot assume anything.

6. Explain that you don't know how it feels, but that you are there to listen
If you don't know how it feels to experience pregnancy loss, you could ask the parents if they would like to explain how they are feeling. It can often be therapeutic for the parents

to talk openly about the experience, to be able to speak of their unborn baby.

7. *Gently remind someone that their grief is valid*
Many parents apologise for their feelings relating to early pregnancy loss and will often say 'I was only ___ weeks pregnant, so it isn't as serious as a later loss.' Remind those who are apologising that their grief is as valid as anybody else's. They have experienced pregnancy loss and should never feel the need to apologise.

8. *Ask if the parents would like to talk about their loss*
Some people are happier not talking about grief, while some may feel as though they are burdening others if they speak too often of their loss. To give someone the chance to talk about their loss is a huge relief to many and greatly appreciated. Find a time to meet with the parents, and follow their lead in how they would like to speak of their loss. If you can find a time where you have no commitments afterwards, this eliminates the feeling that you need to wrap up the conversation before its natural end. To give the parents the time they need without them feeling as though you are rushing off is a kindness they will appreciate.

What not to say when someone has experienced late pregnancy loss

1. *At least you can get pregnant*
Yes, they were pregnant. But now they're not and they don't know when or if they will be again. It's a fact that

the person who has lost a baby was indeed pregnant, but with loss comes uncertainty and a chance that they may not conceive again. There is also the possibility of another pregnancy loss.

2. Maybe you shouldn't have exercised

Try not to place imagined blame on someone who is already likely to question whether they did something to cause the pregnancy loss. Exercise as a reason for pregnancy loss is tied in with the incorrect assumptions that a heavy workload, or stress level, can result in a premature end to a pregnancy. It is unlikely that a healthy level of exercise will cause any reasons for loss.

3. You're still grieving?

It may be hard to consider the depth of grief a parent is experiencing if you have not lived through a pregnancy loss yourself. Not meeting a living baby can make it harder for friends and family to understand the significance of the loss, but to the parents, it can be extremely painful and the grief may be prolonged. Nobody can fully understand the grief of another, but in all cases being sensitive and sympathetic will be appreciated.

4. Remember that others have it much worse

In other areas of life – mentally, physically – people will likely have it much worse than the parents who have just lost their baby. However, after a pregnancy loss, it is about them and how they feel. How bad their experience is compared to others' lives is irrelevant at this time. After a pregnancy loss, they are allowed to acknowledge their feelings of sorrow, hopelessness and grief.

5. I'm sure it won't happen again

Perhaps it will, hopefully it won't. As well-meaning as this comment is, nobody knows the likelihood of another pregnancy loss. Most people who offer condolences try to make things seem a little less bleak and don't mean to offend. Following pregnancy loss, parents will want to be comforted, not fixed.

6. It was for the best, something was obviously wrong

Whether there was a medical reason concerning the baby's health or not, commenting on such a personal detail after late-stage pregnancy loss can feel hurtful and invasive. To assume anything, and to comment on those assumptions, can carry too much emotional weight for those who experienced the loss.

7. Everything happens for a reason

This is a frequently heard comment following pregnancy loss and often one of the most hurtful. Losing a job and finding a new, more challenging role is for a reason. Breaking up with someone and finding a more compatible partner is for a reason. It's unlikely anybody would describe this loss as happening for a reason. For most who lose a much wanted baby, there is no reason.

8. When are you going to try for another baby?

This is a question that frequently arises after someone has experienced pregnancy loss. The comment may stem from a gut reaction in others who feel uncomfortable with the subject of loss. They want to say something hopeful, something about the future. To those who have experienced a pregnancy loss, this question can feel quite pressurised and intrusive. Coming to terms with a loss, at any stage, can take time. It can be helpful to simply ask how a parent is feeling at that moment, rather than asking about a hopeful future pregnancy.

9. Thankfully you have other children
It can often be the case that having other children does cause a mental distraction from the grief of losing a baby, but it doesn't take away from the fact that the parents have lost another child. The mental and physical pain they have experienced doesn't go away when they are with their other children.

10. They are in a better place now
It can be hard to think of a single better place for a baby who died than alive with their parents. With the misunderstanding and discomfort that the subject of pregnancy loss brings, there are many unintentionally ill-judged comments that may cause hurt. It can be helpful to consider that the other person is speaking with good intentions, but that doesn't make the comments any less hurtful at the time.

11. How can you miss something you never had?
Almost immediately after a positive pregnancy test, thoughts can turn to how life will change once the baby is here. Visions of the nursery, pushing a pram, clothing he or she will wear. As early as the first weeks of pregnancy, it's natural to talk to those you choose to confide in about your baby, the plans you will make and all that is to come. You have someone there, or if you choose to look at your pregnancy another way in the beginning, something is there. You may not have held your baby, but you had a baby.

Losing a pregnancy is losing someone, or something, you knew you had and that can be extremely traumatic.

What to say/do when someone has experienced late pregnancy loss

1. Ask questions about the baby
Many parents who have experienced pregnancy loss want to talk about their baby. They want to tell whoever will listen how perfect they were, how they looked like a particular parent, or both. I talked for hours about my baby, telling friends about his beautiful face and perfect hands and feet. It can be hard to hear details of a baby who died, but listening is one of the most important and appreciated things you can do for a parent who has lost a baby.

2. Be consistent in your communication
For the first few weeks, or even months, after your friend or family member has experienced loss, try to call or see them regularly. There will naturally come a time when you will pull back a little and not be in such regular contact, but in the immediate period following a loss, there is little more comforting than consistent communication from those who know your story and are able to listen.

3. Make the time
Most people have busy lives and finding time for anything outside of a daily routine can be tricky. During the time a friend or family member has experienced pregnancy loss, it

can be hugely appreciated if you can clear time in your diary to dedicate solely to sitting with them. It doesn't have to be for long, but just knowing you are on someone's mind and that they have made time for you can mean a great deal.

4. *Ask how the parent/s are feeling (and just listen)*
The urge to talk about ourselves is natural. Part of our everyday conversation is telling others what we have been doing, how work is, what our future plans are. Try to resist the urge to talk about yourself, unless the grieving parent asks to have their mind taken off of their recent loss. Often parents will want to talk about their loss and having someone listen can ease some of the weight of their grief.

5. *I don't know how you are feeling, but I am here for you in any way you need*
This can be one of the most comforting comments to receive after pregnancy loss. It is an open statement that carries with it no questions, no expectations and no requests. On hearing this comment, talk to whoever has given you this opening to let them know what you need at this time. You may wish to talk, to go for a walk, to have someone collect groceries for you. Anything you may need, ask. You will not be a burden.

6. *Sit in silence if that is all you are able to do*
Losing a baby in pregnancy can be one of the only times that others simply do not know what to say. Will you say the right thing? Will you upset the grieving parent? Are those questions too heavy at this time? If you cannot express yourself in a way that makes you comfortable, explain that you

are having trouble conveying the right words. Being honest is better than ignoring those who have experienced the loss. Perhaps offer to spend time with the grieving parent/s, explaining that you may not know what to say, but that this doesn't mean you are not there for them.

7. Ask how the parent would like to refer to their baby
Some may not wish to name their baby, while some will have been calling their growing baby by their future name for months. Others may have chosen a nickname by which to call their unborn child, before they expected to meet them at birth. Whether it's The Baby, the name or nickname, or another word the parent chooses, asking the right way to refer to their baby will be appreciated.

8. Don't try to make the parent/s feel better
Most who experience pregnancy loss will not be looking for an emotional quick-fix plan. Although it's natural to want others to feel better immediately, the likelihood that they will is close to zero. Hearing ways to 'get over it', or 'feel better soon' will not be helpful. Nobody wants to feel as though they are bringing others down, but getting over it and getting better will be a long way off in most cases. A grieving parent will want to do just that: grieve. Sitting with them in their grief will offer far more comfort than suggesting ways to move past their loss.

How friends and family can help

There are practical things to consider after a friend or family member loses a pregnancy. The parents will likely be unable to think clearly about the smaller details in their life, details that, if taken care of, will make a huge difference to them. If you haven't lived through pregnancy loss, it's understandable that you may not immediately consider many of the things you can do for those who have. You will need to ask the parents before doing many of the things I have suggested, but it is likely the actions below will be greatly appreciated.

- Unsubscribe from baby apps – you will need your friend's physical phone, so plan to see them and, while there, ask if they would like you to remove any information relating to pregnancy updates.
- Inform doctors. It is not always a given that doctors will be immediately informed of the loss by the hospital.
- Inform NCT groups. Before encouraging pregnancy messages and birth announcements appear, inform the NCT group that your friends have lost their baby and will be leaving the group.
- Inform friends – rather than the parents composing a group email and feeling obligated to respond to each message, with the parents' permission, write the announcement from your email address and answer any responses.
- Log on and buy shopping each week using the parents' account – they won't be expecting you to pay for their

shopping, but taking control of their weekly shopping delivery to ensure they have what they need at home can be helpful.

- Babysit if they have children – don't offer, as the parents will likely say no, but state that you will be taking their children at certain times to give the parents a couple of hours to just sit in silence, or walk and get coffee.
- Inform the school or nursery if they have other children – facing the nursery or school gates when you have lost a pregnancy can feel overwhelming. To know most of the people at the nursery or school have already been told of their loss allows them to say nothing when they next see them and not feel uncomfortable for their silence.
- Attend hospital appointments with them – it's likely parents will go together, but in the circumstance where the mother is alone, be firm, but not overbearing, in your insistence that you will accompany them.
- Sit at home with them – parents may not want to talk, but watching a favourite film in silence can be incredibly helpful. Let them select the film and, even if you hate it, sit through it without an opinion.
- Walk with them – getting them out of the house is a huge and important step. It's incredibly common to want to stay at home, but the fresh air and change of scenery will hopefully be a break in their day.
- In the least intrusive way possible, find grief counsellors in their local area and send them the contact details. Usually GPs or hospitals will refer bereaved parents to general counsellors, who are often not trained in the area of pregnancy and infant loss. I would have loved someone to suggest grief counsellors in my neighbourhood and

believe this would have been the support I urgently needed after Axel died.

- Make meals that are easy to reheat and deliver them. Don't offer, just do it.
- Put on some rubber gloves and clean the house, or, if you can financially, pay for a cleaning service to go to their house once or twice soon after their baby loss.
- Depending on how close you are, take over bath oil and candles, run your friend a bath and then leave them to this self-care for a short while. You may want to wait in their living room, or you may feel it's best to leave after you have run the bath and lit the candles. It's the act of care your friend will appreciate.
- Buy a clothing gift card. You can send an amount personally, or speak to a group of friends and all put a little money towards the card. I hated my pregnancy clothing as it reminded me of Axel, but it's all that fitted after he was born. I would have loved a new jumper and jeans that had no connection to my pregnancy, but would never have thought to buy myself these things after my loss.
- If the bereaved parents have children, donate some of your own children's toys or buy a few new ones. Give or buy the children toys they can easily play with, that are age appropriate and can guarantee the children being occupied for longer than five minutes. You can also loan their children some of your own children's things, politely explaining that your children would love them back in a month or two.
- Find local activities and suggest you take the grieving friend. They may need some persuading, but it can be

helpful to take the grieving parent out of their home for a few hours. The theatre is a good option, as they don't need to see anybody or say anything. A light-hearted film is also good for the same reasons. Check there is nothing likely to upset your friend in the theatre or film content before you book.

- Don't let them down. If you say you are going to call, see them or arrange something for them at a certain time, stick to it. There is enough disappointment swirling around their head, without the need to add to it.

I asked author and doula Latham Thomas how those close to the grieving parents can be an effective support system.

There's nothing you can say to someone that makes them feel better necessarily, but there are things you can do. Move away from the substance of speech and into the presence of being; what it means to show up, what it means to just be there. It's about the other person saying 'Can I just hold your hand and sit with you?' It's about the people around you not trying to quiet you in the emotional eruptions that come up around the process. Healthy processing is going to look different for every person, but it's not going to be neat. When grief happens, it comes in waves and it can be messy and hard to contain. What those around the mother often want more than anything else is to contain her experience so it doesn't spill on to them. They don't want to hold it. They don't know what to do with it. It's really important to have those around you who can support the bereavement. Having elders around, who have seen a lot. They have the longer time horizon on this earth and they're on the other side of their life, so they know what's ahead. Those people can have perspective and a gentleness that makes you feel supported.

Spiritual leaders, or those from your spiritual community or religion as support can be very anchoring through a period of loss. Ritualising your loss can be powerful. Is there a ceremony that can be done to send off the spirit of the baby? Is there something you can do annually, something that symbolises this particular life? Is there a way to create an altar space in your home that is dedicated to this spirit? Having dependable family members and friends around to support is critical. Perhaps a friend messages and says they're on their way over with food, that they know of a new film you may love and they're coming to be with you and rub your feet. Sometimes it's just that, not being alone. It's the other person not making it about them, about fear, it's letting you move through your loss and the friend not focusing on themselves, but on you. When I'm going to hold space for people, I have to move my stuff out of the way and just make sure I can be present.

The way that we would support folks during the post-partum period, we would swaddle someone to make sure they have the support they need during loss. The maternity period is largely devoted to centring the needs of the baby; we would never leave a newborn alone, we would never let it go an extended period without feeding, the baby would always be held, changed, swaddled, etc. You would always be tending to the baby, meeting its needs. The same should be true for new mothers, they should be tended to through recovery, and the same should apply for those who have experienced loss. Swaddle them up so they feel closeness, they feel tenderness and love. They should not be alone experiencing or processing the loss, they should not be alone after a procedure, there should be people in the house 24/7 making sure the mother's needs are met. As something comes up emotionally, there should be someone there saying 'Tell me', allowing them to let it out. That village keeping has to be at every life stage, including loss, because loss is also part of life. We often compartmentalise grief, making it seem like a failure, putting it out of the way to not really think about it. We have to honour it, because it does happen.

In your role as a doula, when one of your mothers has a pregnancy loss, how do you prepare yourself mentally to take her through the experience? This would be great advice for friends and family members wanting to know the best way to support someone in their lives who has lost a pregnancy?

When I know I am heading into a sacred space, I do my own rituals. It's fortification, building myself up so I know I can show up and feel full and abundant. So I can just give in that time when I am with my client. And when I come back home, I do the closing out of that experience. I take off my clothing, I wash my clothing, I shower, light a candle. I do all these things to ritualise, opening and closing the experience. With the mother, or parents, I try to help them process the experience. It's usually some days later, weeks or months later, that they start to process the experience. It's an important component for people to be able to put one foot in front of the other and try to take steps into this new phase of their life. What's necessary is being able to make space for people, listen, create a haven and a community for them.

As somebody who cares for and guides women through pregnancy, what is your immediate pathway when one of the mothers you are guiding experiences a loss?

I don't think anyone is ever ready for the devastation of a loss, whatever stage it comes. What happens initially when I hear the news, or there's a feeling things are heading in a less optimal direction, I am not always in the same room as the person. The first response is to minimise that distance and find a way to be in the same space together. With the weight of the news while they are going through the experience of shock, I will ask if it's appropriate for me to be with them. So many mothers and birthing people are alone in their experience of loss and it can be incredibly isolating.

It's important to configure a village for them in the aftermath of the loss. If you were going through pregnancy and had a baby, people would show up to village keep and make sure you were eating, help with breastfeeding and recovery. If you were going through a divorce, people would show up and help you process the emotional brunt of that experience. At any major life juncture, people would show up for you, or they should. Yet, how come during the most painful time of your life, when you're grieving, do people not have the capacity to show up?

There often aren't social supports, or educational tools, or even cultural or policy-driven actions that create the space for someone to process pregnancy loss in a way that is healthy and is supportive of their needs, emotionally and mentally. Because we don't have those supports, a doula can bridge the gap. It's about the recognition that this is a really critical time in somebody's life. You need someone to hold your hand as you move through it and you need to feel you are being witnessed in your unique experience.

Pregnancy after loss

Sex and intimacy

Although desperate to be pregnant again, having sex in the immediate mourning period after losing our baby was something neither my husband or I felt ready to do. I was emotionally drained from my grief. I would cry for hours each day. Any desire for sex was halted not only by my mental state, but by my body's exhaustion. My husband was managing his own grief, trying to console me, and he was also the one giving most attention to our six-year-old son. Even though it would be a route to greater intimacy and a possible pregnancy, I felt a deep level of anxiety whenever I considered having sex.

The way I viewed my post-pregnancy body was another barrier. While some women embrace their changing shape during pregnancy, during this second pregnancy, I didn't. The

IVF cycle, plus low-mood over-eating, had caused almost immediate weight gain. This weight, coupled with a lack of regular exercise due to the cold winter months, meant I was left with a body that not only looked pregnant, but that also felt unhealthy. If I didn't like looking at my body, I couldn't see how my husband would either. My husband is by nature very kind, so I don't feel as though he would have viewed my body the way I did, but it was nevertheless another hurdle to get over after our loss.

Following a pregnancy loss, most doctors will advise that it is safe to have sex once any vaginal bleeding stops. This usually indicates that any tissue from your previous pregnancy has left your body, which can be confirmed with a negative pregnancy test three weeks after any pregnancy tissue has left your body, or has been surgically removed. A further indication that your body has returned to a pre-pregnancy condition is by the return of your menstrual cycle (this can take months to return in some women). During the time your body is experiencing this bleeding, particularly in the early stages of your loss, your cervix may be dilated, which can result in a higher risk of infection within the uterus. It is important that all the pregnancy tissue has left your body, or has been surgically removed, due to this risk of infection. It is advisable to consult your doctor if you experience severe lower abdominal pains or foul-smelling discharge.

Sex and intimacy were blocks for me during the most intense first months of my grief. When speaking to therapist Claire Bidwell Smith for this book, she gave me some advice I wish I had known in the first months after losing my baby:

There's such a deep intimacy and vulnerability that comes with sex that you don't want to share that much of yourself with your partner after loss. You want to keep your body to yourself and you don't want to open yourself up to that. You may also feel resistance to feeling pleasure. Your womb and your whole pelvic area has become a place of sorrow at that time, and there's a resistance to allowing that area to become a place of pleasure again. It's a big deal. That space is where your baby died, you're keeping that place sacred and you don't want anything else coming into that place. It can often be unconscious. There's also hormonal things happening, and you're sad and you're grieving. Sex isn't something you want to do at that time necessarily, but often women want to get pregnant again. When you're ready to have sex again, I would suggest making it a ritual. You can do this with your partner, or alone, but take some time to acknowledge that you know that space held your baby and you're going to keep that always, but you're also going to open up again. Continue to expand that space, have a self-ritual around it.

Trying for another baby

I thought that having another baby soon after my loss would be a way to move forward from the grief and sadness I was feeling. I assumed being pregnant soon after losing Axel would take away some of the pain. I was conscious of being forty and the challenges my husband and I had encountered in getting pregnant a second time, so, just weeks after my loss, I began to consider another round of IVF. Desperate to escape my worsening depression, I saw this as a way of finding hope in a situation that was anything but hopeful.

With sex not being something I felt ready for, I knew the structure of an IVF cycle and felt I could cope with the procedures of assisted conception. I began the process of another round of IVF, even though I had been advised it was likely too soon after losing Axel. With my understanding and control concerning the injections, appointments and pills, I chose not to listen.

Due to the negative result of this IVF cycle, I realised it had been too soon after Axel's death. Had the result been positive, I would of course be here telling you that it was perfect timing. Unless there is a medical reason obstructing your path, I don't feel there is a right or a wrong time to begin trying for another baby. I was broken, so if there was a way to ease the unbearable pain, I was going to try it.

A few months passed, we had returned to trying naturally, but with no luck, so my husband and I decided we would revisit IVF. Cycle three was scheduled and I was feeling far more positive than I had ahead of cycle two. I felt like a seasoned professional walking into the assisted conception unit at the hospital. Nurses greeted me by name and I could feel they were rooting for my future pregnancy. With this renewed hope, I was certain this was my time.

For those who have gone through the process of IVF, and those trying naturally, when I say 'the two-week wait', you will know the true meaning of waiting. The two-week wait during IVF is the time in which the embryo/s have been implanted in the womb and you are waiting to see if the embryo/s have embedded in the lining. In a pregnancy without medical assistance, it is the wait to see if an embryo develops. I can honestly say that, on a personal level, I have never watched minutes or hours in the way I did through this waiting period during my six rounds of IVF.

Through IVF, you are encouraged not to take a pregnancy test before the end of the two weeks, as the result could be inaccurate. If anybody has managed to abstain from taking a test for the entire two weeks, let me know. I need to be taught your powers of restraint.

I felt that by day 11, my body would be producing the necessary hCG levels to indicate all was well, if I was indeed pregnant. After this third round of IVF, I was, once again, sure this would bring us our baby.

I did a pregnancy test. I am very certain I am not alone in saying that this is the point in my life when I finally experienced a mirage. The ones you see in films, where water can be seen in the faint distance of the desert by a weary traveller who is close to collapse. Only I was imagining a second blue line, not a watering hole in Arizona. I could see a faint second line. Or could I? Yes, there it is. Or is it? I called my friend Charlotte, the friend who answered my call at 4 a.m. the night Axel died. I needed a second opinion. I wrapped the test in tissue and walked over to her house at a faster than average pace. We placed the test on her kitchen counter and stared at the lines. Yes! We hugged one another and two utterly delusional women agreed that there were definitely, possibly, two blue lines. Of course there weren't. But a great friend combined with a desperate woman can create spectacular mental illusions when there is enough will. On day fourteen, with at least some hope left, I did four further pregnancy tests. All were negative.

Getting pregnant again wasn't something that came easily, and only after five rounds of IVF since Axel had died and months of trying naturally did I become pregnant. The positive pregnancy test we so desperately wanted came over a year after losing our baby. I am unsure if getting pregnant sooner would have made a difference to the time in which I began to lift out of my grief. Another pregnancy may have brought further emotional, and physical, complications. I don't believe things happen for a reason when it concerns loss, but I did come to accept that I had little control over the timings of a hopeful future pregnancy. Finding acceptance in my situation allowed for a partial release of the pressure I had put on myself to become pregnant again.

I spoke to Anjali Patel about her multiple pregnancy losses and how changing her approach to fertility treatment allowed for a more positive experience.

My husband and I met when we were both very young, we dated for seven years before we got married. After a year of marriage, we wanted to expand our family, we were both ready to be parents so decided to start trying. Looking back, we were somewhat naive, as we thought when we stopped using contraception we would fall pregnant. After a couple of months of trying, however, we found out that we were pregnant. It was over the Christmas holidays, we were seeing all our family and friends and I was desperate to tell everyone, but we waited. In January, I returned to work. I was seven weeks pregnant at the time and, while I was at my desk, something didn't feel right. I went to the toilet and there was blood everywhere.

I immediately called my husband and made my way to the nearest hospital. When I arrived, they took a urine sample and asked me to wait to be called in by the nurse. They called me in, but my husband arrived a few minutes later and missed me. The nurse told me that I was no longer pregnant, that our baby had died. The nurse comforted me and called for my husband to come in. We were given the textbook speech that we were young, that we could try again and that miscarriages are so common. I didn't want to hear that, I wanted our baby.

A few months after losing our first baby, we fell pregnant again. Only, the same thing happened and I began to bleed again. My doctor confirmed that I had lost another pregnancy.

Was there a point where you thought you may want to get tested to see if a doctor could give a possible reason for your losses?
We couldn't lose another baby, we were so angry when we were told I had to have another miscarriage before we could be tested. When I met with my GP

I pushed back and she agreed to refer us to the hospital for tests. At the clinic, I was repeatedly told I was young, not to worry and that we should keep trying: it was frustrating. My husband and I had tests and there were no obvious issues, other than my egg count wasn't as high as it should have been for my age, but the doctors didn't consider it to be a huge factor for us. The doctors concluded that we had unexplained infertility, which to us was even worse than being given a reason. I would have preferred something being wrong with one or both of us so we could devise a plan of action. The consultant suggested we begin fertility treatment.

What did you decide were your next steps after being given this news?

My husband and I immediately began IUI before our funding came through for IVF. We did three rounds of IUI treatments, but nothing stuck. Looking back, we shouldn't have done fertility treatment at that time, I wasn't prepared for the toll it took on my mental and physical health. Through some miracle we did fall pregnant from our first round of IVF. We were being monitored, we had science and medicine on our side, so we didn't think anything could go wrong. We went for a scan at around ten weeks and the sonographer fell silent. We knew what had happened before she even said anything. Our baby was there, but there was no heartbeat.

How did you feel after being given this news of a third loss?
Heartbroken. I felt like a complete failure. It's often instilled in us that the more productive we are, the more we're worth. The homes we own, the cars we drive or the careers we've chosen – these are the metrics by which we are judged especially within South Asian communities. So, when I lost our third baby, I began to feel worthless, as though I wasn't fulfilling my duty in giving my husband and our families a baby.

At that devastating appointment I remember immediately wanting to put my clothes on and get out of that room. We were given options of whether to let our baby come naturally, or book an appointment for a D&C. I didn't want to wait, so chose a D&C.

Leaving hospital carrying your baby inside you and knowing they had died must have been incredibly hard.
It is the most intimate form of death you will ever experience in your life. You have someone physically dead inside of you, and that's something no one can understand unless they have gone through it. This loss felt more real than our first two, because we'd seen our baby on the early scans and their little flickering heartbeat. I was so numb, I had so many thoughts in my head, but I couldn't get the words out. As we left the hospital, we felt completely defeated and I remember telling my husband I couldn't do this again, and that we weren't going to have children.

For the days leading up to the D&C, I stayed in the house, I became a recluse. When we went back to hospital, I realised how naive I had once again been. I didn't realise I would be put to sleep through the procedure. My husband wasn't allowed in the room, but I asked for him to be with me until I fell asleep. All I remember is holding his hand and crying until I drifted asleep.

When was the point you felt you could try to get pregnant again?
It was about eight months after our third loss when we felt we would begin trying again. We went back to the same fertility clinic and chose to do another round of IVF. This time my husband and I were in a much better place, we had done a lot of research and we went in with our eyes wide open. We had frozen embryos at the clinic and had one transferred, but it didn't stick.

We chose to do another round of IVF from the beginning, but this time we would split the responsibilities. I would be the body and my husband would be the brain. He tracked all of the dates, took care of all of the medications and let me focus on staying physically and mentally well. This new approach made a huge difference to my mental wellbeing.

Did this IVF experience differ from your first?
During this round of IVF my body exceeded what the doctors expected it to do. On the day of embryo

transfer, the doctors advised we only put one embryo in, but I was adamant that I wanted a greater chance of having a baby, so insisted we put two back in. An early scan showed that one embryo had stuck, so I knew I was right to transfer two. A few weeks later, we had another scan and the sonographer went quiet. I thought we were going to be told there was no heartbeat, but we were told there were two heartbeats. In the first scan, one baby had been hidden. We burst into tears of joy when we were shown the screen, as we could clearly see our twins, Krish and Bodhi.

When trying for another baby, being mindful of getting pregnant three months after your loss can be a consideration. If you become pregnant three months after the loss of your baby, the new baby's due date can be on, or very close to, the due date as the baby you lost, just a year later. Having a baby due on or around the date of your last baby introduces a whole new dynamic of emotions that people can struggle with. You may want to mourn the due date of your baby who died, but that is now the birthday or birth week of your new baby.

The due date can also be a big issue for parents who lose a twin in pregnancy. There can be a feeling that they should be grateful for the baby who survived, but also they will be mourning the loss of the twin who died. Every birthday of your living child is also the birthday of the twin who didn't make it. There are emotional challenges that parents face after pregnancy loss that may not be immediately obvious to those not personally living through the experience.

While trying for another baby, protecting yourself from anything that may cause negative emotions will make the journey a little easier on yourself. Social media, as we have discussed, is a great way to stay connected with others, but can also be a main source of unwanted triggers. Pregnancy announcements, growing bumps and newborns are regularly posted to online accounts, so a break from certain apps can be advisable.

I asked doula and author Latham Thomas for her advice when trying for a baby after loss. I found her words surprising at first, but the more I thought about what she said, the more it made sense. This was a new approach to anything I would have considered at the time I was trying to get pregnant myself, but I would have loved to lean into this way of thinking as a way to overcome many of my fears at the time.

> I advise going to a prenatal yoga class if you intend to get pregnant again. To be amongst women who are like your elders in this process, they're sisters you can look up to.
>
> I think part of the healing is to feel into what comes up for you when you're in that space. You need to know when it's appropriate to go, which is not within the first weeks after you experience your loss. You might be a couple of months in, a year in, and you know having another baby is something you would like to be on a path towards again. Then you say, let me be in spaces with people who are carrying life. Immerse in

that energy. It's not just a class, it can be other group situations. When you go and you're in that and you explain that you're on a fertility journey, or that you experienced pregnancy loss, you say you're there to learn, to be a student of what that is and to nurture your body. It can be triggering and guess what, you can always leave. You don't need to go in, but look at you, you were committed, you almost went. That's huge, that you made a commitment to go. Feeling the sensation in your body is really important, because it's energy, it's information and it helps us to heal. Then you ask yourself why you are afraid, what's coming up for you, why you don't want to walk into the room. What is it that you think will happen? You might cry, and that's okay. If we go, then we realise it does feel good to be there, and the people around us treated us so well, I got so many cheers of confidence when I announced myself and my experience. The fear is of judgement, is of having to feel pain, being reminded in that moment, being triggered. More often than not, when someone does put themselves in a situation and they're not ready, they may feel jealous, all kinds of things, but they're still feeling. The importance is that we feel. We are living in a society that turns us away from feeling, we get really used to tucking away our feelings. We get used to not processing them, not living them, not finding a place to locate them in our bodies. We need to process our feelings to come out the other side of the experience.

Belief

Through my loss and fertility challenges, I had to stay as optimistic as possible and believe that I would have another baby. By thinking positively, you're not going to miraculously cure a medical condition, or ensure the next time you have sex or transfer an embryo at the ACU you're going to find yourself pregnant. Instead, belief and positive thinking may help you to create the lighter thoughts that will get you through another month of trying to get pregnant. For me, it was about finding a way to focus my thoughts on what may happen, rather than focusing on what wasn't happening.

Being told to stay positive and believe you will get what you want in life is hard to hear from others when you have lost a baby or are trying to get pregnant. I can understand why the act of positive thinking and manifesting could seem improbable for some. I disagree with those that say if we all focus our minds we get exactly what we want in life, but I do believe in focusing with intent. For me, it was saying, 'I believe this is going to happen', even if the monthly negative pregnancy tests were showing me otherwise. During the years of trying for a second child, I would consider my choices in daily life and how they would affect my ultimate wish to have a baby. I would see myself holding my baby, and believe that my vision was a probability. My unexplained infertility caused great sadness and disappointment at times, but I would do my best to override the negative thoughts that often swirled around my mind.

I spoke to Deborah Joseph, *Glamour* UK Editor in Chief, on her experience of surrogacy and pregnancy loss and how she believes the negative narrative often surrounding fertility can cause psychological blocks.

I discovered I had endometriosis when I was about twenty-two. I was told at the time that I might struggle to have children in the future. My mother had it too, and never struggled to conceive, so I didn't really think too much about it.

I was thirty-one and had been married for a year when we began trying for a baby. I was quite relaxed about it, but, after a few months, I still wasn't pregnant, so we went for a scan. I was told my fertility age was ten years older than I was, so, at this point, I had the reproductive levels of a forty-two-year-old. Not infertile, but not very fertile either. Combined with my endometriosis, we were advised to start IVF soon after. I was devastated.

After researching IVF clinics, we found one that came highly recommended and began getting checked and finding out what to expect through the process. Our first appointment was terrible; our IVF doctor was awful, negative and unhelpful, and I cried the whole way through. I spoke to a holistic specialist years later, who theorised that being told you may struggle to have children when you're younger, as I was, can cause a psychological block. In my case, that block was my fertility.

I didn't respond well to the IVF drugs. I later understood that I hadn't been given high enough doses of medication to stimulate my eggs. That first round was such a negative experience. After that, I moved clinic, and had better success as my body produced more eggs, but the two cycles of IVF didn't work. I had various scans, which showed my endometriosis was worse than ever. I had two operations to laser off my endometriosis, which we hoped would give our IVF the best chance of working.

We moved IVF clinics again for our fifth round of IVF. The new clinic was more positive, more encouraging that we would have a baby and that helped my confidence greatly, and I did fall pregnant, but unfortunately had an early miscarriage. To be told that it was a possibility made a huge difference. I began having acupuncture, reflexology, anything I felt could help.

Do you feel holistic treatments made a difference?
Mentally, 100%. Each time I had acupuncture, I would go in as a nervous wreck and leave relaxed and feeling more positive. I continued to have these appointments through the following cycles of IVF.

Was there a way that you mentally prepared yourself for the fertility treatments ahead?
We were given some great advice when we first began IVF. We were told to make a decision on how many

times we would go through it. Whether that's based on emotions or finances, it was great advice. Have a plan. Our plans were based on financial, physical and emotional resources. We decided to have six rounds and that would be it. I was approaching thirty-five when we reached the time for our sixth round. It took some of the pressure off, knowing this would be the final time we would do it. It was in some ways a relief.

My last round of IVF, in my mind, was the last time we would try for me to carry our own biological child, then we would explore surrogacy and after that egg donation, in that order. Our sixth round didn't work but we had two frozen embryos left over, so we decided the best chance of having one implant would be to have a surrogate carry our baby. We were matched with a surrogate through a surrogacy charity in the UK.

Soon after our embryo was implanted, she fell pregnant. She called me after she took a positive pregnancy test and, for the first time in my life, I felt I was going to have a baby. I was so happy.

My husband and I went with the surrogate for her six-week scan. Everything looked great, our baby was growing as it should. With the positive news that our baby was finally coming, my husband and I booked a holiday. I needed a break from the years of IVF and to decompress from the experience of hoping our surrogate would get pregnant with our baby. While away, our surrogate had another scan. She was told there was no heartbeat. I was devastated. I felt terrible that our surrogate was on her own. I still regret it now. I carry huge guilt for being away.

How was your emotional state after your surrogate had experienced pregnancy loss?

It was a few days later when we received a text to say she was bleeding, that she was experiencing a pregnancy loss. Before I had fully had time to come to terms with our pregnancy loss, I noticed that I had missed my period. I was convinced I was having early menopause. My mind went back to the time I was told my fertility levels were ten years older than my actual age. Both my mother and grandmother had experienced the menopause in their mid-forties, so, with my fertility age, it made sense. The thought of being pregnant was so far from my mind.

I was due to take a flight for work soon after we returned from holiday, but the morning before my flight I was free, so I booked in to have acupuncture to try to bring on my period. Before I got there, for some reason, I decided to take a pregnancy test instead because the chemist was next door to the acupuncturist. I was furious for putting myself through this test, expecting more disappointment, but an instinct was telling me to take the test. I was telling myself I was an idiot, that I was wasting time and money doing it. I did the test, and waited. It showed I was seven weeks pregnant. I was pregnant at the same stage my surrogate would have been in her pregnancy with our embryo. Initially, when I had missed my period, my husband had said I might be pregnant. I was so angry with him for saying it, crying, knowing it was so unlikely. But now, here I was, pregnant.

Now you were pregnant yourself, how did you feel about your experience of loss through surrogacy?
Honestly, I think I mentally put aside the pregnancy loss of our surrogate for the first part of my pregnancy, I think I was in total shock at being pregnant myself. But there is something inherently disconnected that a woman miles away is miscarrying your baby. I don't think I have fully processed it, even now. It's such a devastating thought. The fact that I was pregnant myself was all-consuming. I have asked myself many times over the years, how did I fall pregnant naturally? I do think the negative conversation between your head and your body is detrimental to anybody trying to get pregnant. When I knew I was pregnant through a surrogate, I had released some of the pressure I put on myself. The tension and stress subsided. Perhaps my mind and body then allowed me to get pregnant? I must have become pregnant within three or four days of being told our surrogate was pregnant. I felt positive this pregnancy was going to work out. I gave birth to my first child eight months later. I went on to have two more children naturally, my last when I was forty.

> **With all you went through, what advice would you give to others?**
> I had a friend recently who was going through IVF. I made her promise me that however she was feeling, she would look at herself in the mirror every day and tell herself: 'I am going to have a baby.' It may seem counter-intuitive and you may not believe it at first. Tell your body every day that you are going to be pregnant, even if you don't believe it, keep saying it. Remove the negative narrative that surrounds most of us who experience pregnancy loss. I would never tell anybody to 'stay positive'. I hated those words when I was trying to get pregnant, they are so flippant and the reality is, when you're experiencing infertility, staying positive is very hard. But I do believe the connection between your mind and your body is an important one.

Reading positive affirmations, for me, resulted in hopeful feelings, even if sometimes those moments were brief. I followed Instagram accounts that posted daily positive affirmations. I downloaded an app to my phone and set a timer to send a positive affirmation each morning, which I would read just as my day was beginning. I bought books that focused on affirming the future you want as your reality. The affirmations didn't create a miraculous change in my mood, but the constant reminders to stay positive and hopeful worked to keep my head just above water.

Through the four years of unexplained infertility, which included six rounds of IVF, I had to believe it was going to happen for me, even if that was against any dominant thoughts that told me otherwise. I celebrated the news of others' pregnancies, because I had to believe that it was going to happen for me too. Being angry and thinking it was unfair was only going to damage me, and I was feeling damaged enough. I continued to visualise a future with a baby. It wasn't easy and it almost broke me at times, but I had to remain hopeful. Hope was all I had.

I spoke to designer Melissa Odabash about late-term pregnancy loss and how a positive mindset allowed her to move through her grief.

I had experienced a normal pregnancy, it was no different to my pregnancy two years before. I was twenty-three weeks pregnant when I inadvertently ate a piece of raw chicken at a restaurant, which led to food poisoning. I spoke with my doctor and was told it wouldn't affect my baby and that I shouldn't be concerned. I had been vomiting all night, but, as with most of us, I trusted my doctor's word.

Did you instinctively feel something wasn't right?
Through pregnancy I felt bad anyway and was vomiting, so after the food poisoning, I assumed I was feeling terrible due to my hormones. I didn't think I had anything to worry about. A week later, I wasn't feeling any movement. I went to the hospital and it

What Next?

was confirmed that my baby had died. I'm sure if I had gone into the hospital when I had called my doctor, they could have given me something and it would never have happened.

After you were told your baby had died, did you stay at the hospital, or were you advised to return home for a few days?
I stayed at the hospital that day. It was all very clinical and straightforward, there was little compassion. I was told I would have to give birth, although I don't remember the exact details. I blanked it out of my mind. I remember I had a nurse with me when I was given the pills for the induction of labour. It took time, it was ten hours later when I gave birth to a baby boy. It was Valentine's Day.

I'm a strong person, but it was devastating, heartbreaking. When a baby is growing inside of you, you feel so attached to it. Then the bleeding afterwards is a constant reminder of what you have lost. I felt fortunate that it wasn't my first baby as I could focus on my daughter at home, I had to continue being a mom to her.

Did you have a support system around you, friends who were there for you after your loss?
A difficult part of my experience was that I had four close girlfriends who were all pregnant at the same time. I continued to see them regularly, I wasn't going to stop seeing them, they were my best friends. They

289

all gave birth within two weeks of when my baby had been due. I went to the hospital to see them all when they were giving birth; it's difficult as you wish you had a baby at the same time. As sad as it was, I think it helped. I was happy for my friends and had to stay positive that it would happen again for me.

Did you throw yourself back into work, or did you take time away from your business at that time?
I went back to work immediately. I had to get on with life, I needed distractions so I wasn't thinking about what had happened all the time. I blocked much of what happened out of my mind, it's part of a coping mechanism, you just keep moving. I spoke to so many friends who told me they had also experienced pregnancy loss, so in one way you feel more confident when you hear that it's so common, it makes you feel as though you are not so alone out there trying to get through it.

How did you navigate the weeks after your loss?
My husband was great and took care of everything. He arranged a burial. I couldn't do anything at that time. My girlfriends were so kind, they were very good to me. I kept myself busy. I had to move forward and be grateful for all I had. It was awful, a horrific thing to go through, but I had to put my mind in a perfect mindset that in the future I would get pregnant and have a healthy baby. I visualised a great future and had to

believe that this wasn't my time. It was something that happened and I had to accept the experience.

From hearing the way you speak of your experience, it's clear that you're an incredibly positive person. What advice would you give to others who have experienced pregnancy loss?

Understand that pregnancy loss is not your fault and try to move forward. When you dwell on what happens in life, you get stuck focusing on the negatives of your past and not the positives of your future. When you have multiple pregnancy losses in a row, it can be hard to stay positive and actually think it's going to work. Sometimes, changing your mindset can help. It may take a year, longer, but you're changing the way you look at your experience. I believe in visualisation, thinking of a great future. Believe that you will have kids. It can help to have a beautiful visualisation board, put it where you can see it every day and visualise that's your future.

Language surrounding fertility, pregnancy, birth and loss

During my fertility journey, I encountered many medical terms that felt outdated and uncomfortable. Being described as geriatric wasn't encouraging. I also felt that 'late miscarriage' did not accurately describe the baby I delivered at five months into my pregnancy. I soon realised my fertility journey was frequently being relayed to me in negative terms.

Without question, medical staff are not intentionally trying to offend anybody with terms that feel outdated and hurtful. There has simply not been a challenge on the textbook terms that have been used for years. Times have moved on, but medical terminology has not.

In early 2021, Peanut app founder Michelle Kennedy worked with medical experts and linguists to create a Renaming Revolution glossary in order to suggest more empowering terminology that could be used.

I asked Michelle why she felt the Renaming Revolution would be a positive step forward if the terms were used by the medical industry.

All of the words relating to fertility, pregnancy, birth and loss tend to have failure associated with them. The reframing of the wording that many women find offensive and upsetting needs to happen at the point of educating young medics. There is reluctance in some areas of the medical community to change the language. This is not seen as a priority. Often it is not considered that women have mental-health issues as a direct, or partial, result of how their experience is managed by medical professionals. Women mostly blame themselves for things that are out of their control. They already feel like a failure, and the terminology that is used is confirming these unhelpful and inaccurate beliefs. If women at the starting point are made to feel less of a failure, there wouldn't be such an impact on their mental health.

What Next?

Some of the most widely used, and problematic, terminology relating to fertility and loss is detailed below, along with the changes Michelle suggests. The below are extracts from the full Renaming Revolution:

Fertility

Current term: Failed Embryo Transfer/Implantation Failure
Suggested term: Non-Implantation
When an embryo doesn't implant or transfer to the uterine lining.

Current term: Hostile Uterus
Suggested term: Uterine Lining Implantation Struggles (ULIS)
When cervical mucus makes the movement of sperm challenging.

Current term: Incompetent Cervix
Suggested term: Early Cervical Dilation
When the cervix shortens and opens early without any other symptoms of labour.

Current term: Infertile
Suggested term: Reproductive Struggles
Struggles to conceive after twelve months of unprotected intercourse.

Current term: Viability Scan
Suggested term: Six-to-Ten-Weeks Pregnancy Scan
Determines if embryos are present and if the pregnancy is progressing.

Loss

Current term: Evacuation of Retained Products of Conception
Suggested term: Compassionate Removal
Removal of the pregnancy tissue from the womb.

Current term: External Mass
Suggested term: Ectopic Pregnancy
A pregnancy where the fertilised egg implants outside the uterus.

Current term: Habitual Aborter
Suggested term: Recurrent Miscarriage
Three or more consecutive pregnancy losses before twenty weeks of gestation.

Current term: Late Miscarriage
Suggested term: Early Stillbirth
Loss of a pregnancy between fourteen and twenty-four weeks.

Current term: Non-viable Pregnancy
Suggested term: Pregnancy Unable to Continue
When the fetus or baby is unable to be born alive.

Current term: Products of Conception
Suggested term: Pregnancy Tissue
The tissue derived from the union of an egg and a sperm.

Current term: Spontaneous Abortion
Suggested term: Pregnancy Loss
Loss of pregnancy naturally before twenty weeks.

Release expectations from yourself and from others

In this section are the main points I took from my own experience, from the first month through to a time when I could see that there was renewed hope for the future. It can be a long journey through the grief process. I hope my words will allow you to release any expectations you have on yourself during this time.

Let go of any friends who are not there for you. This is not to say for ever, but, from experience, I wasted energy thinking of those who simply did not contact me more than once, or did not contact me at all. Any focus during the first months after loss should be on healing and trying to navigate life after your loss. If, in the future, you choose to let the friends who were not there for you back into your life, then that will be something to consider down the line. I have let several friendships go, but have grown closer to those who were there for me when I needed the most compassion. Allow yourself to cry and allow yourself to talk about your baby and your experience. Those that are meant to be in your life will accept your tears and your story, no matter how long they have to sit with you or how many times you repeat your story.

Soon after my baby had died, I went back to work. I owned my own store at the time and felt I had to be there to run my business. I had to wash my hair and do my make-up, I had to get dressed and leave the house. This to me was partially masking what had happened, but also a forced way to return to living my life. It was very soon after Axel had died, possibly too soon, but in the long run it helped me to regain some form of normality. If you have no reason to leave the house, stay in if that is what will make you feel better for that day. I found that getting dressed and leaving the house at least every other day was, albeit temporarily, a way to release the extreme focus on my loss.

When I was at home, I would try to lose myself in a favourite film or show. While reading a book, I couldn't concentrate for longer than a page without thinking of my baby, so I watched television. I don't think my emotional state could have coped with anything other than romantic comedies. I found the best thing I could do for myself was not think past the next hour of time. There was no planning and no projecting how I would feel the next day. I simply kept my focus on what I would do for the next hour, then the next, until I got through the day. I watched reruns of a favourite show that focused on friends and their lives. I escaped my own life by watching others living theirs. The distraction worked, to a degree. Whenever I see this show now, it takes me back to the months after I lost Axel, huddled on the sofa with a blanket. I find the memory strangely comforting, perhaps as a way to feel closer to Axel. Ordinarily I wouldn't have spent so many hours in front of a screen, but I saw this escapism as part of my grief therapy. Categorising my hours in front of the TV as therapy allowed me to release any guilt about 'wasting' my days. I can highly recommend taking the time to sit with favourite and familiar films or television programmes. To me, it felt similar to sitting quietly with friends, only without the need to say anything at any time.

For weeks afterwards I would frequently read online information about pregnancy loss. I would spend time typing in keywords, trying to make sense of things in my mind. As I read stories, facts and theories, it just made this grossly unfair situation all the more confusing. The answers I was looking for weren't out there. Or perhaps they were, but I found there was simply too much information. It became utterly overwhelming. A government site would give condensed medical guidance, while a mother-focused forum would have hundreds of opinions beneath a pregnancy loss post. My mind was already filled with grief, guilt and possible causes of loss from the hospital. This almost addictive searching contributed to my already delicate emotional state. After a month, I made the decision not to search online any longer. If I had a question, I would write it down and wait until I had a call with my doctor or a community midwife. My anxiety levels improved. My head was still clouded due to my grief, but at least my thoughts became a lot clearer.

I called friends and talked for as long as I felt was appropriate; they had lives too and I didn't want to overwhelm them with my grief. Whenever I spoke to anybody, I was honest and didn't try to brush over the fact that I was in incredible pain. I was fortunate in that certain friends showed me just how loved I was. I had a feeling I had true friendships, but until something as enormous as this happens in your life, you can never really know who will be there for you. I will never forget the kindness from friends who took the time to sit with me, offer help and just be on the end of the phone to listen. One friend explained that she was terrified of talking about death, particularly of a premature baby, but that she wanted to be there for me. We ended up sitting on the phone in silence, as that is all she was able to do. I appreciated her for her honesty and just knowing that she was there for me, even in silence, meant so much.

Try to stop thinking of how things could have been different. I spent countless hours asking myself if I should have listened to my instincts and gone to the hospital hours earlier. Or whether I should have booked additional scans, just in case. In the majority of cases, there is no knowing when pregnancy loss will occur. To have your thoughts on a constant negative loop with imagined scenarios of what you could have done differently is only going to make you feel more traumatised. Unless you were given clear information that you should have done something differently in your pregnancy to prevent pregnancy loss, try to redirect your thoughts to what is happening in your present moment.

Make a choice to only spend time with those who make you feel like you can be yourself around them. It will be hard enough to make it through each day, so behaving in a certain way to make others feel more comfortable will add unnecessary pressure. There may be friends, family or colleagues who are well-meaning, but continue to say things that make you feel awful. Make polite excuses to not speak to or see them for a while. You are living through one of the most traumatic periods you are ever likely to experience, so now more than any other time you can choose who you spend time communicating with.

Explain why you appear angry or upset all the time, if this will make things easier on you. I found through my trauma I became angry for a period of time, which is a normal part of the grieving process. I could hear when I snapped at my son, or became frustrated when people around me were not considering my situation. If possible, it can be helpful to explain to whoever you have directed negative energy towards that you are dealing with a pain-ful issue and apologise if you have caused upset to others. Explaining your situation (very briefly if it's someone you don't know) can lighten the situation and allow for some understanding.

Try not to pressure yourself into responding to calls and messages. One mistake I feel I made was to force myself to respond to kind messages, but also work emails. You may think that people will be offended if you don't respond to them, perhaps you are right in some cases, but now is the time to do exactly what feels right for you. If you feel you cannot answer work-related emails, place an out-of-office message on. Friends will understand if it takes you days, weeks, possibly months, to respond. If they don't understand, it can be helpful to explain, when you are ready, just how bad things have been and why you were unable to respond. It comes back to the point that unless you have lived through pregnancy loss, it can be difficult to understand this form of trauma.

Your outlook will change, often for the better. Before I lost my baby, I would focus heavily on the things that didn't matter greatly in my life. I would allow minor negative situations to occupy my thoughts for far too long. Since Axel died, I have found truth in the saying 'Don't sweat the small stuff'. Five years on and it is impossible for me to spend too long on the small stuff, as I have experienced the overwhelming huge stuff.

I spoke to Lina Chan on how pregnancy loss led to a significant life shift, leaving a career in finance to set up Parla, a leading wellness and women's reproductive health company

Can you tell me about your journey to motherhood?
My firstborn was Mia Tianshi Christie. Mia means My in Latin and Tianshi means Angel in Chinese. Mia was

born still at twenty-six weeks. My pregnancy with Mia wasn't straightforward and from the early weeks of pregnancy, I experienced recurrent bleeds. I attended every scan thinking the worst, but each time the sonographer would detect a heartbeat. I hung on to every hope that I would make it to forty weeks. At twenty-four weeks, my waters broke.

Where were you when your waters broke?
I was at home in bed. At first I thought I had wet myself, but I knew that something wasn't right. I woke my husband up and we rushed to the emergency room at the hospital. A few hours after we arrived, I was examined by an obstetrician. It was confirmed that my waters had broken, but that my baby's heart was still beating. I knew the odds were stacked against us, but I clung to the hope that our baby would make it.

How were you cared for from this point, knowing there were concerns for your baby?
I stayed in hospital on bed rest and had frequent scans to monitor her condition. I had been in hospital for almost two weeks, when in the middle of the night I woke up feeling very cold and scared. I waited patiently for the nurse to arrive in the morning and check for a heartbeat. Only this time, she couldn't find one. Our baby girl had died in the night.

Knowing our baby no longer had a heartbeat, I was told I would have to be induced to bring Mia into the world. I laboured for over eight hours to deliver her. I couldn't hold her, so my husband did. I was scared. I felt guilty and ashamed. I felt like a complete failure, so I couldn't bring myself to hold her. My husband stayed with her for a few hours while I rested.

Was there a point where you felt you could hold Mia that day?
When I woke up a good friend of my husband had sent him an email. Her boy was born still at forty weeks and even though I had never met this friend, she shared her experience with me. She encouraged me to spend as much time as I could with Mia, as it would help me in my grieving process. When I finally held Mia, my heart burst open. The combination of pain and love was unbearable. I loved and kissed her, yet the tears and sobbing wouldn't stop. I was in hospital for three days, where we got to spend precious time with Mia. We tried to cherish every minute with her. Mia was our perfect, first, beautiful baby girl. Still today, after almost nine years, I can still feel that tightness in my chest. The pain doesn't knock me off my feet any more, but it's still there.

How did you navigate life after losing Mia?
Once I recovered physically, I wanted to try to get pregnant again as soon as possible. Unlike with Mia, conceiving was not straightforward. It took us over a year to conceive only to lose our pregnancy at eight weeks. I felt that the universe was working against me.

In losing my babies, I lost my sense of self and my confidence. On the outside I seemed fine, but I felt lonely, isolated and completely broken. The lack of control was also hard for me to deal with. Up until that point, everything that I applied myself to I would achieve. When it came to pregnancy, the opposite was true. I had no control. I thought that after one year of grieving the loss of Mia I would feel better, but my second pregnancy loss opened the wounds back up. That's when I realised grief is not linear.

Did you feel you wanted to try again soon after your second loss, or did you need time to process all that had happened?
I stopped trying to get pregnant and focused instead on rebuilding my confidence. I needed to regain that trust in myself and let go of what I could not control. I remember thinking that I have lost two children, I cannot lose myself or my husband. My husband and I made a commitment to healing, rather than trying to get pregnant again. I also started speaking more openly about my losses. I do believe that there is growth in loss. It is the last thing you want to hear while you are in it, but with the right support and mindset, you can become stronger and more resilient.

Along with rebuilding the confidence and trust in your body, did you make any other changes in your life?
In the period after my second loss, I was still working in finance, but I trained to be a yoga teacher. I also did

a nutrition course and a mindfulness course. While these activities helped me navigate my grief and gave me a structure to follow each day, when I look back, I realise that they were the building blocks of how I became resilient and gained trust in my body and mind again. This life shift also set the foundation of the business I launched in that time.

Rebuilding my resilience initially began as a simple gratitude practice. Eventually, after many years of this practice and with the support of family and caregivers, I went on to have three healthy children. After having my second child, and seeing that now I had two living girls to take care of, I started reflecting on all that I had gone through. I want to make sure that if my daughters ever have challenges building their family, they won't feel the confusion, isolation and shame that I felt.

Communicate your feelings to your partner, taking the time to ask how they are feeling through their grief also. I am unsure how great I was at taking my own advice. I know I talked about my baby to anybody who would listen, including my husband. Looking back, I probably didn't give him the attention he needed and the chance to explain how he was feeling. We cried together, then, after a while, he stopped crying and I continued being the one needing him to comfort me. It is so hard to think of anybody other than yourself when you are engulfed in grief. When possible, remember that two of you lost a baby.

You will be happy again, and you will laugh again without feeling guilty. It can be hard when you begin to feel a little lighter as it can seem as though you are letting go of your baby. I felt awful when I laughed for the first time about something a friend had said. I felt I would be judged and people would assume I was getting over my loss. Feeling happy is the best possible thing, even if it's only for a brief moment. Try to embrace those moments and don't try to prove that you are still hurting. Laughing for a while won't lessen the love or grief you have for your baby. The only judgement will likely be that you place on yourself (unless you have very judgemental friends, who possibly shouldn't be with you at this time).

You are a mother. You are a mother to the children you carried. If you don't have children that people can see, saying you are a mother can mean you have to explain your journey. Discussing your loss is something you may only wish to do with people you know well. Saying you are a mother to strangers can be too much of an emotional investment. I choose the moments in which I tell people I have two children, or three, based on how much I want to give myself to whoever I am talking to. Not acknowledging Axel in conversations with strangers is not dismissing his existence, it is simply a way of preserving my emotional reserves.

There is no right or wrong way to navigate your way through pregnancy loss. Decisions will need to be made concerning your baby, your body and your wellbeing. Advice will be given, solicited or otherwise. There is the potential for judgement of the decisions you make. At this time, more than any other, you have to cancel out the noise of anything that may add to your trauma.

What Next?

Grief will come in waves. There were times when I felt as though I was recovering from the emotional hold grief had on me, then I would fall straight back down to my lowest ebb once again. I would be consumed with sadness and feel as though time hadn't moved on at all. These moments gradually became less frequent and now, a few years on, I only get very affected by Axel's death on his birthday, or other dates that are connected to my loss. I find that as I have spoken so openly about Axel, he is with me. By talking about him with family and friends, or just thinking of him by myself, it keeps him close. I feel that talking about my loss is very healthy. I used to be conscious of mentioning him when out for dinner or bringing him up in conversation on the phone to a friend, but I no longer feel that way. He's a part of me, so now I simply speak of him when it feels natural to do so.

FOUR

Life After Loss

Two years on – a personal experience

On our fifth IVF cycle since Axel died, it was confirmed that I was pregnant. I wanted to share my news with the world, to post an image of my growing bump on Instagram, a place where so many had reached out to me following the loss of my second baby. Although this third pregnancy had been labelled high risk, I decided that by the three-month mark I would announce that our baby was due in the spring. By week ten I started to ease into the pregnancy. My confidence that this baby would make it had grown. The Harmony Test told us our baby was a girl.

At almost three months pregnant, my husband, never home during the day, had landed late morning from a business trip and had decided to come home before heading to the office. He had been home for just a few minutes when I felt a small rush of fluid. I looked inside my underwear to see a substantial amount of blood, enough to let me know that something was wrong. I managed to make it to the toilet before a greater rush of blood came, carrying with it a large blood clot that forcefully hit the water beneath me. Through tears I told my husband I had miscarried, we had lost another baby. Strangely, when I saw what I believed was my baby lying in the water, at that moment my tears were not of sadness, but of anger and frustration. For two years I had been injecting myself with drugs, had been pregnant, or grieving for the baby I had watched pass away in the summer of 2017.

With a mix of emotions, I walked downstairs to the kitchen. I took a pair of rubber gloves and found a small freezer bag in which to place what I thought was my baby. To me this was a second baby I would quietly bury. I placed what I believed to be my baby in the small clear bag, wrapped it in tissue, got into the car and called the hospital as my husband drove us to A&E. I called the IVF clinic on the way to ask when I could start the process again.

We signed in at the hospital and were rushed through. The tests were done and standard procedures were checked off by nurses. I was told there was no availability for a scan, either within the NHS or the private clinic close by, so we would have to come back in the morning to confirm whether I was still pregnant. Those hours were hell – not knowing if I should be grieving another loss, or be thankful my baby was still alive. The next morning, the sonographer placed the ultrasound on my stomach. There was my baby. Her heartbeat was strong. I had experienced a subchorionic hematoma – relatively common, I was told. And so we left the hospital. My husband kissed me as he left for the tube station. I drove home with the ultrasound image of our daughter clearly in view on the passenger seat.

Nothing I ever thought about pregnancy was this complicated. You had sex, you made a baby. Until our attempts to get pregnant with a second child, this was how easy I assumed my fertility journey would be. No IVF, no child loss, no pregnancy loss.

My twelve-week scan proved to be another hurdle. Laying on the bed, the sonographer excused herself and walked back in ten minutes later with an obstetrician. Confirming a problem with my mucus plug, it was explained that my baby would be here shortly if I didn't have an operation to fix a cerclage; stitching that would hold the top of my cervix together for the remaining six months of my pregnancy. At 6 a.m. the next morning I was back in the hospital, leaving later that day with the security that would, I hoped, get me safely to the forty-week mark.

Tempting fate by announcing the bump on Instagram was something that no longer felt like an option. I felt too fragile to expose myself, knowing what fate could bring. Thankfully, it wasn't difficult to hide my stomach until at least six months. I liked it this way, my news only shared with those I met. In a world of sharing our every move, it made the nine months more special because it became my little secret.

With a growing bump came growing anxiety. Most days, my mind would create negative scenarios, both terrifying and exhausting. I regularly saw a healer who had helped me when Axel died. I tried guided meditation, hoping it would calm my mind. I steered clear of any online communities that discussed possible problems during pregnancy. Although helpful for some, I found the forums caused me further confusion and distress. I chose instead to save any questions I had and wait to ask medical professionals at antenatal appointments. This worked to eliminate at least some of the unwanted noise in my mind.

Finally, she came. Audrey. A planned date and planned operation. I chose the first caesarean section of the day, just before 7 a.m. I knew that if I had the entire day to consider the operation to bring my baby daughter into the world, I would likely break from the anxiety that had been building over the past nine months. The hospital had an eerie silence in those early hours that I knew only too well. I was rushed there two years prior, following the night I prematurely gave birth to my son at home and watched him pass away. I was certain this baby was going to die too. A terrifying vision of my daughter lying lifeless on my stomach had frequently entered my mind in the days leading up to the operation.

It should have been an occasion of happiness. Moments that should have been filled with love instead filled me with terror. Tears fell as my bed was wheeled to the operating room. I asked for my caesarean to be postponed, could we wait another day? I wasn't ready to face the fear that, like him, she might not make it. I closed my eyes through my surgery, choosing to block out what was happening. I sobbed quietly as my body was manoeuvred by the surgeon. The few minutes on the operating table felt endless as I waited to hear a cry, confirmation that I would finally get the baby I was unsure would ever come. And then I heard her. My husband held her to my face and my fists unclenched with relief.

With the relief that came a few days after her arrival came a sadness that I hadn't expected. I had a beautiful daughter, but I had still lost a son. Those initial days in the hospital when Audrey would cry, I would imagine the sounds Axel would have made. She opened her eyes and I pictured her face as his. I knew she was here and that my son was gone, but those split seconds when my mind allowed me to imagine the 'what if?'s left me with an almost unbearable longing for the baby I had lost.

My arms wanted to hold the son I met, whose mouth I watched trying to breathe the air that would keep him alive. With the happiness my daughter brought, there was initially guilt for every moment that Axel was not there. I had to find a way to let him go, while still being able to hold him close. His freedom was my freedom, but my chest tightened when I thought I may need to loosen my hold on him, to say out loud that I will never forget him, but that I am moving forward. I felt somehow overwhelmed by my love for him and the pain that saying he could now rest brought.

I waited a few days after Audrey had been born to announce the news that I had been pregnant, and now had a daughter. I didn't lay blame on the friends and well-meaning strangers who, without truly understanding, commented that I finally got my happy ending. There is no happy ending. I realised how lucky I was to have two healthy children, there was a new life and deep love for a baby who I thought might never come, but I still lost a son. The happy ending would have been that he lived too.

Moving forward doesn't mean forgetting

Try not to feel guilty as your grief begins to lessen. You're not forgetting your baby or moving on, you're just finding ways to manage your trauma. When I began to feel a little more positive, I almost wanted to revert to crying each day to honour my baby, to show him I wasn't moving on. I often felt conflicted; I wanted to be happy again, but I felt that being sad kept me closer to my baby. It did become easier to have positive moments without feeling guilty, but it took time.

Each morning for months after my loss, I woke with anxiety and a physical chest pain where the reality of what happened would hit me over and over again. This was the most draining and emotionally painful time each day, when I realised that what had happened was a reality. It's hard to live with what is happening, but it does become less painful as the months pass. I didn't love people telling me that time was a healer when I was in my deepest period of grief, but they were right, for me it was. In time I understood that I wasn't forgetting my baby, I was simply learning to live with my loss.

I spoke to Chloe Regan about second-trimester loss and how she honours the memory of her son.

I fell pregnant with Leo in June 2019. I have to say I was nervous and felt I had to abide by the unwritten rule of not telling anyone until I hit twelve weeks. At ten weeks, I did the Harmony Test and found out we were having a boy. His due date was my thirtieth birthday. I remember my husband and I visualising weekend football practice and visits to the playground in the early days of my pregnancy.

In the early weeks, was there any reason to think your pregnancy was high risk?
At seven weeks, I was told that I had a bicornuate uterus (something that affects 1 in every 200 women), that it was nothing to worry about and that many pregnancies are unaffected by the condition. I felt

reassured by the sonographer and didn't think too much about it. In retrospect, I mourn this blissfully unaware version of myself, and think how uneducated I was about pregnancy complications.

At twelve weeks, I woke in the middle of the night with severe bleeding. We went straight to the hospital, where they diagnosed a threatened pregnancy loss. The hospital didn't have ultrasound equipment there, so I would have to wait for an appointment. I managed to secure a private scan that morning, but those hours of not knowing were just excruciating. The idea that I could have had to wait longer didn't sit right with me. The kind sonographer very quickly said she could see a healthy heartbeat, explaining that I had a hematoma by my placenta and that we should monitor it.

How did your pregnancy progress in the weeks after this news?

The bleeds continued and I remember the sinking feeling in my heart that came with each episode. At twenty weeks, I woke in the night due to an intense feeling of pressure in my stomach. I went to the loo and there was a huge gush of water. Some people say when your waters break it's not like in the movies, but for me, it was. We rushed to the hospital where they tested the fluids and I had an ultrasound. The ultrasound showed I had lost almost 80% of the amniotic fluid, but our baby's little heart was still beating away and I could still feel his light flutter kicks. We named our baby Leo. I will never forget the face of the doctor, shoulders slumped, saying they were 'So sorry'. It was explained that I had a preterm premature rupture of the membrane.

I was admitted to the labour ward, which seems like the cruellest form of torture to any family who has to go through the heartbreak of losing a baby. The midwives were incredibly kind, but it was excruciating to hear the very distinct newborn cries close by as I lay there knowing my son may not make it.

I was seen by a consultant. He told me that a baby at twenty weeks needs amniotic fluid to help their lungs develop and these next four weeks were the most crucial. I had read there were many parents whose babies had survived preterm premature rupture of the membranes (PPROM), which I found to be a great source of hope. I was placed on bed rest and just needed to get to twenty-four weeks pregnant, then there was a far greater chance of Leo surviving.

Did you stay in hospital for the next four weeks, or were you told you could go home?
We stayed in the hospital for three days, Leo and I fighting hard. On the third day we went down for a scan with the consultant. As I was wheeled into a lift, I remember feeling the biggest sense of peace. I don't know if that was just being out of our room, or Leo gaining his wings. I like to think it was the latter. It is a great source of comfort for me in reflection.

My husband said he knew straight away, from our consultant's face, as he tried and failed to find a heartbeat. I can't remember too much of what happened after hearing the words 'I'm sorry, I can't find a heartbeat.' We walked back to the ward through a sea of pregnant women, where I was greeted by a bereavement midwife. Spending time with the bereavement midwife made a huge difference to my experience. I was gently told that my next steps were to go home and come back in two days to deliver the baby.

How did you feel, knowing you would have to leave the hospital, while still carrying your baby?
I was shocked. My world had shattered into a million pieces. The idea of leaving the hospital and continuing as normal was unfathomable. I just wanted everything to be over and to be in my safe space at home with my two cats, who have been so healing. Living, breathing, existing with my little bump in those days before going back into the hospital were inexplicably difficult.

I went back to the hospital two days after Leo died to be induced. I saw the same consultant and remember him saying that he hoped it didn't take too long. Within three and a half hours, Leo was born. Those hours were the hardest of my life. My body had a very strong reaction to the induction medication, so everything went from 0–100 super quickly. The hospital was short-staffed and I remember begging for some pain relief. The staff prioritised the women who were delivering living babies. I recall myself pleading with a doctor, saying that I couldn't take my baby home, and could someone who gets that privilege please sacrifice their anaesthetist. A few minutes before Leo was born, someone did come to administer pain relief. I was given fentanyl, which was allowed, as Leo was not alive.

Did you spend time with your baby in the hospital?
The next twenty-four hours we got to meet and spend precious time with our beautiful boy. When I look back at some of the pictures, the grief and heartache is so clearly etched in my face. I find it hard to look at myself. I am so glad we have these memories with him and his blanket that smells like him. I keep his blanket sealed in a transparent plastic bag in his memory box. I want to try and preserve that beautiful smell.

How have you learned to live alongside your grief since Leo died?
We miss Leo every day and I always wonder how different our life would be if he was with us. We visit the cemetery where we held Leo's funeral on his birthday each year, on his due date and whenever I feel grief creeping up. I often light a candle to let him know we are thinking about him. It is my way of feeling I can care for him and honour him, even without him being here.

I am sure other women who have been through pregnancy loss can relate to seeing that positive test and spending days daydreaming about their new baby and making plans. I wish the only event we had planned for Leo wasn't his funeral and I wish the only pictures of him were not the ones we have. However, I am so grateful that he graced us with his short life and we feel so blessed to cherish these memories. I find joy in the little things, practise gratitude daily, and have a humble outlook on life and loss. Despite it being the most traumatic and testing experience of my life, it has shaped me as a person and as a mother in more ways than I could possibly imagine.

Understand that life goes on. People will stop asking how you are, friends will call and the conversation will no longer be all about you and your baby. There is an unspoken time limit for how often people will call to ask how you are, and that's okay. Those around you won't have forgotten about your grief and trauma, but there will naturally come a point where your experience won't be the first thing people will talk about when you speak to them.

Let go of resentment or anger towards those who no longer ask about your baby. You are living through the experience, but they have their own lives and possible problems of their own. Remember that you are not the only one who is trying to navigate a situation that is out of your control.

In navigating a future without my baby, I found it interesting and hugely comforting to discover the phenomenon of Microchimerism. This occurrence results in a small amount of cells from a previous pregnancy being identified within

the mother. In some cases, these cells can be detected dec-
ades after that pregnancy. I love to think that part of the
baby you lose is within you for ever, and could possibly be
within a future child. Nancy Shute, Editor in Chief of *Science
News*, put it beautifully when she wrote of Microchimerism:
'Mother and child are engaged in a silent chemical conversation throughout pregnancy, with bits of genetic material and
cells passing not only from mother to child but also from
child to mother.'

I came to realise that there was no right or wrong way of
looking at my experience of baby loss. I didn't want to move
forward without my baby, but I knew I needed to release
parts of the experience I was holding on to. I didn't want to
live my life either trying to forget my baby, or holding him
so close that it would prevent me from moving forward in
a positive way. I found that if I accepted Axel would live
alongside me, he would always be with me. This acceptance
of my experience allowed me to release much of the hold
grief had over me. We are not being forced to slot ourselves into categories of grieving, depressed or recovered. I
found a great deal of peace in saying I was living alongside
my baby, rather than explaining to people that I felt better,
or that I was still unable to move forward from the initial
intense grieving period.

Living alongside your loss and finding a way to move forward with the inclusion of your baby, or babies, may be
difficult at first. Knowing when to include or speak of your
losses can be hard to navigate, as this is not something you
were prepared for in life. I know I found it incredibly tricky in
the first year after losing Axel to know when to include him.

There were feelings of guilt if I didn't mention him, and I could also feel uncomfortable when I did. It took some time to find a rhythm where he naturally lived alongside me.

One of the things I found most confusing to navigate was the inclusion of my baby in everyday events. We would book a restaurant for a family dinner, but to my husband and son I would speak of the three of us going, not the four of us. Should I always say the four of us? Or is it a given that it's the four of us? I'm not going to book a table with four seats, but am I dismissing Axel's existence if I don't at least include him in our conversation? Am I being crazy? Unkind? Both? Will Axel hear me saying he's not really coming? There were always so many questions swirling around my head. None of us really knew where to go with this, but, after a while, we naturally stopped including Axel when talking of booking restaurants, or going to events. I'm pretty sure we were all looking at each other, wondering who was going to say the other hadn't mentioned Axel's place, but after a while, things just became more simple. We knew Axel was with us, and that was enough.

Family birthdays are a little different and Axel is always included. For mine and my husband's birthdays, all three children's names are signed on the cards. The same with my two children: everyone is there. When signing cards for others, it's the names of the four of us who are attending in person, then five kisses at the end. Sometimes I just like to keep Axel to myself and it's enough that I know he's on the card with that kiss. I am the first to say don't dismiss the children that people cannot physically see, but sometimes I don't want there to be any questions, or polite acknowledgements of Axel's name on the card.

Leading up to Axel's birthday is a tricky time. I can feel the date approaching and it always brings back vivid memories and emotions. There is a lot I can't remember from that time, but waking up on the night he died, my waters breaking and giving birth to him is still fresh in my mind. I can feel a lower mood begin to take hold at least a week before his birthday. I find that making lots of plans that week can be helpful. To have a full schedule of work and social occasions takes my mind off of the dread I feel leading up to Axel's birth date.

For Axel's birthday, there's a small breakfast celebration with my husband and children each year. Presents for Astie and Audrey (they have cleverly tricked us into buying them presents to make it a 'real' birthday celebration) and a birthday cake. Not a monumental layered cake with chocolates pouring out from the middle, just a simple cupcake with a candle. We visit the tree in the cemetery where we scattered Axel's ashes. It's a place I love to sit, even when it's not his birthday. It's peaceful in the perfectly manicured grounds, a welcome break from the noise of the city. I find Axel's birthday mostly thoughtful, rather than sad. I often think of how he would look, how different our lives would have been if he had stayed.

My husband and I have never been big on celebrating Mother's and Father's Day. To many, those who have children at home and those who have children who have passed away, the day signifies a moment to acknowledge and appreciate parenthood in all its forms. I found this day even trickier to navigate after Axel's loss, so now choose to bypass these occasions altogether.

How to talk about pregnancy loss in the future

I lost my son in 2017, and although so much is still required to bring the system and its understanding of the trauma up to date, there has been some progress in how people treat and discuss pregnancy loss. The conversation is opening up, I agree, but not to the point where we can openly discuss pregnancy loss without the feeling we are often making others uncomfortable. This form of loss is still so connected to secrecy, emotional discomfort in others and even judgement.

Soon after I experienced loss, I felt fraudulent saying I had lost a baby. I was, on occasion, made to feel uncomfortable. I was corrected on more than one occasion and the words 'my baby' were swiftly replaced by 'your miscarriage'. I personally feel the term miscarriage lessens the reality of what actually happens when you experience pregnancy loss. To me, when your pregnancy ends prematurely, it is the loss of your baby. With the doctor's words in mind, whenever I called Axel my baby who died, I believed others were judging my words. I honestly believed people were saying my son wasn't actually a baby and I was making too much of what had happened to me. Whenever I posted on social media, I pictured people saying I was exaggerating that I had lost a baby. Now I say with great conviction that my baby passed away. I met him. He was perfect. Small, but perfect. How you choose to refer to your experience is your choice. At any stage, your baby is your baby, so however you speak of your pregnancy loss will be right for you.

I often question whether I should say I have three children, or the two that people can see in front of them. Depending on my confidence in the situation, I either say three, or two. When excluding Axel, I do this purely to save an uncomfortable moment with whoever I am speaking with. I do feel guilty for occasionally hiding his existence. Pregnancies end and it is painful both mentally and physically. We shouldn't feel any need to silence our experience, or conceal the babies who are very much a part of us. The conversation is still one that can cause feelings of unease in others, so many who have experienced loss often choose to stay quiet.

Due to the reaction I have seen in some people's faces when I mention my baby who died, it can be easier, emotionally, to simply say I have two children. When standing in a group, you don't want to be the person to take the conversation from holiday plans to babies we lost, but equally we shouldn't be shamed into feeling as though we cannot be honest about our experiences.

I asked therapist Claire Bidwell Smith for her advice in speaking of the babies we lost, without it being awkward for those around us.

> You pick and choose your moments. When you choose not to include the full number of children you have carried, you give yourself that forgiveness. It can be a case of just letting yourself get through the conversation with whoever you're speaking to. Of course you are always acknowledging your baby or babies, but you can choose whether to give others all the information. When you do speak of the babies you lost, let

those around you deal with it. That's how we change culture – we stop hiding it so much and we talk about it. It may not be something you can do straight away; it can come later in your grief when you feel more comfortable. In the first year or two after a loss, it can be difficult as it brings up so much, so you really do have to be gentle with yourself. You do it as a way to honour yourself, take care of yourself. It's not that you're not acknowledging your baby, you're taking care of yourself. We have to integrate loss into our lives, we have to make space for it. I don't believe in getting over a loss, moving on. We move forward with it, we take it with us. Two things can be true at once, we can be grieving and horrifically sad *and* still live a meaningful life. You don't have to pick one. It's about finding a way to hold both at the same time. You don't only have to be happy or sad. You can be both.

With the time that passes, it can be more difficult to broach the subject of your loss with those around you. There can be an internal build-up in the need to speak of your baby, to get the words out of you. It is helpful to be able to speak out loud and to share memories of your baby, at whatever stage you lost a pregnancy. If an opportunity doesn't arise, or you feel uncomfortable initiating a conversation about your loss, arranging an appointment with a counsellor or healer every few months can be incredibly helpful in letting all of your emotions and thoughts out to someone who will be there to listen. I no longer find it comfortable to speak at length with friends and family about my loss, so, every six months, I see the healer who I saw for the year after Axel died. We talk about Axel, about my grief and experiences since losing him. The chance to speak about him without concern that I am placing too much weight on a friend allows me to connect clearly with my emotions and the memories of my baby.

My hope is that you will find great empathy from those around you, but there may be misunderstandings from others, a lack of compassion, or possible judgement on how you live through your grief. You are living through your experience and only you can know the truth of all that happened and all you feel. Perhaps it is because I have always been very open about the loss of my pregnancy at five months that I now feel pride when speaking of my baby. It's certainly a way of coming to terms with Axel's death, to speak openly about him with love and warmth. The way in which we choose to speak of our losses must be exactly as we feel it to be. There will never be a greater time to be honest with yourself and with others. Navigating your journey of pregnancy loss is not loving less, moving on, or forgetting. It is reaching a point where you find more peace than pain in your experience, when you can feel as though you have moved beyond your grief.

Epilogue

In writing this book, with generous contributions from others, I have learned so much about grief and loss. I thought I knew so much already, but I had merely scratched the surface. In a journey of loss that has spanned five years, I have lost a baby, moved beyond a grief that I thought was impossible to live through, grown closer to some friends, let others go, experienced the intensity of six rounds of IVF and had a baby girl. Having another baby was not the happy ending to the story, she simply introduced a different way for me to find joy after a reality that I never imagined would be mine.

The interesting thing in a life after pregnancy loss is that you often find out so much more about who you are. Maybe not immediately, but in time, you can feel the difference in how you react and how you view situations in life. It may take you some time to find peace, you may never reach a point where pregnancy loss isn't the dominant thought in your mind, but I hope you can live alongside the loss, or losses, that you never imagined would be a part of your story.

When I look back at my life before losing Axel, I see how very different I was. No better, nor worse, just different. The ability to empathise with those who have experienced grief, of any kind, is something I appreciate from my experience. To know the true value of relationships and friendships and to appreciate strangers who offer genuine words of kindness is another positive that perhaps I would not have understood had I not lost my son. This is not to say I am glad I lived through losing my baby, I wish it had never happened, but there are certain things that have come from loss that have greatly improved my understanding of those around me, and myself.

Prior to the summer of 2017, I had been living a life that, apart from secondary infertility, was moving along without me being mindful of everything I valued within my relationships, career and my future. It's easy to move through life in this way, but I was forced to stop and really focus on each area of my life, something I am certain I would not have done had I not lost my baby.

I don't believe things happen for a reason when it concerns pregnancy loss, but I do believe in the positive of being shown another way to view life and the experiences we face. As time has moved forward, the memory of the night my baby died has become one of love, rather than a memory I would rather not revisit. Thinking of all that happened in detail brings too much pain, so I think of the night with a lighter touch, with the beauty of meeting my son, rather than of losing him.

The trauma wasn't a lesson or an experience that was sent to teach me something. Instead, it was a moment that shifted my direction, my thoughts and how I viewed life. There are few positives in the experience of pregnancy loss, but to understand pain, to realise your own strength and to have a compassion for others that you may not have had without this trauma can help to bring a level of inner peace. Nobody would wish to live through pregnancy loss, but it is finding a way to appreciate your strength once you have moved beyond the first stages of grief.

The kindness shown from others during and after my grief will be something I hold in my thoughts for ever. In times when you need others the most, to be shown who is truly there for you results in a bond that is stronger than you may never have known was possible. It is in times of need that people will show up for you in a way you never expected, and you are shown a kindness that is unconditional. There are transition points in life with friends, when you move forward with them, or allow them to move away. For me, losing my baby and not being the person I once was, for a long while anyway, was a key moment for this transition. It was another point of acceptance in my experience of loss.

I have moved beyond my grief with a love I wouldn't have known without my loss. I grew up with a mother who I know deep down was loving, but who was emotionally distant. She had her own challenges, which included depression, and I remember few moments of feeling close to her, or being hugged or told how much I was loved. She died before I asked many of the questions I wish I had been able to ask about her own relationship with love.

I have come to understand that to show love is not always easy, it is a huge emotion that requires the giver to first love themselves, or be shown a way in which to love. My heart was ripped apart when I lost Axel, I experienced unimaginable pain, but also the greatest force of love for my baby and those close to me. The blocks I had carried from my own childhood, along with the emotional distance inherited from my mother, lifted. The ways in which I had unconsciously learned to not show love in its fullest form had been replaced by a greater understanding of what it is to show and receive love.

While in the final stages of writing this book, considering my own mother and my relationship with love, I happened to watch an interview with the actor Andrew Garfield. He spoke movingly of his mother's recent death and his own grief from that loss. Although a different form of loss, he expressed how he hoped his grief would stay with him for ever, because ultimately that grief is all the unexpressed love he had for his mother. The words resonated with me greatly, as, in losing my baby, I found a way to really see love. My loss will for ever be a reminder to love more.

After loss, you deserve to love yourself more than ever, to care for yourself deeply and to know that what happened wasn't your fault. To experience pregnancy loss is not your failure, it is a part of who you are. Allow the love you are shown to absorb deep within you and believe that you are worthy of that love. Your own force of love is there for you and for those who couldn't stay with you. Allow yourself to feel that love deeply when you need it the most. There is no greater time for you to love yourself and all you are than when you experience loss. You created life, and no matter how long you carried your baby, you loved them uncondi-tionally as their mother. You will always be their mother.

Acknowledgements

Thank you to my agent Juliet Pickering, for your kindness, clarity and confidence. Thank you to my editor Anna Steadman, for your compassion and taking such care with the words on these pages. Thank you to each contributor who gave their time and emotional energy to allow me to share their story; Kate Bryan, Jools Oliver, Katherine Ormerod, Elizabeth Day, Melissa Odabash, Leandra Medine Cohen, Deborah Joseph, Charlotte Sinclair, Kitty Galsworthy, Shema Tariq, Marina Guergova, Simi Lindgren, Michelle Kennedy, Alexandra Stedman, Rhiannon Smith and Nico Taylor, Aimee Baron, Chloe Regan, Grace Mortimer, Kraig Wiedenfeld, Sarah Gwonyoma, Courtney and Sabrina, Holly Scott Lidgett, Anna Walker, Lina Chan, Anjali Patel. To Gubby Ayida, Latham Thomas and Claire Bidwell-Smith, to have your expertise and experience within this book means so much, thank you. Thank you to the friends who supported me when I lost Axel, and encouraged me through the process of writing this book; Amma Amihyia, Gabriele Hackworthy, Charlotte Graham, Silvia Steffen-Ehl, Madeleine Macey, Alec Maxwell, Paris Lees, Billy Daley, Brian Reyes, Fenella Bates, Candice Lake, Jane Gentle, Tom Montgomery, Susan Bender, Rebecca Suhrawardi, Indre Serpytyte, David Pagliaro, Alex Eagle, Vanessa Kingori, Sandra and Gary Waterston, Caroline Bar, Sadie Mantovani, Danielle Soder Kent, Ava Thomas. Thank you to Bozoma Saint John, Lael and Eve. Thank you to Edward Enninful,

Acknowledgements

Sarah Harris and Giles Hattersley, for your friendship and support while writing of my pregnancy loss experience for British *Vogue*. To Ariel Levy, whose own story of losing her son made me feel less alone when I lost mine. To Jay, I am so lucky to have a brother like you. Thank you to my husband Nils and son Astie for living through the loss of Axel with me, and for showing me what true love really is. And to my daughter Audrey, who makes each day brighter.

Resources

The Miscarriage Association
The Miscarriage Association provides information and support for those who have experienced pregnancy loss
miscarriageassociation.org.uk

Child Bereavement UK
Support for families and education of professionals for when a child dies or when a child is bereaved
Childbereavementuk.org

Tommy's
Tommy's is dedicated to finding causes and treatments to save babies' lives, along with providing pregnancy and baby loss information and support
tommys.org

Sands
The Stillbirth and Neonatal Death Society works to support anyone affected by the death of a baby and improve the care bereaved parents receive
Sands.org.uk

Borne
Borne's mission is to end premature birth. The charity funds research to advance the knowledge of pregnancy and childbirth, and improve the lives of mothers and babies through challenging pregnancies and births
borne.org.uk

Resources

Petals
Counselling for trauma or loss during pregnancy and birth
Petalscharity.org

Five X More
Five X More focuses on empowering black women to make informed choices and advocate for themselves throughout their pregnancies and after childbirth
Fivexmore.com

ARC
Antenatal Results and Choices provides information and support to parents before, during and after antenatal screening, when they are told their baby has an anomaly
Arc-uk.org

Twins Trust Bereavement Support
Twins Trust Bereavement support helps parents who have lost a baby or babies during a multiple pregnancy or at any stage after birth
Twinstrust.org/bereavement

Samaritans
Samaritans provides emotional support to anyone in emotional distress, struggling to cope, or at risk of suicide
Samaritans.org

CBT Questionnaire – see page 137
getselfhelp.co.uk/docs/ThoughtRecordSheet7.pdf

Index

Index